SUSTAINABLE BUILDING
SYSTEMS AND CONSTRUCTION
FOR DESIGNERS

fb

Sustainable Building Systems and Construction for Designers

LISA M. TUCKER

Virginia Polytechnic Institute
and State University

FAIRCHILD BOOKS

New York

Executive Editor: Olga T. Kontzias
Assistant Acquisitions Editor: Amanda Breccia
Editorial Development Director: Jennifer Crane
Senior Development Editor: Joseph Miranda
Associate Art Director: Erin Fitzsimmons
Production Director: Ginger Hillman
Production Editor: Jessica Rozler
Cover Design: Erin Fitzsimmons
Cover Art: © ArchPhoto, Eduard Hueber
Text Design and Page Composition: Tom Helleberg
Interior Illustrations: Lisa Tucker

Library of Congress Catalog Card Number: 2009926331
ISBN: 978-1-56367-712-0
GST R 133004424
Printed in the United States of America
TP11

Contents

Extended Contents

Preface

I HAD SEVERAL goals in mind when I initiated this project. The first of these goals was to gather in one place all the information an interior design educator needs to provide an overview of construction and building systems as it relates to interior design. Over the past ten years of teaching building systems courses under a variety of different course names, I was continuously struck by the need to use multiple books to really touch on all the subjects that a student needs to learn within a CIDA accredited interior design program. Coupled with this was the need I felt to emphasize sustainability.

Few books covered general building systems and construction, and none of these addressed sustainable design directly. Those that do exist were intended for architecture audiences specifically. Many of the books addressing sustainable design were technically oriented, and relied on scientific and technological approaches to making buildings more energy efficient, smarter, and more complex.

I believe it is important to show students that sustainability is not a problem of science, but one of values and ethics first. Our way of building in North America is fundamentally obsolete. We do not have the resources to continue along this path. It is destined for failure. I have tried to include a variety of approaches to sustainable design. Underlying this are some basic assumptions. First, the most sustainable approach is not to build new buildings in every case. Building reuse should always be considered before new construction.

Second, less is more. In this case, what I intend is less square footage. Smaller space that is optimized through excellent interior design far outweighs throwing square footage at design problems. Finally, I come from an historic preservation background. A sensibility for how we built in the past can provide a simpler and more sustainable approach to building construction—new methods and materials are not always the answer.

This book is formatted to include a wide variety of visual components. I have sketched as many of the details as I could to encourage students (and faculty members) to think graphically in the design process and about how materials are assembled and shown in drawings. The designer must communicate his/her design intent through drawing. The computer is a tool that is relied upon heavily today. The skill to be able to sit down and think through a connection using paper and pencil is disappearing. Despite this, I have stressed this as a pedagogical tool of this book. I cannot ask students to do that which I will not attempt. Mastery of the details of how one can have what occurs first as an idea and later in actual form comes from knowing materials and their tolerances, and through thinking through the connections based on this knowing. Any good designer needs to practice and master this. Hand sketches are supplemented by a wide variety of interior photographs that demonstrate the application of the text in actual project samples.

If I have been successful, this book will be the one that interior design educators charged with teaching building systems and construction as well as new graduates who need to know how to do something for a project will use. It is my hope that it will sit at the desks of students and practitioners and inspire designers with the confidence to create beautiful and sustainable interior spaces that enhance our health, safety, and overall welfare.

Specifically, this book addresses accreditation criteria in Standards 6 and 11, and covers in detail Standards 12, 13, and 14 of the 2009 CIDA Standards. All of this has been underscored using a sustainability approach.

To use this book effectively, I would encourage you to create a building detailing sketchbook, and to actively sketch building details and components throughout the process until it becomes second nature to dissect what you see and create what you intend when detailing any aspect of an interior space.

Acknowledgments

AS IT TURNS out, writing a book is a much bigger undertaking than I could have even imagined. It is also the product of the efforts of many people, not just the author. First, I would like to thank Olga Kontzias for always believing in this project and me. I would also like to give a special thanks to Joe Miranda, my editor, for always cheerfully answering a lot of questions about the process and for allowing me to make changes as the project developed.

I would like to give a special thanks to Tama Duffy Day, a principal at Perkins + Will for sharing my request for images and case studies with all of the Perkins + Will offices. Thanks to Tama, I heard from her colleagues around North America and was able to include an amazing collection of case studies that illustrate the green design principles of this book. Thank you to J.D. McKibbon, AIA, AMA, LEED AP in the Chicago office, Lora Ingram in the Seattle office, Howard Weiss, principal in the San Francisco office, Joan Blumenfeld and Abigail Carlen, LEED AP in the NYC office, Melissa Radatz in the Vancouver, British Columbia office, Cathy Falwell in the D.C. office, and John Morris, project manager in the Charlotte, North Carolina office.

Thank you to Todd Ray, a principal of studio27architecture, for sharing information about their projects.

Thank you to Linda Segerson (OTJ) and Steven Sorrells (RTKL), two former students of mine at Virginia Tech, for providing case studies from the offices where they work. Thank you to the marketing department at RTKL and Laura Knox at OTJ Architects.

I also want to thank current students Amrita Raja, Hyun-Jun (Steve) Chang, Lauren Shaw, Katherine Johnson, and Britney Bishop for their generosity in sharing current projects with me to inspire future students along the path of sustainable design. A special thanks to Dana Ricci my graduate student assistant who has spent an entire semester scanning and working with the hundreds of images for this book.

Most importantly, I want to thank my husband, Jim, who has put up with all of the time and effort this type of project takes away from everyday living. He is an inspiration and walks the talk of a sustainable life.

SUSTAINABLE BUILDING
SYSTEMS AND CONSTRUCTION
FOR DESIGNERS

CHAPTER 1

A Holistic Approach to Building Design and Construction

Many species around the world are now threatened by climate change, and some are becoming extinct—in part because of the climate crisis and in part because of human encroachment into the places where they once thrived. In fact, we are facing what biologists are beginning to describe as a mass extinction crisis, with a rate of extinctions now 1000 times higher than the normal background rate.

Al Gore, An Inconvenient Truth

OBJECTIVES

- Identify the designer's role in a building design project
- Differentiate among green building rating systems, theoretical approaches, and guidelines
- Apply an integrated approach to a design project
- Compare the roles of the architect and designer in a project
- Compare green product certifications and identify which ones are first party, second party, and third party

INTRODUCTION

The building design and construction industries are in the midst of great changes. As global warming and skyrocketing oil prices have become everyday topics of conversation, the way in which buildings are made has become central to these important issues. As a major source of energy use and material depletion, rethinking buildings may provide part of the solution to the mounting resource and planetary issues.

The design and construction of a building is a complex process and involves many different people. Traditionally, an architectural firm has overseen the process and has coordinated other professionals (engineers, interior designers, and specialists) to produce a complete set of drawings that are then put out to bid by a collection of contractors. This linear process has been the model for many years. The public bid process has several inherent problems from a quality control perspective: contractors bid only on what they see, knowing they can later submit change orders to make up for anything the architects left out of the drawings; the low bidder wins regardless of quality; and in many situations, the people building the building are not involved in the design of the building. By its very nature, this leads to a contentious and often litigious process.

A new method of building design is on the horizon. Several firms are switching to a **Building Information Modeling (BIM)** approach. This requires all stakeholders in the building to be involved earlier on in the process. A three-dimensional computer model is constructed that includes rich data from all subcontractors and suppliers early on in the process. Because this model incorporates structural, mechanical, electrical, plumbing, lighting, and other information during the design process, interference between systems can be discovered well before a building is under construction. Corrections made on the computer model are far less costly than those made in the field. Suppliers, such as the steel manufacturer, can also provide detailed information. This means the actual **shop drawings** come from the three-dimensional model, and waste is significantly reduced during fabrication and building assembly.

Not only does the BIM method to design help reduce errors, but also can be used to generate materials take offs, pricing information, energy modeling, and many other services. Thus, the budget of a building is an integrated part of the design, and decision making occurs throughout the process, rather than through the use of **value-engineering** after the design is complete. Ultimately, the BIM approach creates a building that has been carefully designed from multiple perspectives, has involved all of the key players in a building project, can be designed on budget, and significantly reduces waste. This is a much more sustainable way of designing.

TEAM APPROACH

As with BIM, the **U.S. Green Building Council (USGBC)**'s **LEED (Leadership in Energy and Environmental Design) Green Building Rating System** relies on an integrated team approach to building design in order to be successful. What makes LEED Rating Systems work is having multiple stakeholders present in the decision-making process for a building from the beginning. Various people assume the many different documentation responsibilities associated with this type of building. A **LEED Accredited Professional** participates in the process to help facilitate it. The building which results and that has been reviewed to meet the LEED criteria is then a **LEED Certified Building**. Ultimately the team will determine which level of LEED Certification they hope to obtain for the project. The current levels of compliance are from highest to lowest: Platinum Certified, Gold Certified, Silver Certified, and Certified. The number of points accumulated determines the ultimate certification classification. The USGBC and most LEED Accredited Professionals recommend that a project team try for more points than it actually needs for the desired level of compliance in the event some points are not awarded in the end. Although there are many other green building rating systems and evaluation tools, the LEED Rating Systems have been the most widely adopted in the United States.

OTHER LEED RATING SYSTEMS

In addition to LEED for New Construction (NC), there are several other LEED Rating Systems in place, including: Existing Buildings, Commercial Interiors (CI), Core and Shell, Schools, Retail, Healthcare, Homes, and Neighborhood Development. For the past few years, separate examinations have been given for LEED CI and LEED NC, although beginning January 1, 2009, the USGBC returned to offering only one examination.

TABLE 1.1 SUMMARY OF LEED RATING SYSTEM POINT ALLOCATIONS

NEW CONSTRUCTION VERSION 2.2	POSSIBLE POINTS
Sustainable Sites	14
Water Efficiency	5
Energy and Atmosphere	17
Materials and Resources	13
Indoor Environmental Quality	15
Innovation and Design Process	5
26–32 CERTIFIED 33–38 SILVER 39–51 GOLD 52–69 PLATINUM	

Source: Lisa Tucker, based on LEED NC.

OTHER GREEN BUILDING RATING SYSTEMS

Although many other green building rating systems have been developed, few have gained the momentum of the LEED systems in the United States. Thus, while a brief listing of other systems will be included here, a list of other resources discussing these systems in more detail will be added for further information.

GREEN GLOBES

Green Globes (www.greenglobes.com) provides a building assessment tool in an online format. The system covers building design and operation through a third-party certification process.

BEES

Building for Environmental and Economic Sustainability (BEES) is a Windows-based energy software tool that allows the user to make decisions based on life-cycle information and consensus standards.

STARS

Sustainability, Tracking, Assessment, and Rating System (STARS) is a self-reporting framework developed by the Association for the Advancement of Sustainability in Higher Education. The current version, STARS 5.0 is available as a pdf and can be downloaded at www.aashe.org/stars/. The categories for self-reporting include co-curricular education, curriculum, faculty and staff development and training, research, buildings, dining services, energy and climate, grounds, materials, recycling and waste minimization, purchasing, and transportation.

GREEN GUIDELINES FOR HEALTHCARE (GGHC)

These guidelines outline the best practices for sustainable design in healthcare, including basic practices and principles, design, construction, and operation. Points are used for self-improvement purposes only, and are not tied to level of achievement. More information can be found at the GGHC website www.gghc.org.

INTERNATIONAL ORGANIZATION FOR STANDARDIZATION (ISO) 14000

This group of standards holds as its goal "to provide a framework for a holistic strategic approach to the organization's environmental policy, plans and actions" (www.iso.org). This framework, created in 2004, establishes a common reference point for a variety of customers and companies.

PRINCIPLES OF SUSTAINABLE DEVELOPMENT FOR MINNESOTA

Written in 1999, this document looks at five principles for sustainable development. The document is available at www.eqb.state.mn.us.

LIFE-CYCLE ASSESSMENT (LCA)

According to the U.S. Environmental Protection Agency website, **life-cycle assessment** is "a technique to assess the environmental aspect and potential impacts associated with a product, process, or service by:

- Compiling an inventory of relevant energy and material inputs and environmental releases;
- Evaluating the potential environmental impacts associated with identified inputs and releases;
- Interpreting the results to help you make a more informed decision"

Life cycle assessment is a critical component for selecting specific materials in a building project. All parts of the life cycle contribute to the overall sustainability of a product. The **embodied energy** of the product includes its extraction, manufacture, transportation and ultimately, disposal.

GUIDING PRINCIPLES

Several groups and individuals have created guiding principles for sustainable design.

THE NATURAL STEP

According to www.naturalstep.org, "since 1988, The Natural Step has worked to accelerate global sustainability by guiding companies, communities, and governments onto an ecologically, socially, and economically sustainable path. More than 70 people in 11 countries work with an international network of sustainability experts, scientists, universities, and businesses to create solutions, and innovative models and tools that will lead the transition to a sustainable future."

ECOLOGICAL DESIGN BY SIM VAN DER RYN

Ecological design can be defined as "any form of design that minimizes environmentally destructive impacts by integrating itself with living processes."

—from *Ecological Design* by Sim Van Der Ryn and Stuart Cowan

This integration implies that the design respects species diversity, minimizes resource depletion, preserves nutrient and water cycles, maintains habitat quality, and attends to all the other preconditions of human and ecosystem health.

Ecological design seeks to minimize impact to the environment. By working with natural systems—water, habitat preservation, and local resources—ecological designers try to integrate the built world with the natural one. The term was coined in a book of the same name by Stuart Cowan and Sim Van Der Ryn.

PATTERN LANGUAGE BY CHRISTOPHER ALEXANDER

Christopher Alexander created a series of patterns that he says represent different design conditions in the world that people prefer. He draws the patterns from examples in the vernacular and recommends their use in designed places.

HANNOVER PRINCIPLES

Architect William McDonough wrote the Hannover Principles as guiding principles for the EXPO 2000 at the World's Fair in Hannover, Germany. The complete document can be found at www.mcdonough.com.
The Hannover Principles:

1. Insist of rights of humanity and nature to co-exist
2. Recognize interdependence
3. Respect relationships between spirit and matter
4. Accept responsibility for the consequences of design
5. Create safe objects of long-term value
6. Eliminate the concept of waste
7. Rely on natural energy flows
8. Understand the limitations of design
9. Seek constant improvement by the sharing of knowledge

BIOMIMICRY

Biomimcry is the title of a book by biologist Janine Benyus. As adopted by the design professions, it refers to the study of nature a source and inspiration for design problems. According to www.biomimicry.net,

> Biomimicry is a new discipline that studies nature's best ideas and then imitates these designs and processes to solve human problems.

Biomimicry (from bios, meaning life, and mimesis, meaning to imitate) is a new science that studies nature's best ideas and then imitates these designs and processes to solve human problems. Studying a leaf to invent a better solar cell is an example of this innovation inspired by nature.

PERMACULTURE

The permaculture concept, the brainchild of David Holmgren and Bill Mollison in the 1970s, was conceived as a response to global environmental crisis. As defined by Mollison and Holgren, permaculture is "an integrated, evolving system of perennial or self-perpetuating plant and animal species useful to man" (Holmgren 2002, xix). The idea of these consciously designed eco-systems is to create a local solution that is perpetually sustainable.

NATIONAL PARK SERVICE

The National Park Service (NPS) has created its own guidelines for sustainability when working on a NPS-owned property. These are available for download at http://workflow.den.nps.gov/staging/6_Design/Designstandards/DesignStds_sustain_section.htm

The guiding principles of sustainability were drafted under vice president Al Gore, and director of the NPS Roger Kennedy. The primary topics of discussion include natural resources, cultural resources, site design, building design, energy management, water supply, waste prevention, and facility maintenance and operations.

CRADLE TO CRADLE

Cradle to Cradle is the title of a book written by William McDonough and Michael Braungart. The main concept of the book seeks to eliminate waste on the planet. McDonough maintains that waste equals food, and that the elimination of waste creates a cradle to cradle system to replace our current cradle to grave system for human materials and their use.

ECOLOGICAL FOOTPRINT

According to www.footprintnetwork.org, the global footprint network defined the ecological footprint as "a management tool that measures how much land and water a human population requires to produce the resources it consumes, and to absorb its wastes under prevailing technology." Individuals can calculate their individual ecological footprints on the Earth Day website found at www.earthday.net/footprint/index.asp.

PRODUCT OVERSIGHT AND RATING SYSTEMS

In addition, there are several organizations and groups overseeing sustainable building products. These can be divided into three types: first- party certification, second-party certification, and third-party certification. The most rigorous of these is the third-party certification process that requires an independent and outside review process.

THIRD PARTY

Third party certification occurs when an outside agency certifies a product to conform with a set of standards. This approach reduces potentials for conflict of interest and seeks to be transparent. Several agencies provide third party certification of a variety of sustainable issues and products.

Forest Stewardship Council

Forest Stewardship Council (FSC) was established in 1993 and provides accreditation to third-party organizations certifying wood products. It is the only one currently recognized under the LEED Rating Systems.

EnergyStar

Launched by the Environmental Protection Agency (EPA) in 1992, the EnergyStar program provides energy use guidelines for a variety of building products and appliances.

Scientific Certification Systems (SCS)
Sustainable Choice

This third-party certification was initiated in 2003 to recognize carpets conforming to the National Science Foundation 140 standard.

Master Painter's Institute (MPI)
Green Performance

This 2005 standard is based on the EPA's guidelines for volatile organic compounds and is recognized under the LEED Rating Systems.

Sustainable Forestry Initiative (SFI)

Established in 1996, SFI is not currently accepted by LEED Rating Systems. It is a third-party certification standard for sustainable logging and reforestation initiatives.

Greenguard

The Greenguard Environmental Institute (2002) certifies products and furniture and is widely accepted. It meets LEED Rating Systems requirements.

Cradle to Cradle

This system, begun in 2005, has industry recognition and represents the most rigorous certification process in the market place. The program is a comprehensive certification process that looks at the entire life-cycle of products. Few products are cradle to cradle certified.

Planet Positive

Established in 2006, Planet Positive has sought to standardize carbon offset credits within the industry.

Green Seal

Green Seal is the oldest of the current Green Product Certifications. Initiated in 1989, Green Seal is cited by LEED Rating Systems and provides a life-cycle assessment for many products including light fixtures, sealants, flooring, and other materials.

SECOND PARTY

With second party certification, an industry seeks to provide its own method of certifying sustainable features of a particular type of product.

Carpet and Rug Institute (CRI)
Green Label Plus
The CRI Green Label, established in 2004, is a second-party certification mechanism. The carpet industry provides ratings for its own products.

The design and construction of a building involves many different professionals.

Architect

An **architect** is an individual trained in the art and science of building design. Although qualifications for licensure vary somewhat from state to state, an architect has passed the national Architectural Registration Exam (ARE), after having worked for a specific period of time (usually three years or more) and having received a professional degree in architecture (either a 4 + 2, 5-year undergraduate bachelors of architecture or a Masters of Architecture). The term "architect" is a legally regulated term and cannot be used by an individual who is not licensed.

Interior Designer

The term **interior designer** is regulated in some states and not in others. In some jurisdictions, a professional interior designer is identified by the title "certified interior designer." To sit for the National Council for Interior Design Qualification (NCIDQ) exam, an applicant must have a specific combination of work experiences and education. An interior designer designs the interior spaces of a building and works only with non-load-bearing partitions. To work with bearing walls and other structural building elements, an interior designer must work in tandem with an architect or engineer.

Engineer

Engineers are educated and licensed in specific areas of specialization. In general, their specific training does not include aesthetic concerns. Although they *design* structures, they are not designers in the sense that an architect or interior designer is a designer. Areas of engineering specialties related to building design include:

- Structural/Civil
- Mechanical/Plumbing/Electrical

General Contractor

The requirements to be a general **contractor** also vary from state to state. Generally, no specific education requirements exist for contractors, although some may have a postsecondary educational background. Some jurisdictions divide contractors into different classes—A, B and C—based on the monetary value of the projects they can do. There is usually a different level of testing at the different class levels as well.

Owner

The owner is the person paying for the project.

Specialists

In addition to the basic players involved in a standard construction and design project, there may also be a specialized need for experts in particular areas. Examples of these include the following:

- Security
- Acoustics
- Lighting

LEED Accredited Professional

A **LEED Accredited Professional** has passed the LEED exam administered by the U.S. Green Building Council. This accreditation attests to a person's familiarity with green building practices in general and the LEED Rating System in particular.

PURPOSE OF THIS BOOK

The purpose of this book is to provide a holistic overview of the building construction process with an emphasis on the design and construction of sustainable interiors for interior designers. Table 1.2 shows a breakdown of the traditional interface between the interior designer and the rest of the design team. This will also provide the overall framework for the chapters of the book and the way in which information will be organized therein.

TABLE 1.2

INTERFACE OF INTERIOR DESIGNER'S ROLE IN A BUILDING PROJECT

ARCHITECTS/ENGINEERS	INTERIOR DESIGNER
Site and foundation	Understanding of orientation and how that will impact interior
Structure	Space planning within the existing structural walls and grid
Mechanical	Indoor air quality—off gassing of interior materials and finishes; coordination of lighting with ducts, supply and return locations
Electrical	Electrical needs of specific equipment; locations of open office systems; location of switches; lighting design
Plumbing	Coordination of lighting, signage, and other ceiling-mounted items with sprinkler heads; interior space planning that accounts for stacking and grouping of plumbing and allows for plumbing vents
Wall systems	Interior partitions, non-load-bearing partitions
Roof systems	Ceiling systems
Floor systems	Flooring materials
Acoustics	Interior finishes NRC; interior partitions STC; interior doors STC; open plan systems furniture layouts
Fire safety	Location of fire safety equipment and exit signage; compartmentalization and egress route
Data, voice telecom	Locations
Security	Space planning for visual sight lines; space allocation for specialized equipment

Source: Lisa Tucker

KEY TERMS

architect

Building Information Modeling (BIM)

contractor

embodied energy

engineer

interior designer

LEED (Leadership in Energy and
    Environmental Design) Green
    Building Rating System

LEED Accredited Profession

LEED Certified Building/Project

life-cycle assessment

shop drawings

U.S. Green Building Council (USGBC)

value engineering

ASSIGNMENTS/EXERCISES

1. Take a specific state or jurisdiction
   and find the actual requirements for
   interior designers, architects, and
   contractors within that location.
   Compare these with other states
   and jurisdictions.

2. Visit the Department of Energy's
   website and look for information
   on BIM.

3. Think of three things you can do for
   the rest of the semester that would
   make the world a more sustainable
   place, and do them.

4. Begin a journaling process about
   your experiences of building interiors.
   How do they make you feel?
   Emotionally? Physically? Spiritually?
   Can you identify why? Evaluate a
   new space each week as you move
   through the various components
   of the building you will be learning
   about. Sketch and keep a record
   of what you are learning for future
   reference.

RESOURCES

Fortmeyer, R. (2007). (Mis)Understanding Green
    Products. *Architectural Record,* 11/08,
    173–180.

Interiors and Sources. (2008). Ecolibrary Matrix.
    Interiors and Sources, Green Guide, 2008.

United National Environment Program, (2003).
    International Life Cycle Partnership. *Life
    Cycle Initiative.* Retrieved March 15, 2008
    from www.uneptie.org.

An excellent resource for additional
information on rating systems is *The Sustainability Revolution: Portrait of a Paradigm Shift*
by Andrew R. Edwards.

www.biomimicry.net

www.epa.gov/ord/NRMRL/access/. Retrieved
    12/7/07.

www.footprintnetwork.org. retrieved 12/7/07.

www.naturalstep.org. Retrieved 12/7/07.

www.patternlanguage.com

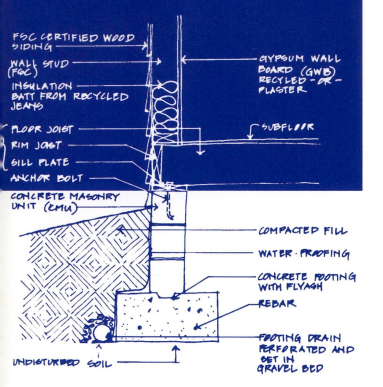

FSC CERTIFIED WOOD SIDING

WALL STUD (FSC)

INSULATION BATT FROM RECYCLED JEANS

FLOOR JOIST

RIM JOIST

SILL PLATE

ANCHOR BOLT

CONCRETE MASONRY UNIT (CMU)

GYPSUM WALL BOARD (GWB) RECYLED - OR - PLASTER

SUBFLOOR

COMPACTED FILL

WATER · PROOFING

CONCRETE FOOTING WITH FLYASH

REBAR

FOOTING DRAIN PERFORATED AND SET IN GRAVEL BED

UNDISTURBED SOIL

CHAPTER 2

Site Considerations and Foundations

This cyclical, cradle-to-cradle biological system has nourished a planet of thriving, diverse abundance for millions of years.

William McDonough and Michael Braungart, Cradle to Cradle

OBJECTIVES

- Identify shallow and deep foundation systems
- Assist in the analysis of a building site as it relates to interior design concerns
- Participate in site design discussions with a knowledge of the breadth of issues related to building placement on a site

INTRODUCTION

As mentioned in Chapter 1, the processes of building design and construction are changing. Traditionally, the major buildings systems have been divided as follows: structural systems; mechanical, plumbing, electrical systems (MPE); enclosure systems; and interior systems.

THE BUILDING SYSTEMS OVERVIEW

A building is composed of multiple **building systems** that all work together and must be carefully coordinated. These include the structural systems, the mechanical systems (mechanical, plumbing, and electrical), the enclosure system, and the interior system.

The structural systems are the component members that make the building stand. *Mechanical, plumbing, and electrical (MPE) systems* are the combinations of systems that make the building comfortable for and usable by human beings. *Enclosure systems* are the materials used to keep water and weather out of the building, and keep heat and cool air inside the building. The enclosure systems include all of the exterior finish materials. **Interiors systems** are the materials used to finish the inside.

A building combines all of the systems and is ultimately responsive to a particular site.

THE SITE

The architect is responsible for placing the building on the site. This process might also include a landscape architect or civil engineer. How the building is placed with relationship to the sun, prevailing winds, and other site appurtenances will impact the energy use of the building as well as the natural daylight that enters the interior. The amount of electric lighting and how it is switched will be directly affected. Because these are interior concerns, the interior designer should be involved in the design process as early as possible.

According to the Architecture 2030 website (www.architecture2030.org), the most effective way to improve energy efficiency and reduce our reliance on fossil fuels is through good design. By simply placing a building to take advantage of natural ventilation, passive solar and daylighting strategies, as well as air sealing, proper insulation, and materials selection, building energy use can be reduced by 50 to 80 percent as was done during the energy crisis of the 1970s.

OVERALL SITE CONSIDERATIONS

Most issues related to site design and building placement can be divided into three basic categories: regulatory, aesthetic, and environmental.

Regulatory

Regulatory concerns address the various man-made conditions imposed upon a particular site as a result of zoning, building codes, and accessibility requirements.

Aesthetic

Each site has its own aesthetic characteristics. These include views as well as site features to be preserved and highlighted.

Environmental

Each site has its own eco-system that contains a variety of life forms as well as weather characteristics. Man's intervention on the site might also create specific environmental issues for a specific site.

Natural. Natural site features include species to be protected or reintroduced to the site; prevailing winds; sun patterns; and the existence and location of water bodies.

Man-made. Man's interventions can include issues such as access to site; utilities; previous landscaping; and the need for noise barriers.

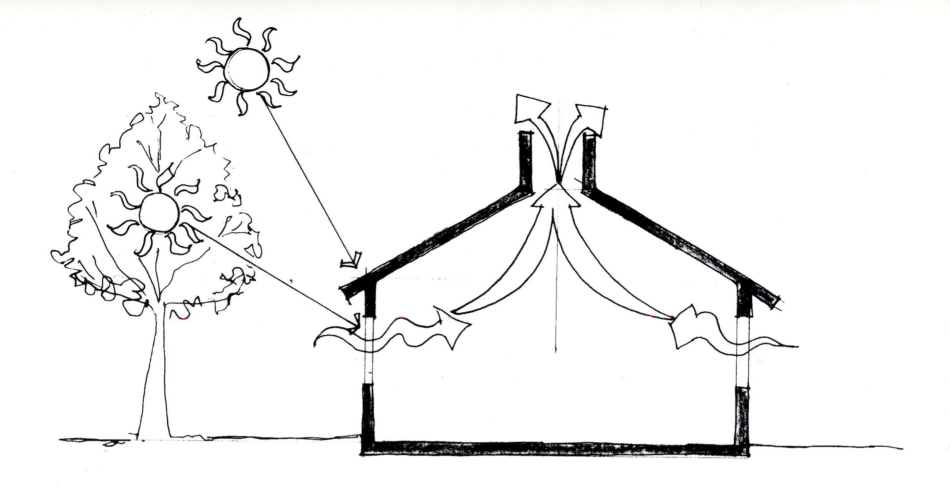

HOW THE SITE IMPACTS THE INTERIOR

The Sun

The sun rises in the east and sets in the west. During the winter months, the sun dips towards the southern exposure in the northern hemisphere. As a result, the interior spaces will experience more direct sunlight on the south side of the building. Similarly, the north side of the building will have no direct sunshine, and will tend to be the colder side of the building. In the southern hemisphere, these conditions are reversed. Buildings designed to take advantage of daylight use less energy.

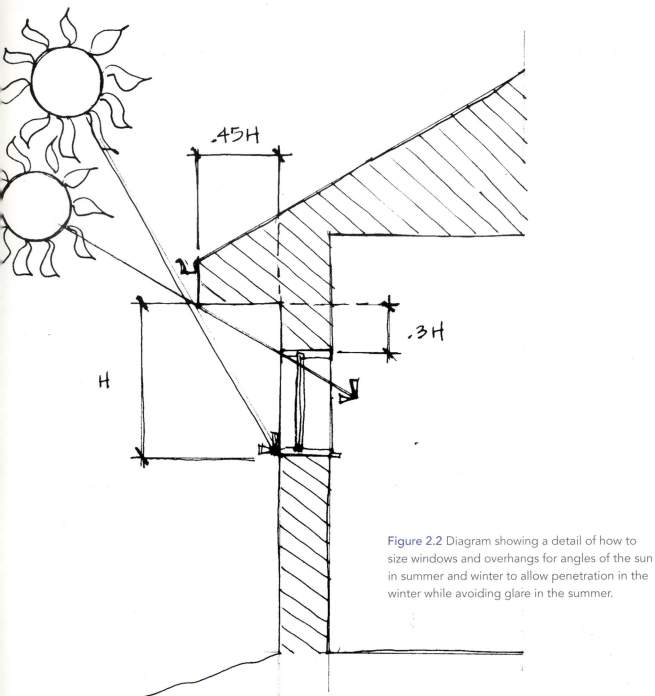

.45H

.3H

H

Figure 2.2 Diagram showing a detail of how to size windows and overhangs for angles of the sun in summer and winter to allow penetration in the winter while avoiding glare in the summer.

The amount of natural daylight entering the space will have an impact on several factors: the electrical lighting (amount of and switching considerations), the health and welfare of the building occupants, and the potential for glare in the space. Simply stated, glare is unwanted, disruptive light, coming from a given source. Sunlight coming through windows can potentially create glare on computer screens, for example. Possible solutions to this condition include operable window treatments, interior and exterior light shelves, and space planning solutions that take potential glare into account. Electrical light switching also needs to respond to the available sunlight. Light fixtures located near a window may be on solar sensors, or simply switched separately from those located deeper in a space. This provides flexibility within the space and energy savings for the building user.

Wind, Cold, and Rain

In addition to general space planning and lighting concerns, the entry into a space needs to be handled carefully. In particularly cold and windy areas, the use of an **airlock** is desirable. The airlock allows people to enter into a

This keeps the majority of the wind and cold separated from reception areas, seating areas, and building lobbies, thus providing increased levels of human comfort. Both thermal comfort and lighting will be discussed in more detail in later chapters.

Views

The interior design will respond to where the windows are located and what can be seen through them. Important views may be showcased using interior design elements. If the interior designer is on board early enough, he or she can also have input into the placement of windows because they impact interior needs such as sunlight penetration, furniture placement, and glare minimization.

Outdoor Rooms

Oftentimes, a building design may include outdoor spaces that are designed as "rooms." Examples include outdoor terraces, patios, breezeways, porches, and other outdoor rooms.

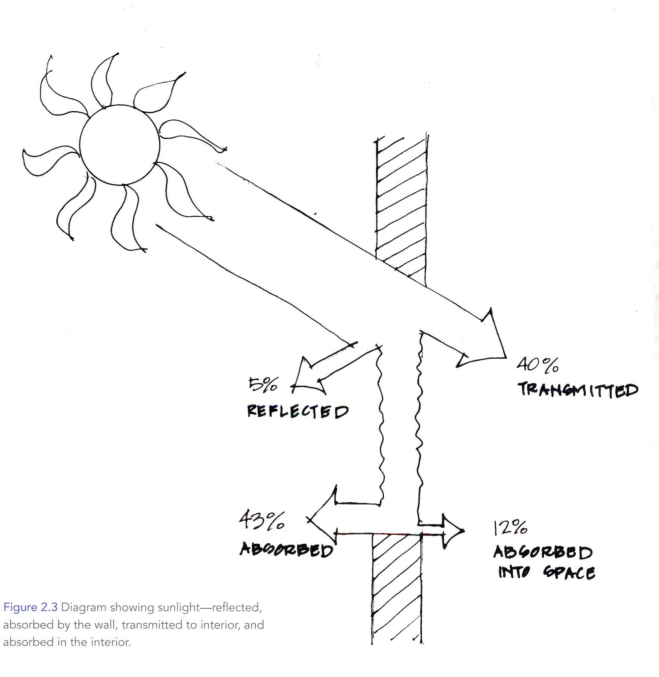

Figure 2.3 Diagram showing sunlight—reflected, absorbed by the wall, transmitted to interior, and absorbed in the interior.

5% REFLECTED

40% TRANSMITTED

43% ABSORBED

12% ABSORBED INTO SPACE

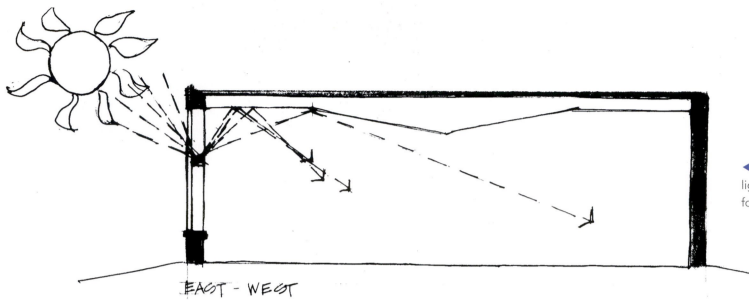

EAST - WEST

◄ **Figure 2.4** Diagram showing light shelf and ceiling formation for an east or west exposure.

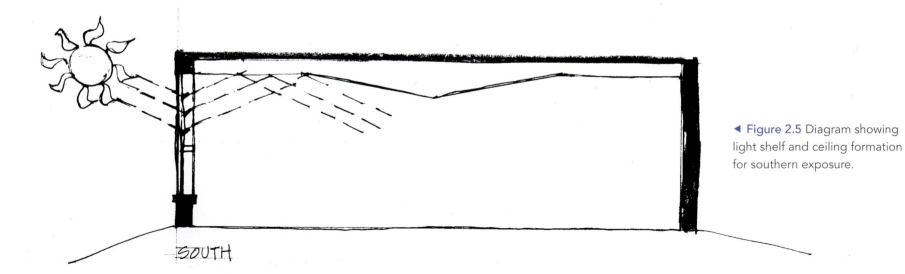

SOUTH

◄ **Figure 2.5** Diagram showing light shelf and ceiling formation for southern exposure.

FOUNDATION SYSTEMS

Although interior designers do not design foundations, a working understanding of the terminology is helpful. The primary purpose of the foundation system is to carry all the loads in a building safely to the ground. Ideally, this will be distributed evenly or uniformly. When the loads are not evenly distributed to the ground, the building will have differential settlement, meaning that the settlement is not uniform. The assumption is that all buildings will settle, and to make this settlement uniform is the goal of the foundation design. A second purpose of a foundation is to resist lateral forces (coming from the side). These might be from either hydrostatic pressure from water in the soil, or from earthquakes.

All buildings settle over time. Settlement is a key factor in the design of a foundation system. An improperly designed foundation system can result in differential settlement as seen in Figure 2.6.

Depending on where a building is located and the soil conditions found there, different

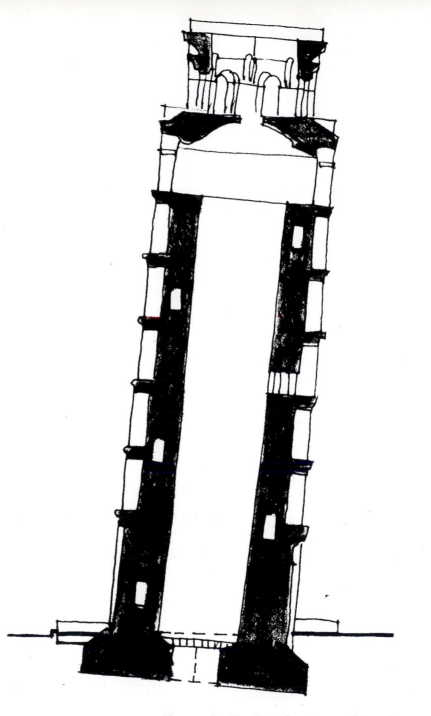

Figure 2.6 Diagram of the Leaning Tower of Pisa demonstrating differential settlement.

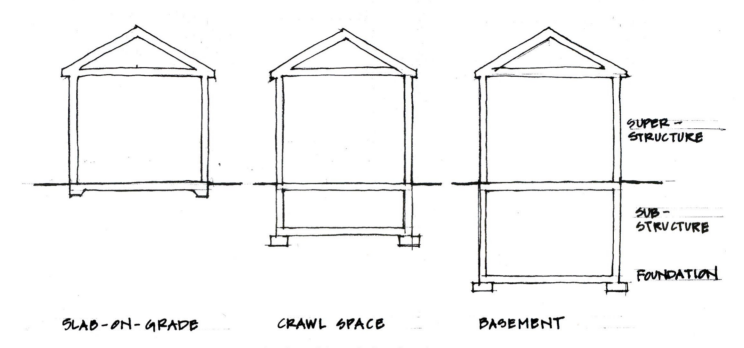

SLAB-ON-GRADE   CRAWL SPACE   BASEMENT

Figure 2.7 Sketches of three shallow foundation types.

types of foundations might be used. These can be divided into two overall types: shallow and deep. Shallow foundations include slab-on-grade, crawl spaces, and basements.

Typically, in residential construction, one of these three systems is used. The foundation wall might be composed of either concrete block or cast-in-place concrete and rests on a reinforced concrete footing pad.

Large buildings have significantly higher loads, and deep foundations are often used to counteract the forces associated with the greater weight of the building. Two types of deep foundation systems are piles and caissons. A pile system is mechanically driven into the soil whereas a caisson is generally reinforced, cast-in-place concrete. A caisson relies on both end-bearing as well as side friction. The piles system relies exclusively on side friction.

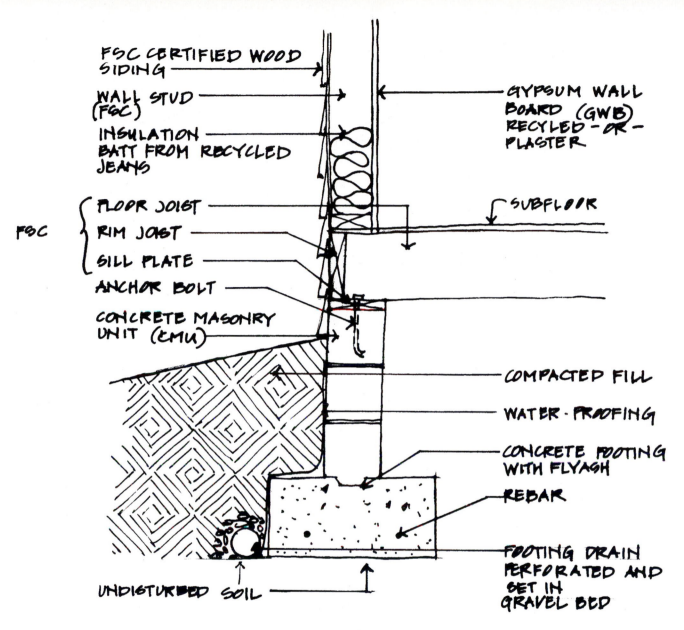

FSC CERTIFIED WOOD SIDING

WALL STUD (FSC)

INSULATION BATT FROM RECYCLED JEANS

GYPSUM WALL BOARD (GWB) RECYCLED -OR- PLASTER

FSC {
FLOOR JOIST
RIM JOIST
SILL PLATE

ANCHOR BOLT

CONCRETE MASONRY UNIT (CMU)

SUBFLOOR

COMPACTED FILL

WATER-PROOFING

CONCRETE FOOTING WITH FLYASH

REBAR

FOOTING DRAIN PERFORATED AND SET IN GRAVEL BED

UNDISTURBED SOIL

Figure 2.8 Wall section showing continuous concrete wall footing and concrete block foundation wall.

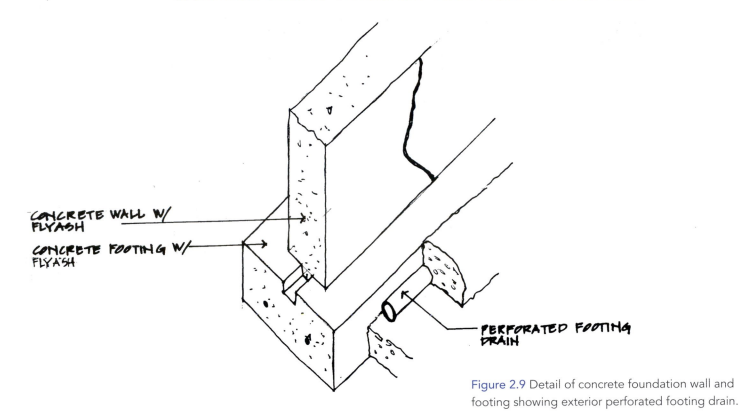

CONCRETE WALL W/
FLYASH

CONCRETE FOOTING W/
FLYASH

PERFORATED FOOTING
DRAIN

Figure 2.9 Detail of concrete foundation wall and footing showing exterior perforated footing drain.

TABLE 2.1 SHALLOW FOUNDATIONS AND DEEP FOUNDATIONS TYPES

SHALLOW FOUNDATIONS	DEEP FOUNDATIONS
Slab-on-grade	Caissons
Crawl space	Piles
Matt/raft foundation	Sub-structure
Continuous wall footing	
Basement	

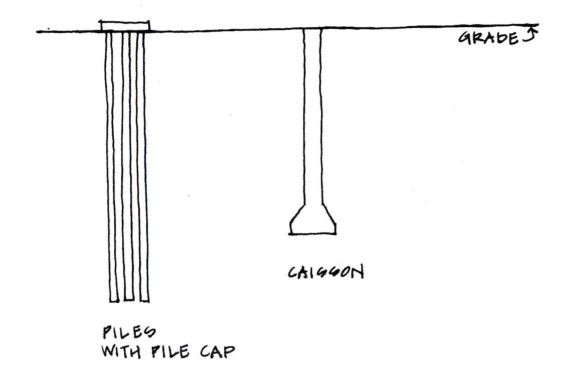

GRADE

CAISSON

PILES
WITH PILE CAP

Figure 2.10 Sketch illustrating two deep
foundation types—piles with a pile cap
and caissons.

SUSTAINABILITY ISSUES

The way in which a building is sited has direct consequences to the sustainability of the building. First, it is important to ask if a new building is needed at all. The most sustainable building is one that already exists. This has the least impact on resource use and the availability of land. Assuming a new building is required, several site conditions should be assessed. The USGBC's LEED Rating System asks designers to carefully consider the site with respect to existing infrastructure, transportation routes, and proximity to urban areas. Brownfield sites might also be considered as a preferable option to previously undeveloped land. A **brownfield** site is one that has been designated by the Environmental Protection Agency (EPA) or other agency as one requiring some remediation due to previous contamination. The less negative impact the new building can have on existing eco-systems, the better. To even consider LEED certification for a project, all of the prerequisites must be met. The project team makes strategic point selections from the possible points available beyond the pre-requisites, depending on the desired level on LEED certification.

As mentioned earlier in this chapter, a brownfield is a previously developed site that contains toxins that must be abated. An example of this is a former gas station site where buried tanks have begun to leak into the soil. Points are awarded for remediation and then building on such a site. By building on a site that has already been in use, existing infrastructure may be available, and prime agricultural land and other undeveloped land is preserved.

The addition of a building and its accompanying parking areas, sidewalks, and other hardscape changes the microsystem around the building. Where the site once absorbed heat naturally, the introduction of the building tends to retain more heat. For example, blacktop parking lots, black roofs, and other low albedo surfaces raise the median temperature of an area. This is called the heat island effect. A light-colored surface with a high solar reflectance index (SRI) is a high albedo material. Potential interventions awarded points under the LEED system include green roofs, pervious pavement, and reduced impervious hardscaping.

The way in which a site is landscaped and developed will directly impact the water usage. The LEED Rating System responds to these issues in several ways. The use of indigenous plants reduces and possibly eliminates the need for irrigation. Rainwater catchment systems that collect storm water runoff can be used as an irrigation source if needed. Several technologies have been and are being developed to reduce water usage. Examples of these include waterless urinals, grey water usage, composting toilets, and low-flush toilets.

TABLE 2.2 CURRENT LEED NC RATING SYSTEM 2.2—SUSTAINABLE SITES

NEW CONSTRUCTION VERSION 2.2	POSSIBLE POINTS
SUSTAINABLE SITES	14
Pre-requisite: construction activity pollution prevention	
Site selection	
Brownfield redevelopement	
Alternative transportation: public transportation access	
Alternative transportation: bicycle storage and changing rooms	
Alternative transportation: low-emitting and fuel efficient vehicles	
Site development: protect or restore habitat	
Site development: maximize open space	
Stormwater design: quality control	
Stormwater design: quantity control	
Heat island effect: non roof	
Heat island effect: roof	
Light pollution reduction	
WATER EFFICIENCY	5
Water efficient landscaping: reduce by 50%	
Water efficient landscaping: no potable use or no irrigation	
Innovative wastewater technologies	
Water use reduction: 20% reduction	
Water use reduction: 30% reduction	

LIVING MACHINE

The **Living Machine** is a wastewater treatment system that mimics a wetland environment. It is designed to treat raw sewage through a natural purification process. In doing so, it takes wastewater from a building and processes it naturally. Biosolids are broken down by bacteria and separated from the water. In a **hydroponics** system, bacteria and the resulting wastewater nutrients are diverted to plant roots. The resulting effluent can be used for either site irrigation or toilet flushing.

WATER BASICS

Whitewater: potable (drinkable) water.
Graywater: suitable for flushing toilets, but not for drinking.
Blackwater: raw sewage.
Xeriscape: involves conserving water through landscaping, especially through the use of native plants and the reduction of the amount of grass that is planted on a site. Mulching is used around the plants. This approach keeps water in place and allows the site to drain easily.

SUMMARY

This chapter has reviewed some of the basic
site considerations when planning a new
building. Although interior designers do not
necessarily deal with these specific issues, it
is important to understand how a building is
sited and the possible ramifications of siting
on interior considerations such as natural
light, heat gain, and views. The following case
study illustrates the application of LEED site
design criteria to a new building.

Figure 2.11 Wetlands system to process sewage.

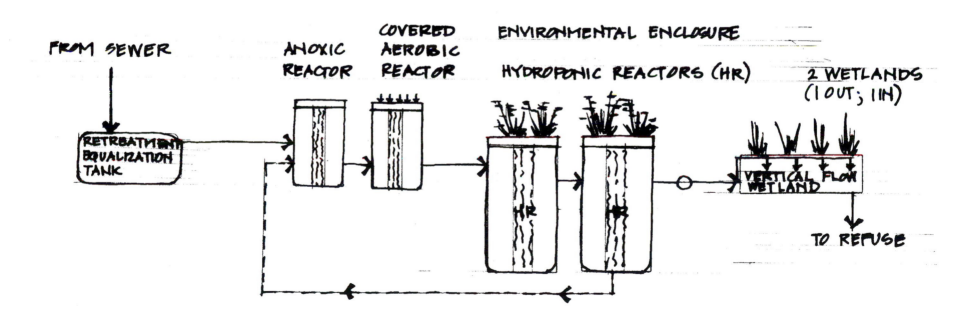

CASE STUDY

WHITE ROCK OPERATIONS CENTER BY BUSBY PERKINS + WILL

Several of the sustainable site strategies discussed in this chapter were implemented into this project to help it achieve a LEED Gold Rating. These include grass and gravel parking areas; indigenous vegetation; a planted roof; the use of photovoltaic panels; exterior sun control grills; and a water collection and use system used for flushing toilets with rainwater collected onsite.

◀ Figure 2.12 (*opposite*) Exterior view of White Rock Operations Center showing exterior overhang and shading devices. **Photo credit: Colin Jewall.**

▼ Figures 2.13a–c (*this page*) Exterior sustainable features including grass and gravel parking, planted roof, and indigenous vegetation. Grass and gravel parking and indigenous vegetation. **Photo credit: Busby Perkins + Will.**
Green roof photo credit: Enrico Dagostini.

▲ Figure 2.14 Rooftop photovoltaic array.
Photo credit: Busby Perkins + Will.

◄ Figure 2.15 Exterior sun louvers.
Photo credit: Colin Jewall.

KEY TERMS

airlock

albedo

blackwater

brownfield

building systems

differential settlement

glare

graywater

hardscape

heat island effect

hydroponics

Living Machine

solar reflectance index (SRI)

whitewater

xeriscape

ASSIGNMENTS/EXERCISES

1. Visit the Architecture 2030 website (www.architecture2030.org) and view the online PowerPoint slideshows.
2. Record your responses to each.
3. What can you, as an individual, do to reduce your energy consumption/ ecological footprint?
4. Use two buildings that you see every day as examples, and analyze if and how they respond to the site.
5. Sketching assignments: Look for construction site examples of foundations in your area. Identify the method and type(s) of foundations being used.
6. Photograph or sketch examples of framing a view.
7. Photograph or sketch examples of outdoor rooms.

RESOURCES

www.architecture2030.org/regional_solutions/ homeowners.html. Retrieved February 1, 2008.

LEED NC Version 2.2 available at www.usgbc.org

Ching, Francis D. K., and Cassandra Adams. *Building Construction Illustrated.* 3rd edition. New York: John Wiley and Sons, 2001.

Sustainable Sites Initiative (www .sustainablesites.org/index.html)

Living Machines (www.worrellwater.com/ products_lm.html)

In addition to the United States Green Building Council, several of the groups and individuals mentioned in Chapter 1 have created guiding principles for sustainable site design. For additional information on guiding principles for site design, research the following:

- *Ecological Design*, Sym van der Ryn
- *Pattern Language*, Christopher Alexander
- Hannover Principles
- biomimcy
- permaculture
- National Park Service
- Cradle to Cradle

CHAPTER 3

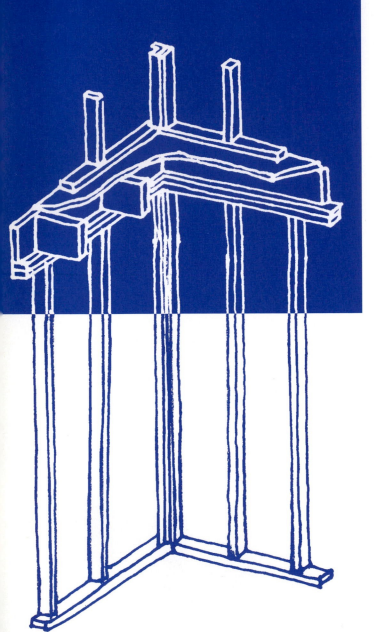

Structural Systems

I have been, as the physicist Victor Weisskopf once said of himself, a happy man in a terrible century. My preoccupation was not, however, with nuclear swords and breathtaking technological advances, but of a wholly different kind: I have served as a close witness to fundamental changes in Nature.

E.O. Wilson, *naturalist*, A New Edition for a New Generation

OBJECTIVES

- Identify a building's structural elements
- Compare the roles of an interior designer and an architect or engineer in regards to building structures
- Compare structural frames, stud wall systems, and bearing walls

INTRODUCTION

By definition, interior designers do not deal with structural systems; however, it is still important that they recognize the building's structure and know when an engineer or architect is required on a project. The National Council for Interior Design Qualification (NCIDQ) provides the most detailed definition of the interior designer:

Interior design is a multi-faceted profession in which creative and technical solutions are applied within a structure to achieve a built interior environment. These solutions are functional, enhance the quality of life and culture of the occupants, and are aesthetically attractive. Designs are created in response to and coordinated with the building shell, and acknowledge the physical location and social context of the project. Designs must adhere to code and regulatory requirements, and encourage the principles of environmental sustainability. The interior design process follows a systematic and coordinated methodology, including research, analysis, and integration of knowledge into the creative process, whereby the needs and resources of the client are satisfied to produce an interior space that fulfills the project goals.

Interior design includes a scope of services performed by a professional design practitioner, qualified by means of education, experience, and examination, to protect and enhance the life, health, safety and welfare of the public. According to the NCIDQ website, these services may include any or all of the following tasks:

- Research and analysis of the client's goals and requirements; and development of documents, drawings, and diagrams that outline those needs;
- Formulation of preliminary space plans, and two- and three-dimensional design concept studies and sketches that integrate the client's program needs and are based on knowledge of the principles of interior design and theories of human behavior;
- Confirmation that preliminary space plans and design concepts are safe, functional, aesthetically appropriate, and meet all public health, safety, and welfare requirements, including code, accessibility, environmental, and sustainability guidelines;
- Selection of colors, materials, and finishes to appropriately convey the design concept, and to meet socio-psychological, functional, maintenance, life-cycle performance, environmental, and safety requirements;

- Selection and specification of furniture, fixtures, equipment, and millwork, including layout drawings and detailed product description; and provision of contract documentation to facilitate pricing, procurement, and installation of furniture;
- Provision of project management services, including preparation of project budgets and schedules;
- Preparation of construction documents, consisting of plans, elevations, details, and specifications to illustrate non-structural and/or non-seismic partition layouts; power and communications locations; reflected ceiling plans and lighting designs; materials and finishes; and furniture layouts;
- Preparation of construction documents to adhere to regional building and fire codes, municipal codes, and any other jurisdictional statutes, regulations, and guidelines applicable to the interior space;
- Coordination and collaboration with other allied design professionals who may be retained to provide consulting services, including but not limited to architects; structural, mechanical, and electrical engineers, and various specialty consultants;
- Confirmation that construction documents for non-structural and/or non-seismic construction are signed and sealed by the responsible interior designer, as applicable to jurisdictional requirements for filing with code enforcement officials;
- Administration of contract documents, bids, and negotiations as the client's agent;
- Observation and reporting on the implementation of projects while in progress and upon completion, as a representative of and on behalf of the client; and conducting post-occupancy evaluation reports.

The professional organizations for interior design also provide their own definitions of an interior designer. According to the American Society of Interior Designers (ASID):

An interior designer is professionally trained to create a functional and quality interior environment. Qualified through education, experience, and examination, a professional designer can identify, research, and creatively resolve issues and lead to a healthy, safe, and comfortable physical environment.

A decorator fashions the "look" of a space and its outward decoration—paint, fabric, furnishings, light fixtures, and other materials. In addition to enhancing the total visual environment, an interior designer creates a space that is functional, efficient, and safe.

According to the ASID website, among the many areas of expertise a professional designer commands are:

- Space planning and utilization, including organizational and storage needs
- Long-term project and lifestyle planning
- National, state, and local building codes
- Safety and accessibility
- Ergonomics
- Design for people with special needs
- Conservation and "green" design
- Historic restoration
- Interior detailing of background elements, such as wall and ceiling designs
- Custom design of furniture, drapery, and accessories
- Selection of appliances, plumbing fixtures, and flooring materials
- Acoustics and sound transmission
- Audiovisual and communication technology
- Construction documents and specifications

The International Interior Design Association (IIDA) provides both a long and a short definition for an interior designer:

SHORT DEFINITION

The Professional Interior Designer is qualified by education, experience, and examination to enhance the function and quality of interior spaces.

For the purpose of improving the quality of life, increasing productivity, and protecting the health, safety, and welfare of the public, the Professional Interior Designer:

- analyzes the client's needs, goals, and life and safety requirements;
- integrates findings with knowledge of interior design;
- formulates preliminary design concepts that are appropriate, functional, and aesthetic;
- develops and presents final design recommendations through appropriate presentation media;
- prepares working drawings and specifications for non-load bearing interior construction, materials, finishes, space planning, furnishings, fixtures, and equipment;
- collaborates with professional services of other licensed practitioners in the technical areas of mechanical, electrical, and load-bearing design as required for regulatory approval;
- prepares and administers bids and contract documents as the client's agent;
- reviews and evaluates design solutions during implementation and upon completion.

LONG DEFINITION (SCOPE OF SERVICES)

The Interior Design Profession provides services encompassing research, development, and implementation of plans and designs of interior environments to improve the quality of life, increase productivity, and protect the health, safety, and welfare of the public. The interior design process follows a systematic and coordinated methodology. Research, analysis, and integration of information into the creative process result in an appropriate interior environment. According to the IIDA website, practitioners may perform any or all of the following services:

PROGRAMMING

- Identify and analyze the client's needs and goals. Evaluate existing documentation and conditions.
- Assess project resources and limitations.
- Identify life, safety, and code requirements.
- Develop project schedules, work plans, and budgets.
- Analyze design objectives and spatial requirements.
- Integrate findings with their experience and knowledge of interior design.
- Determine the need for, make recommendations, and coordinate with consultants and other specialists when required by professional practice or regulatory approval.

CONCEPTUAL DESIGN

- Formulate for client discussion and approval preliminary plans and design concepts that are appropriate and describe the character, function, and aesthetic of a project.

DESIGN DEVELOPMENT

- Develop and present for client review and approval final design recommendations for space planning and furnishings arrangements; wall, window, floor, and ceiling treatments; furnishings, fixtures, and millwork, color, finishes, and hardware; and lighting, electrical, and communications requirements.
- Develop art, accessory, and graphic/signage programs.
- Develop budgets.
- Presentation media can include drawings, sketches, perspectives, renderings, color and material boards, photographs, and models.

CONTRACT DOCUMENTS

- Prepare working drawings and specifications for non-load bearing interior construction, materials, finishes, furnishings, fixtures, and equipment for client's approval.
- Collaborate with professional services of specialty consultants and licensed practitioners in the technical areas of mechanical, electrical, and load-bearing design as required by professional practice or regulatory approval. Identify qualified vendors. Prepare bid documentation, collect and review bids.
- Assist clients in awarding contracts.

CONTRACT ADMINISTRATION

- Administer contract documents as the client's agent.
- Confirm that required permits are obtained.
- Review and approve shop drawings and samples to assure they are consistent with design concepts.
- Conduct on-site visits and field inspections.
- Monitor contractors' and suppliers progress.
- Oversee on their clients' behalf the installation of furnishings, fixtures, and equipment.
- Prepare lists of deficiencies for the client's use.

EVALUATION

- Review and evaluate the implementation of projects while in progress and upon completion as representative of and on behalf of the client.

In all the previously mentioned definitions, interior designers are prohibited from doing structural interventions on a building and must work with the proper trained professionals when considering structural changes. This chapter will present a broad overview of the various types of structural systems a designer is likely to encounter when working with those professionals licensed and trained to design and alter them—including traditional systems, historic systems, and alternative systems.

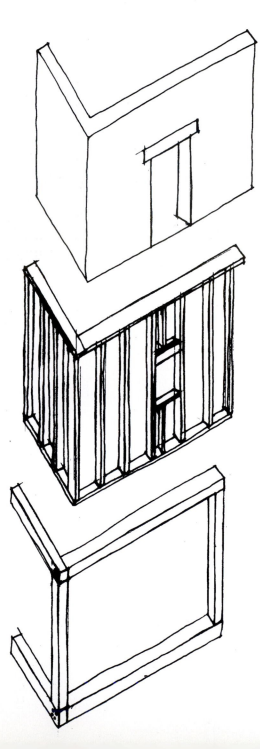

PURPOSE OF STRUCTURAL SYSTEMS

The main purpose of a structural system is to carry the load of a building and transfer them to the foundation. The way in which this takes place depends on the type of structural system. Generally speaking, structural systems can be divided into three primary types: **bearing wall**, **structural frame**, and **stud wall** systems. The three basic materials from which structural systems are composed are wood, steel, and concrete/masonry construction.

BEARING WALL

Bearing wall construction relies on the entire wall to carry all loads to the foundation beneath. When an opening is made in a bearing wall, a steel, concrete, stone, or brick lintel or arch is needed to carry the load of the wall above the opening. Bearing walls are most frequently constructed of concrete, stone, brick, or concrete block.

STUD WALL

The stud wall system relies on several small members to carry loads to a horizontal sole plate that in turn distributes the weight to a sill plate. Both light gauge steel and light frame wood construction use stud wall systems.

STRUCTURAL FRAME

The structural frame system is composed of columns and beams that transmit loads to the foundation. Heavy timber, structural steel, or pre-case concrete can be used to create a structural frame.

Figure 3.1 (*top*) Bearing wall with lintel over door opening.

Figure 3.2 (*middle*) Stud wall with cripple studs below window opening.

Figure 3.3 (*bottom*) Structural frame with columns and beams.

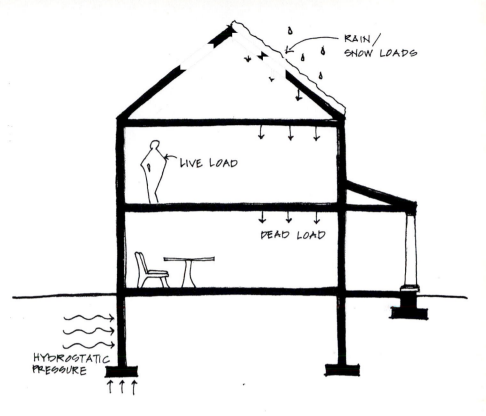

STRUCTURAL BASICS

The three primary characteristics of a structural system are as follows:

- Stability
- Strength and stiffness
- Economy

LOADS

There are several types of loads that act upon a building and to which the structural system must respond. These include live, dead, uniform, concentrated, static, and dynamic loads. **Live loads** are those loads that move. Examples include people and furnishings within a building. **Dead loads** are those loads associated with gravity and include the building materials and the weight of the building itself. A **uniform load** is distributed evenly. For example, stone flooring materials would be a uniform load on the floor framing system.

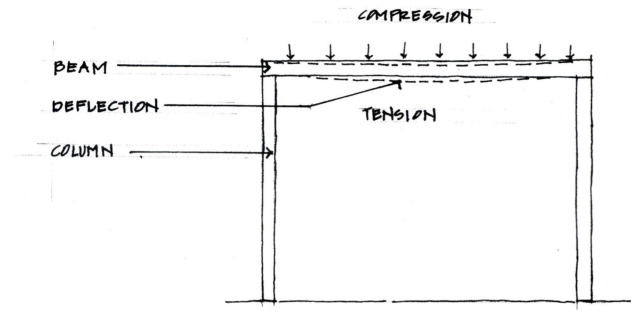

COMPRESSION

BEAM

DEFLECTION

TENSION

COLUMN

Figure 3.5 Columns and beam illustrating compression, tension, and deflection.

By contrast, a concentrated load acts on a single point. An extremely heavy safe or piece of equipment would exert a concentrated load. Static loads are those loads that move slowly over time. Sudden jarring movements are called dynamic loads, as exemplified by both earthquakes and wind loads.

These various loads put the building under different types of stresses that include tension, compression, shear, and bending.

Tensile stress occurs when the building materials are pulled apart under a load. Compression is what occurs when a building material is compacted together under a load. Compressive stress normally occurs on the top of a structural beam whereas tensile stress takes place on the underside of the member. Structural design seeks a state of equilibrium wherein all of these stresses are equalized. Following Newton's Third Law of Motion: *the sum of all the forces (loads) in a building must equal zero*. Shear describes the stress that is caused by sliding forces that are moving in two different directions. Bending stresses occur when a material is deformed under the weight of a load.

Several forms have been developed to resist loads within a building and to respond to tension, compression, and shear forces.

Cable

A cable system operates in pure tension to support a load.

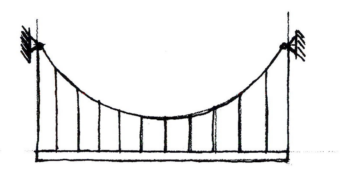

Figure 3.6 Cable structure.

Post and Beam

The post and beam system is designed to work in compression (column or post) and in bending and shear (beam.)

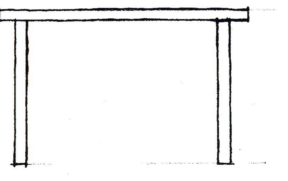

Figure 3.7 Column and beam structure.

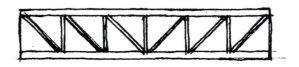

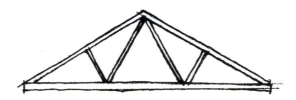

Truss

A truss relies on the principle of triangulation to support loads. The interior members form a series of triangles to maximize the amount of weight that can be carried. Trusses can be constructed of either wood or steel, and come in many different configurations. Some members are in tension and others in compression such that the sum of all forces equal zero.

Figure 3.8 Truss.

Arch

The arch works in compression.

Figure 3.9 Arch.

Shell

A shell system consists of a thin curved membrane that acts in tension or compression, and sometimes both tension and compression. It is usually made of reinforced concrete.

Figure 3.10 Shell.

HISTORIC SYSTEMS

Historically, most buildings in the United States were constructed of wood. The first form of wood construction consisted of a **column and beam** system with intermediate wood members. This is also known as a **heavy timber frame**. Prior to the Civil War, these joints were often **mortise and tenon and pegged** together.

Prior to the Civil War the roof joists most often featured mortise and tenoned joinery as well. The ridge board, to which roof rafters could be attached, began to be used following the Civil War period. Another distinguishing feature of historic framing materials is that a two–by–four was actually 2 inches by 4 inches—both nominal and actual size.

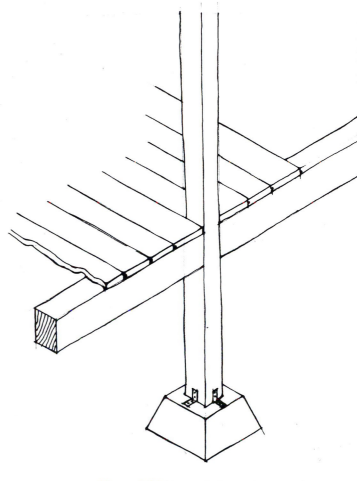

Figure 3.11 Heavy timber column and floor beam with wood decking.

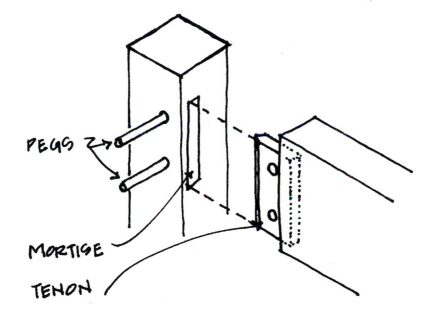

PEGS

MORTISE

TENON

Figure 3:12 Mortise and tenon joint.

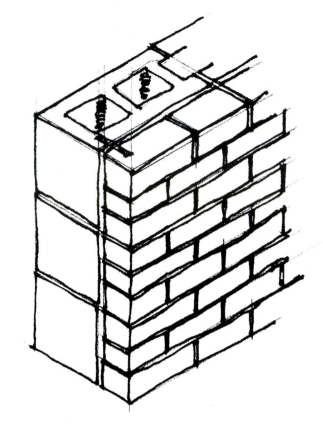

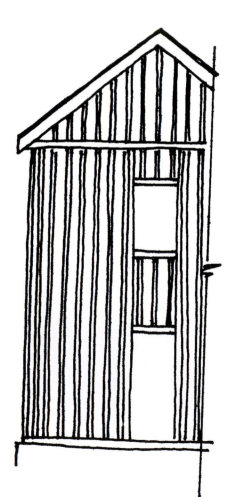

▲ Figure 3.13 Masonry bearing wall.

◄ Figure 3.14 Balloon framing.

Those buildings that were constructed of masonry, such as stone or brick, relied on bearing wall construction. The bricks were hand made on the building site, and stone was quarried locally in most cases.

Balloon framing was introduced during the nineteenth century as a new form of wood framing. The balloon framing method relied on walls studs and floor joists in standardized sizes that were nailed together. Walls studs extended from the foundation level to the roof whereas floor joists extended from front to back or side to side of the building. Floor joists were then hung from the wall framing.

SYSTEMS IN USE TODAY

WOOD

For a variety of reasons, balloon framing was replaced by today's method of light frame construction: **platform framing**. For platform framing, each floor level platform supports the walls for that floor. Platform framing can be used for both residential and small commercial projects. In addition to platform framing using 2 inch by 4 inch and 2 inch by 6 inch stud walls, heavy timber framing is still used in some residential construction, particularly to create a more rustic interior appearance. When wood is used, it should be Forest Stewardship Council (FSC) certified to ensure that it comes from a sustainable managed forest.

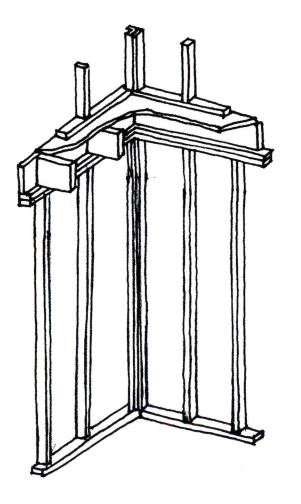

▲ Figure 3.15 Platform framing.

▶ Figure 3.16 Contemporary heavy timber framing.

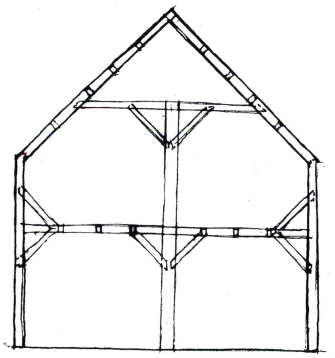

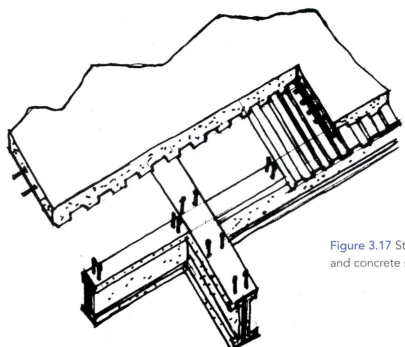

Figure 3.17 Steel floor beams with metal deck and concrete slab.

STEEL

Similar to wood, there are two basic types of steel construction systems: light gauge and structural steel. Structural steel consists of a column and beam type system, and light gauge steel incorporates metal studs and metal joists. It should be noted that steel has a high-embodied energy.

MASONRY AND CONCRETE BEARING WALL SYSTEMS

Masonry consists of a unit member joined together with mortar. Examples of this type of construction include brick, stone, terracotta, and glass block. Both the masonry bearing wall and the concrete bearing wall rely on the entire surface to carry loads. Brick can be made locally from clay and although stone may be quarried locally, it is finite in supply.

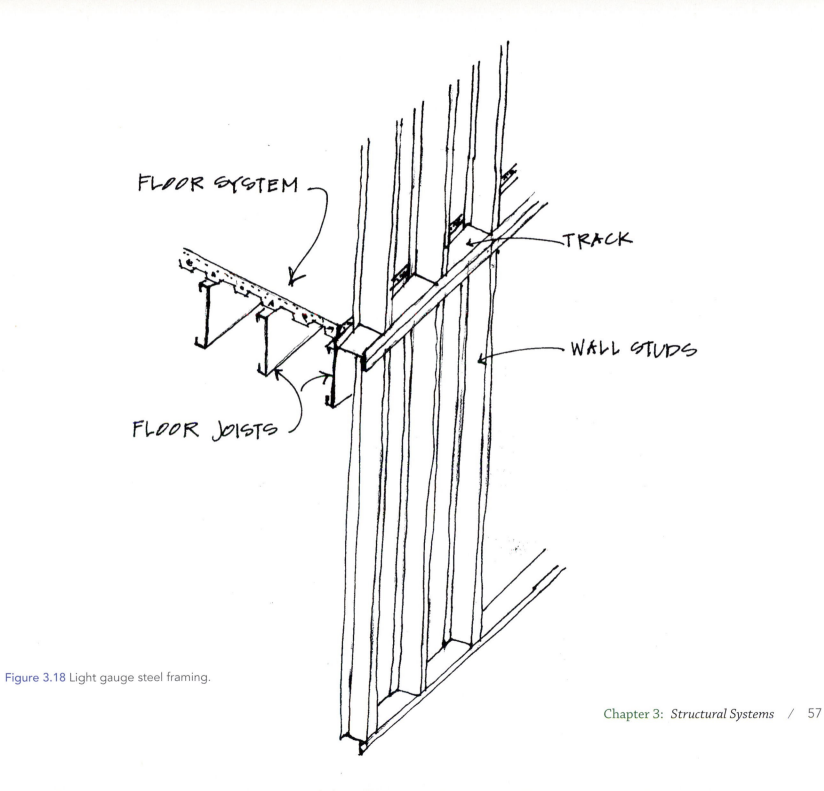

FLOOR SYSTEM

TRACK

FLOOR JOISTS

WALL STUDS

Figure 3.18 Light gauge steel framing.

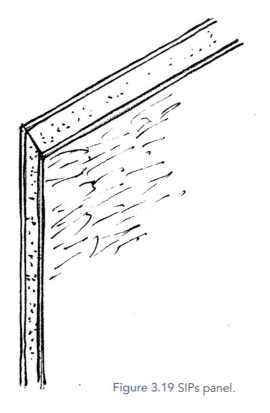

Figure 3.19 SIPs panel.

OTHER SYSTEMS

In addition to these traditional structural systems, several new materials have been introduced and some traditional building materials have been reintroduced. These include structural insulated panels, cob construction, straw bale construction, adobe construction, rammed earth construction, and other alternative building methods.

Structural insulated panels (SIPS) are becoming increasingly popular because they use 30 percent less wood than standard light frame construction. Although they provide no thermal mass, they can be easily assembled on site and contain integral insulation. Agriboard is a sustainable SIPS product made from rice or wheat straw.

Cob construction is produced using earth, straw, water, and sand. This hand-mixed material can be formed into a variety of shapes, and provides a naturally insulated building using earthen construction. Similar to adobe construction, the earthen walls are self-supporting. Oftentimes, those building a cob house will insert decorative windows, bottles, and other forms of glass into the wall, thus enhancing its organic appearance.

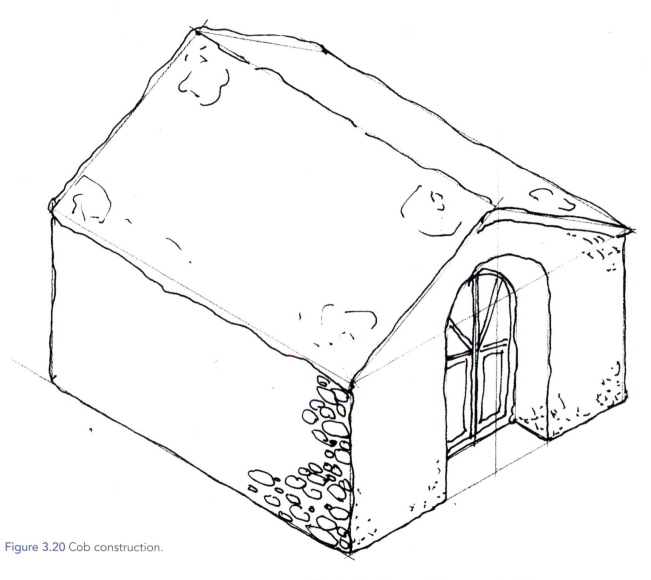

Figure 3.20 Cob construction.

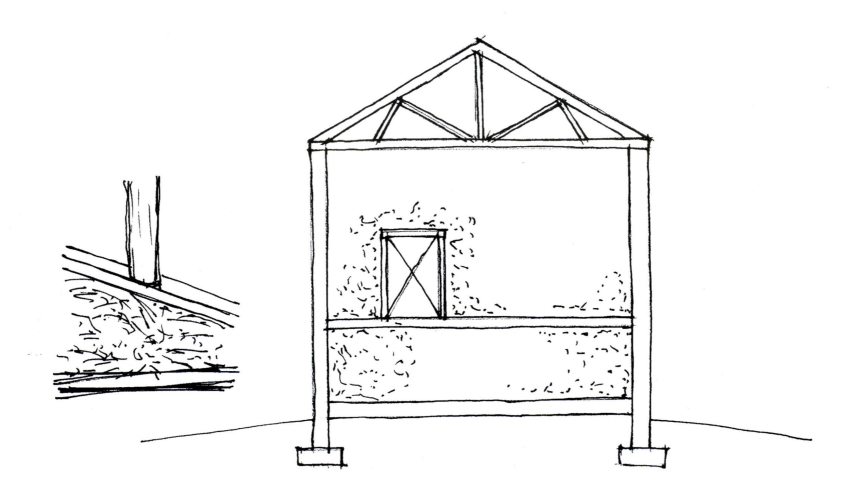

Figure 3.21 Straw bale construction.

Bales of straw are the primary wall component in straw bale construction. A wood frame provides the structural framework within which the straw bales are laid like masonry blocks. Oftentimes bamboo will be used inside the bales of hay to keep them aligned vertically.

Adobe consists of dirt with added water. Some clay in the soil allows for more stable adobe material. Because of its composition, adobe construction should be protected with deep overhangs and by being lifted off the ground by a foundation. As an earthen material, adobe is an excellent insulator, holding in heat in the winter and cool in the summer. Traditionally, adobe buildings were constructed in arid climates with abundant clay-enriched soil and scarce rain.

HAND·MADE ADOBE BRICKS

Figure 3.22 Adobe brick wall with arch.

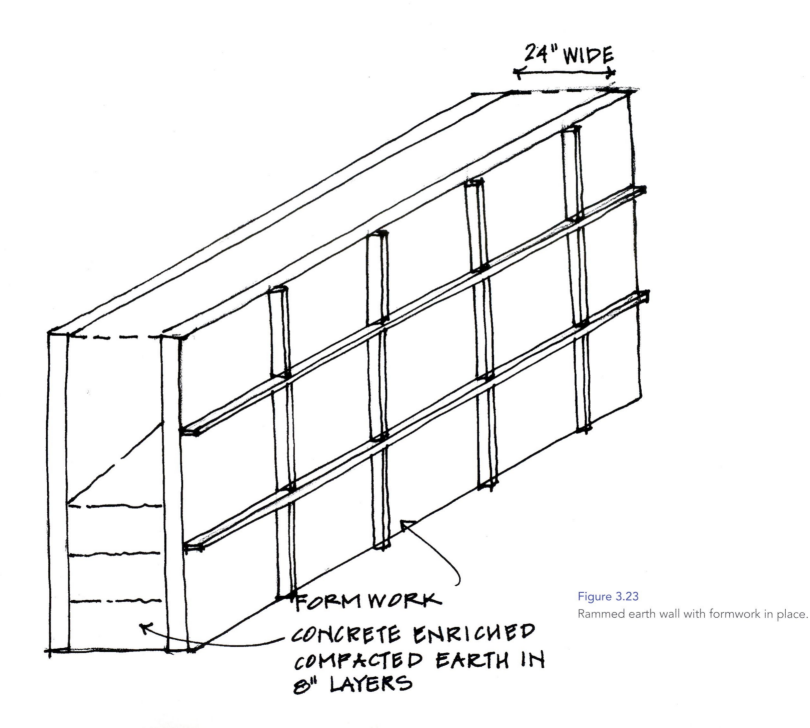

24" WIDE

FORMWORK

CONCRETE ENRICHED
COMPACTED EARTH IN
8" LAYERS

Figure 3.23
Rammed earth wall with formwork in place.

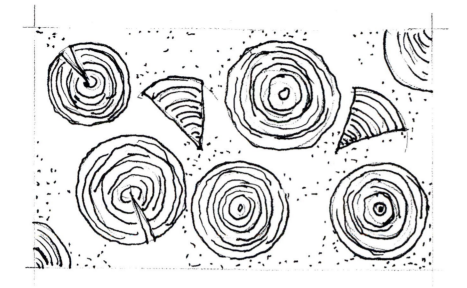

Large, load-bearing walls are used in rammed earth construction. As a self-supporting material, rammed earth also features excellent insulating qualities. The Great Wall of China was built of rammed earth construction. Like cob and adobe construction, the primary material is earth.

As the name suggests, cord wood construction uses "cord" wood, or what appears to be firewood held together with concrete.

Bamboo framing uses bamboo, a rapidly renewable resource, as a framing system. Similar to light frame construction, multiple members are placed at regular intervals. The canes of bamboo must be joined together such that the structure of the cane itself is not undermined.

▲ Figure 3.24 Cord wood wall.

▼ Figure 3.25 Bamboo as a framing material.

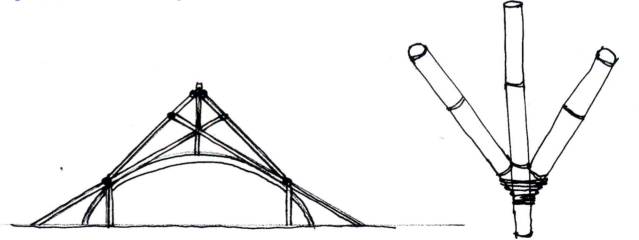

Figure 3.26 Earth sheltered house.

When a building is partially concealed beneath the ground, it uses earth sheltered construction. This form of construction relies on the constant ground temperature to maintain a constant temperature within the interior.

Gabion walls consist of a metal cage containing rocks that are approximately 5 to 6 inches in diameter. Although ordinarily used as a retaining wall, this method of construction has also been successfully used in building construction.

Figure 3.27 Gabion construction.

Sandbag walls use stacked sandbags as the primary wall within a timber frame. The sandbags provide excellent thermal insulation and sound absorption as well as keep water from entering the interior. This is a viable option for vernacular construction in parts of Africa and other places with an abundance of sand and local labor.

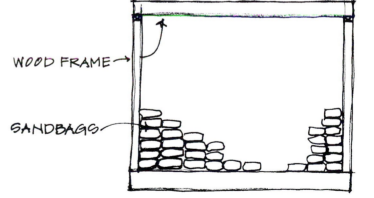

Figure 3.28 Sandbag wall.

RECYCLED MATERIALS

Reclaimed lumber, or lumber from old barns and other buildings, is becoming a common new building material such as for a flooring material and other applications. Massive timber framing members can be planed into smaller members for use in a new building or renovation project.

The structural system of a building is what makes the building stand up. This can be accomplished in many ways using a variety of materials.

TABLE 3.1
COMPATIBILITY OF STRUCTURAL
SUPPORT AND DECK/FLOOR FRAMING SYSTEM

STRUCTURAL TYPE	DECK/FLOOR SYSTEM
Light wood framing	Wood joist with plywood subfloor
Wood post	Wood beam with planks
Masonry bearing wall	Wood joist with plywood subfloor
Wood beam with planks	
Reinforced concrete flat slab	
Reinforced concrete pan joist	
Reinforced concrete waffle pan	
Steel frame	Steel beam with steel subfloor
Bar joist with steel subfloor	or concrete slab
Reinforced concrete precast plank	
Reinforced concrete column	Reinforced concrete flat plate
Reinforced concrete frame	Reinforced concrete flat plate
Reinforced concrete waffle pan	
Reinforced concrete precast plank	

Source: Adapted from Shaeffer, p. 13.

SUMMARY

This chapter provided an overview of structural systems, including those made from wood, steel, and masonry construction. Several sustainable alternatives were introduced, including the use of FSC certified wood, recycled materials, and vernacular solutions such as rammed earth, adobe, and straw bale. The following case studies illustrate some of these techniques within current interior spaces.

CASE STUDIES

AHL SERVICES BY STUDIO27ARCHITECTURE

A late-eighteenth century heavy timber, brick, and stone structure was chosen for AHL Services. One floor of the building was removed, exposing the existing historic hand-hewn heavy timber structure. Additional support was provided for this structure using steel channels.

Figure 3.29 AHL Services showing interior brick and stone wall. Photo Credit: Anice Hoachlander, Hoachlander Davis Photography, LLC.

67

◄ Figure 3.30 AHL Services showing interior heavy timber beams with new steel beams attached to load bearing masonry walls. Photo Credit: Anice Hoachlander, Hoachlander Davis Photography, LLC.

▶ Figure 3.31 (*opposite*) Detail showing connection of steel beams to masonry wall. Photo Credit: Anice Hoachlander, Hoachlander Davis Photography, LLC.

◀ Figure 3.32 a–b (*opposite*)
Load bearing masonry walls with interior non load-bearing wallboard wall. Photo Credit: Anice Hoachlander, Hoachlander Davis Photography, LLC.

▲ Figure 3.33 Historic interior showing original heavy timber floor framing which was removed. Photo Credit: Anice Hoachlander, Hoachlander Davis Photography, LLC.

UNIT DERWIN BY STUDIO27ARCHITECTURE

In Unit Derwin, the original cast-in-place concrete columns and beams were uncovered and left exposed.

◄ **Figure** 3.34 Interior view of bath showing existing exposed concrete column. **Photo Credit: Anice Hoachlander, Hoachlander Davis Photography, LLC.**

▲ **Figure** 3.35 Interior view of living area. **Photo Credit: Anice Hoachlander, Hoachlander Davis Photography, LLC.**

▲ Figure 3.36 Interior of living space showing existing concrete beam.
Photo Credit: Anice Hoachlander, Hoachlander Davis Photography, LLC.

▶ Figure 3.37 Interior view of home office showing
concrete column and beam. Photo Credit: Anice
Hoachlander, Hoachlander Davis Photography, LLC.

DC NAVIGATORS BY RTKL

The architects of the DC Navigator building retained the original cast iron columns and wood beams. Wooden girders and beams as well as the underside of the flooring above were painted white and used as a ceiling for the space.

▲ Figure 3.38 Interior of work space which includes existing cast iron columns with heavy timber beams and exposed mechanical. Historic wood flooring and brick wall are also retained.

◄ Figure 3.39 Detail of cast iron columns with heavy timber beam. View also shows the underside of the wood beams above and underside of wood decking.

75

▶ Figure 3.40 (*this page*) Detail showing the integration of the exposed mechanical system with the existing structure and incorporation of a new curved wall (non-load-bearing).

◀ Figure 3.41 (*opposite, left*) View of existing load bearing masonry wall supporting steel beam with wood decking and new ½ wall partitions to define the space.

◀ Figure 3.42 (*opposite, right*) Existing brick bearing wall with salvaged wood partition and lowered wallboard soffit.

KEY TERMS

adobe	heavy timber frame
agriboard	live load
balloon framing	masonry
bamboo	mortise and tenon and pegged
bearing wall	platform framing
bending	rammed earth
cob	sandbag
column and beam	shear
compressive	SIPs
concentrated load	static load
cord wood	straw bale
dead load	structural frame
dynamic load	stud wall
earth sheltered	tensile
equilibrium	uniform load
gabion	

ASSIGNMENTS/EXERCISES

1. Construct a model of one of the structural systems discussed in this chapter at 1" = 1'-0". Pay particular attention as to what is needed to make the system stand up, support its own weight, and keep from racking. How are windows and doors framed in? You will need to do necessary background research to succeed. When built, your structure should be able to support the weight of one brick in addition to its own dead loads.

2. Research at least one of the alternative building systems in this chapter. How is this system addressed in the International Building Code? If it is not addressed, how would you go about proving that it meets code requirement equivalents?

RESOURCES

www.ncidq.org/who/definition.htm. Retreived February 15, 2008.

www.asid.org/find/What+Does+an+Interior+Designer+Do.htm. Retreived February 15, 2008.

www.iida.org/i4a/pages/index.cfm?pageid=379. Retreived February 15, 2008.

Structures terminology and design basics:

R. E. Schaeffer. *Elementary Structures for Architects and Builders* 3rd ed. Columbus, Ohio: Prentice Hall, 2002.

Alternative Building Systems:

Elizabeth, Lynne and Adams, Cassandra. *Alternative Construction: Contemporary Natural Building Methods*. New York: John Wiley and Sons, 2000.

An excellent source of information on alternative building techniques is www.greenhomebuilding.com.

CHAPTER 4

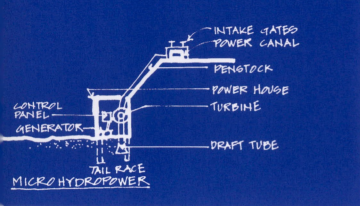

INTAKE GATES
POWER CANAL
PENSTOCK
POWER HOUSE
TURBINE
CONTROL PANEL
GENERATOR
DRAFT TUBE
TAIL RACE
MICRO HYDROPOWER

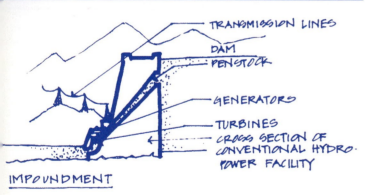

TRANSMISSION LINES
DAM
PENSTOCK
GENERATORS
TURBINES
CROSS SECTION OF CONVENTIONAL HYDRO-POWER FACILITY

IMPOUNDMENT

Mechanical Systems

In our search of comfort, convenience, and material wealth, we have begun to sacrifice not only our own health, but also the health of all species. We are starting to exhaust the capacity of the very systems that sustain us, and now we must deal with the consequences.

Sim van der Ryn and Stuart Cowan, Ecological Design

OBJECTIVES

- Identify sustainable forms of power
- Compare heating systems and cooling methods
- Understand system commissioning
- Identify issues of human comfort with regard to HVAC

INTRODUCTION

Both mechanical and electrical systems require power to operate. The energy used to generate this power comes from several sources, some of which are sustainable, and many of which ultimately are not. The U.S. Department of Energy acknowledges the following energy sources: bioenergy, coal, electric power, fossil fuels, fusion, geothermal, hydrogen, hydropower, natural gas, nuclear, oil, renewables, solar, and wind. These sources can be subdivided into those that fall under the Renewable Energy/Biomass program, and those that do not.

SOURCES OF FUEL

Bioenergy is produced from organic matter such as corn, municipal waste, and wood. In theory, these resources are renewable, but additional energy is required for their production. Furthermore, the recent emphasis on bio-diesel from corn has led to higher prices and concerns over the sustainability of growing corn itself because of intense reliance on petroleum-based fertilizers.

Fossil fuels provide over 85 percent of the fuel for electricity in the United States. These consist of oil, coal, and natural gas. All fossil fuels are finite in quantity and are associated with greenhouse gases.

Coal is a naturally occurring element that can be mined either through underground mining operations or strip mining. Although coal is abundant in some parts of the world, it takes millions of years to form. After this resource has been tapped, it will take millennia to reconstitute. Coal has been long associated with pollution (mercury, nitrogen, and sulfur) and greenhouse gases. New programs are being created to capture these gases as well as to make mining a safer occupation for miners. According to some researchers, this technology will not be resolved until 2030, and by this time, it will be too late with regard to greenhouse gas emissions and global warming (www.architecture2030.org).

Oil, like natural gas and coal, is a fossil fuel and is largely dependent on foreign sources, particularly those located in the Middle East. According to the DOE, in 2007, oil was used in 99 percent of vehicles and represented 40 percent of current energy use in the United States.

Natural gas is a fossil fuel used for some alternative-fuel vehicles and is touted as clean burning.

Hydrogen is a commonly occurring element in the world. Developers of hydrogen technologies seek to reduce U.S. dependence on foreign oil. Hydrogen can be made from fossil fuels and renewable sources such as wind, geothermal, and solar. No emissions result from hydrogen-fueled vehicles.

Nuclear energy has long been the subject of debate in the United States. The primary reason is that radioactive material is produced and must then be stored for millions of years. The DOE is currently working to make nuclear energy a viable, competitive, and environmentally sound choice. A major concern associated with nuclear energy is the possibility of a reactor meltdown and leakage of radioactive materials into the surrounding area.

Renewables are energy sources that are not limited, and can be constantly refreshed. These include solar power, wind power, hydropower, and geothermal sources.

Wind turbines are placed on the landscape to capture the prevailing winds and convert that to energy in the form of electricity. Now commonly used in some parts of the country, the primary concern for environmental advocates is danger to birds.

Hydropower (also called hydroelectric power) is generated by water and is, therefore, a renewable energy source. According to the DOE, researchers are looking for ways to reduce the environmental impact of this power source that has the current capacity to produce the equivalent energy to 500 barrels of oil. The environmental impact associated with hydropower includes the damming of large bodies of water and the subsequent destruction of adjacent land through flooding, as well as the potential for dam breaks and flooding.

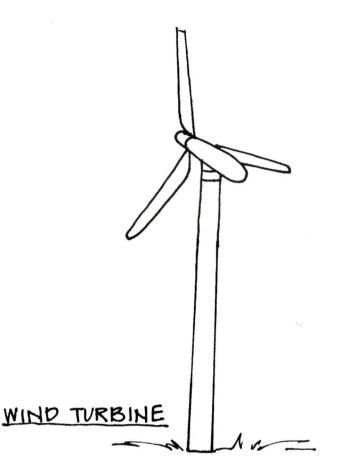

WIND TURBINE

Figure 4.1 Sketch of wind turbine.

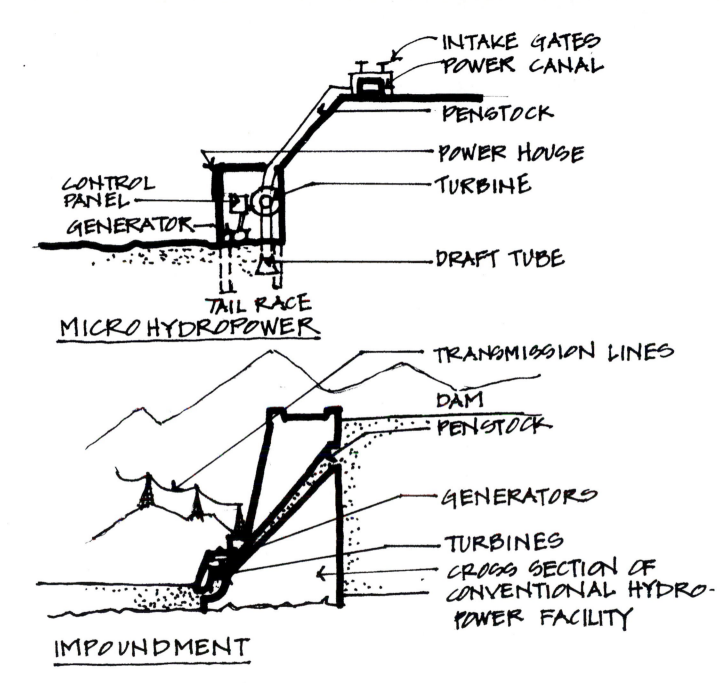

INTAKE GATES
POWER CANAL
PENSTOCK
POWER HOUSE
TURBINE
DRAFT TUBE

CONTROL PANEL
GENERATOR
TAIL RACE

MICRO HYDROPOWER

TRANSMISSION LINES
DAM
PENSTOCK
GENERATORS
TURBINES
CROSS SECTION OF CONVENTIONAL HYDRO-POWER FACILITY

IMPOUNDMENT

Figure 4.2 Two types of hydropower systems.

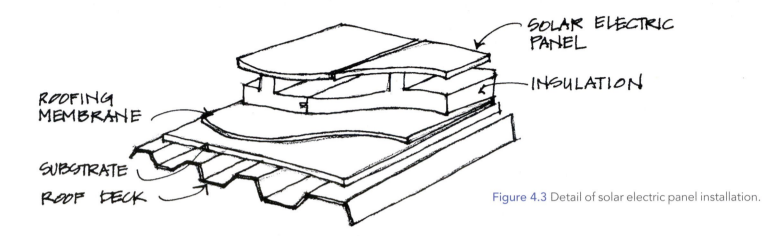

SOLAR ELECTRIC PANEL

INSULATION

ROOFING MEMBRANE

SUBSTRATE

ROOF DECK

Figure 4.3 Detail of solar electric panel installation.

Solar energy comes from the sun. Several methods for capturing this energy exist including photovoltaic cells and solar panels. Solar energy can be stored in batteries and used to generate electricity and heat water for buildings. The primary drawbacks of solar energy include the high cost of collection cells, the use of batteries, and the use of cadmium in photo cells.

Geothermal is an expensive though truly renewable resource. Strategies for geothermal heat range from deep penetration to molten rock through shallow ground water solutions. Geothermal systems rely on the natural heat and cooling of the earth to provide energy. The advantages of geothermal systems include: elimination of boiler and heat rejector installation, operation and maintenance, elimination of all outdoor equipment, elimination of water loop temperature controls, reduced mechanical room size, and increased energy efficiency (Liu, 2007).

Electric power can be made in many different ways. According to the U.S. Department of Energy, over half of it is currently produced with coal. The fastest growing fuel source is natural gas. Similar to coal, natural gas is a fossil fuel and is, therefore, ultimately in limited supply.

Fusion-produced energy is a current area of research as is plasma research. The DOE is exploring both as possible energy sources for the future.

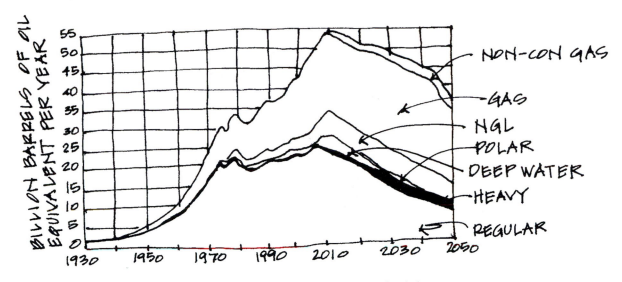

Figure 4.4 Peak oil chart.

FUEL CONSIDERATIONS

The choice of fuels must be tempered by a variety of concerns including cost, availability, and environmental impact. The majority of scientists agree that greenhouse gas emissions as the result of burning various fossil fuel sources has led to global warming. Many scientists also submit that we have reached the point where our consumption of oil is outpacing our ability to extract it from the earth, otherwise known as peak oil. According to these scientists, our availability of oil will continue to decline from this point forward. Coupled with this is the fact that the major sources of oil production are located in the Middle East, a politically unstable area for the United States. Nuclear fuel poses its own set of issues related to the disposal and containment of nuclear waste that is radioactive for millions of years. Communities across the world oppose either the use of or disposal of nuclear waste.

MECHANICAL SYSTEMS

When power is produced from the different fuel sources, it can be used to power various types of mechanical systems. The common term for interior heating and air systems is **HVAC** (heating, ventilation and air conditioning). The goal of HVAC systems is to provide for human comfort, and several different systems exist.

HUMAN COMFORT

Human comfort varies from culture to culture as well as person to person. Some people can tolerate more extreme temperatures than others. In the United States, most have come to expect interior spaces that have a fairly consistent interior temperature. How comfort is experienced is the result of a couple of factors including temperature and relative humidity. Most can tolerate higher temperatures if the relative humidity is lower. A **psychrometric chart** relates several variables—dew point, wet bulb temperature, dry bulb temperature, and relative humidity—to demonstrate what is generally accepted as the comfort zone for most people.

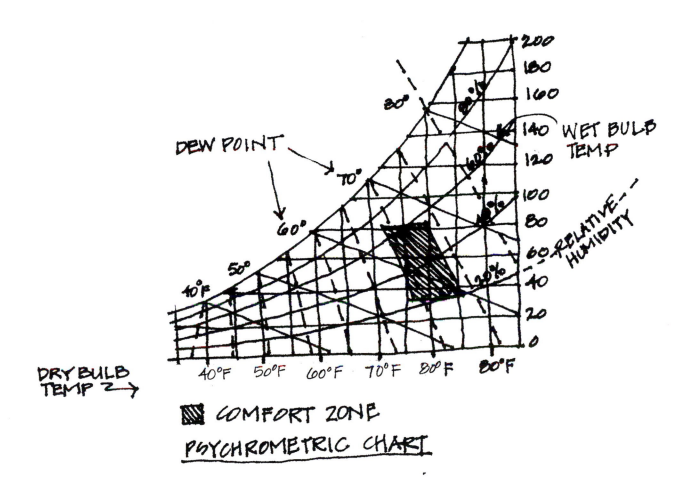

Figure 4.5 Psychrometric chart showing comfort zone.

Creating these conditions in many areas of the world requires mechanical treatment of the air. These mechanical treatments are divided into heating and cooling, and rely on the following methods of heat transfer: evaporation, radiation, convection, and conduction. Evaporation occurs when air moves across a wet surface causing moisture to turn to vapor. An example of this would be standing in front of a fan after jogging a mile and sweating. When a warm body gives off heat this is called radiation. The car engine that has been driven recently radiates heat. Convection involves the movement of molecules. An example of this is the tendency of hot air to rise. Conduction occurs when two bodies are in direct contact. When stepping on a cold tile floor in the middle of winter, heat is conducted from the foot to the cold tile, making the feet become cold.

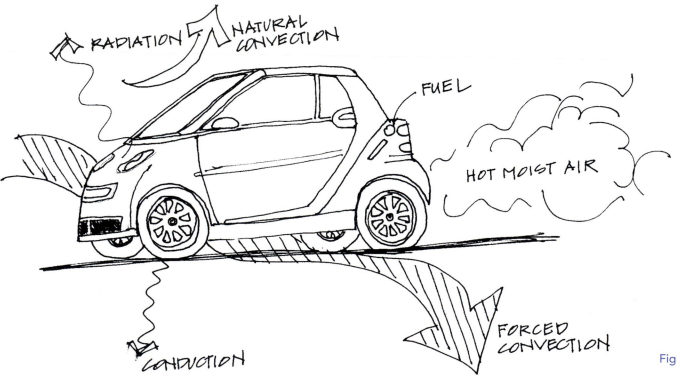

Figure 4.6 Heat exchange sketch.

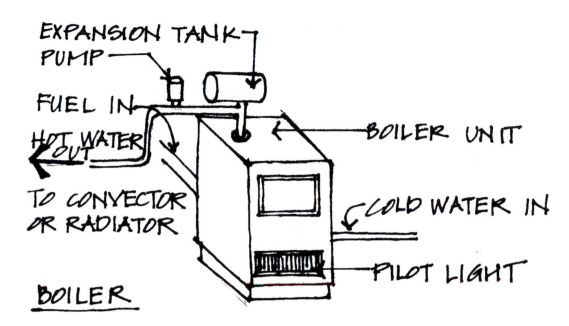

EXPANSION TANK

PUMP

FUEL IN

HOT WATER OUT

TO CONVECTOR OR RADIATOR

BOILER

BOILER UNIT

COLD WATER IN

PILOT LIGHT

Figure 4.7 Boiler sketch.

HEATING SYSTEMS

There are several types of heating systems, and all of them rely on the previously mentioned methods of heat transfer. In general, heating systems can be divided into those that use water (**hydronic** systems) and those that use air.

HYDRONIC SYSTEMS

Boilers are used to heat water to provide either hot water or steam for heat. The hot water or steam is piped through a building and delivered to various room units. This system is commonly used in large building and multi-building complexes. Boilers require expansion tanks for the water to expand, piping to and from unit radiators, and radiators. The hot water may also be used for other applications in the building.

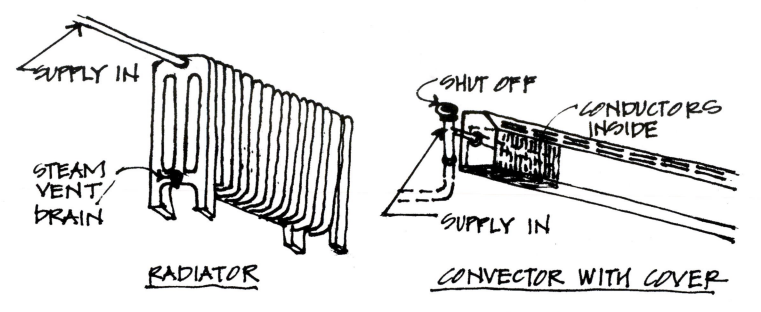

Figure 4.8 Two types of radiators.

Radiators can be divided into two types: steam and hot water. The use of steam radiators oc-curs primarily within historic buildings and has been largely replaced with hot water radiators. According to the DOE, hot water radiators systems are the next most common system after the heat pump in new residential construction in the United States.

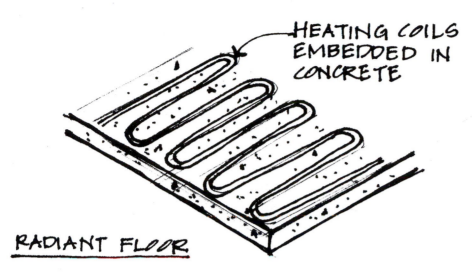

HEATING COILS
EMBEDDED IN
CONCRETE

RADIANT FLOOR

◀ Figure 4.9 Radiant floor with heating coils embedded in concrete.

▼ Figure 4.10 Hydronic radiant flooring system.

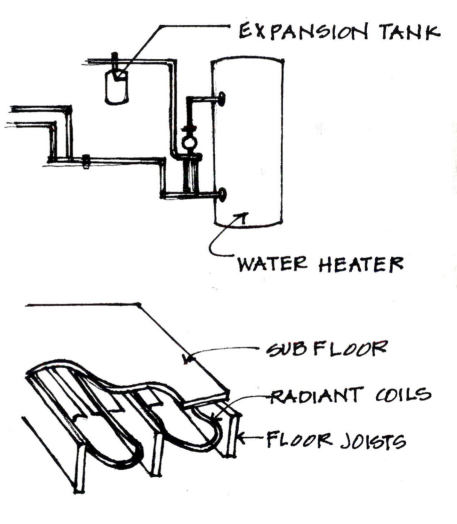

EXPANSION TANK

WATER HEATER

SUB FLOOR

RADIANT COILS

FLOOR JOISTS

ELECTRIC SYSTEMS

Radiant heating relies on heating surfaces of a space—wall, floor, or ceiling. The two primary types of radiant systems include radiant panels and radiant floors. In both systems, heat can be provided using either electricity or hot water. Radiant panels consist of aluminum that is heated using one of these two sources. Similarly, radiant floor systems incorporate either electric cables, or water piping through which heat is distributed to the floor.

Chapter 4: *Mechanical Systems* / 91

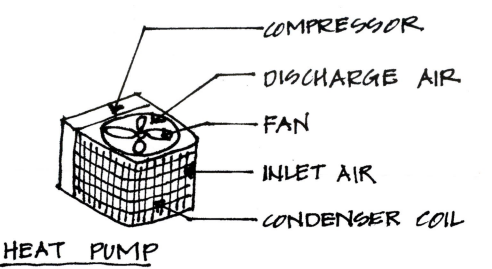

COMPRESSOR

DISCHARGE AIR

FAN

INLET AIR

CONDENSER COIL

HEAT PUMP

Figure 4.11 Sketch of heat pump.

Forced air is the most common system installed within new residential construction. Using outside air, the heat pump moves warm air through the interior in the winter months and reverses to push in cool air during the summer months. Air source pumps are the most common, although other types of systems also exist, such as the ground source heat pump. The ground source heat pump is much more efficient, but it is expensive to install.

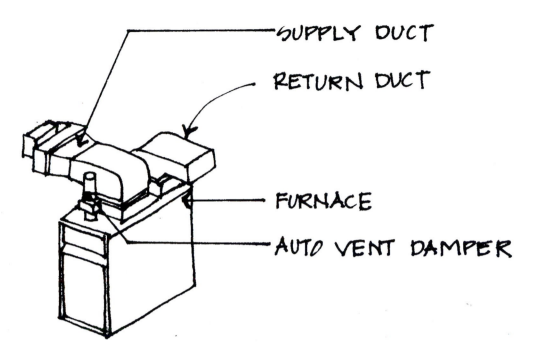

SUPPLY DUCT

RETURN DUCT

FURNACE

AUTO VENT DAMPER

FURNACE

▲ Figure 4.12 Sketch of furnace.

▼ Figure 4.13 Baseboard radiator.

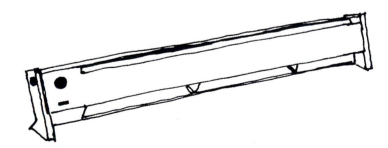

Furnaces are used to heat air that is then distributed through the building using ductwork. If fossil fuels are used to heat the air, a chimney flue is required to vent the gasses to the outside. These contain a pilot light for continuous operation. Depending on the specifics of the system, these can either be inefficient or highly efficient.

Electric resistance is a type of system that uses electricity to produce heat. The electricity itself can be produced from a variety of fuels. Because of the inefficiency of this process, electric heat is expensive. Delivery methods for this form of heat include both forced air systems and individual room units.

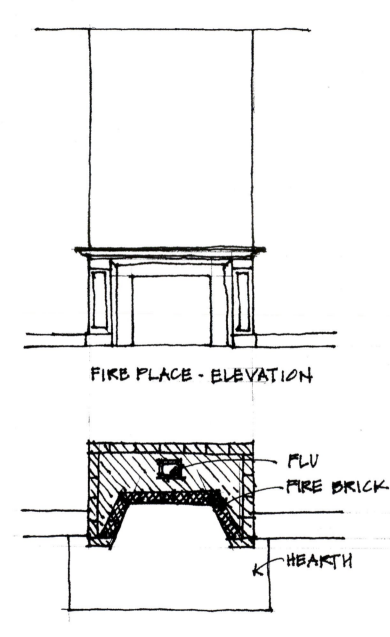

FIRE PLACE · ELEVATION

FLU
FIRE BRICK
HEARTH

EXTERIOR END CHIMNEY
PLAN

HEAT PUMP
(see forced air)

WOOD SYSTEMS

Wood stoves/fireplaces have traditionally been used as a source of heating for historic buildings (prior to coal and electricity) as well as for off-the-grid buildings. Today, it is possible to purchase high-efficiency wood-burning stoves that include catalytic converters that burn the combustible gases, thus reducing the resultant air pollution. Masonry stoves provide **thermal mass** thus adding to the indoor heat that is then radiated into the space. Thermal mass is the capacity of a body to store heat. Inserts can also be purchased to retrofit existing fireplaces.

Figure 4.14 Wood burning fireplace.

Pellet stoves use wood pellets as fuel and are traditionally more efficient than other wood-burning systems. These can also be either freestanding or in the form of a fireplace insert. As with other wood systems, a chimney is required.

Figure 4.15 Wood pellet stove.

GEOTHERMAL SYSTEMS

Ground Loop Heat Pump Systems

These systems use either water or antifreeze that circulates through a closed loop. The pipe loop works as a heat exchanger and can be located either horizontally or vertically. Commercial systems often use vertical placement because of lot size restrictions. A horizontal placement is located three to six feet below grade whereas the vertical loop might go as deep as 300 feet.

Surface Water Heat Pump Systems

In the surface water system, the heat exchanger loop is located a minimum of ten feet beneath a body of water and is considered to be the most cost effective system.

Groundwater Heat Pump Systems

Water pumped from a well is used for the groundwater system. These are divided into three types: open systems, closed loop systems, and standing column systems. The advantage of these systems is that they can be very cost effective.

Hybrid Geothermal Systems

The hybrid system combines geothermal with conventional heat rejectors. This system is both highly efficient and cost effective (Liu, 2007).

COOLING SYSTEMS

Cooling can be provided to a space in three basic ways: avoid heat gain, passive cooling strategies, and mechanical cooling. A heat avoidance strategy involves how the building is sited to take advantage of prevailing winds, avoid direct sunlight, and allow for breezes. Several strategies have been adopted in different parts of the world to take advantage of **passive cooling**. Examples of passive cooling measures include front porches, wrap around porches, towers for ventilation of hot air, central stair halls that are vented at the top, and the use of jalousie, hopper, or casement windows to direct breezes.

TYPES OF MECHANICAL COOLING SYSTEMS

Heat Pump (see forced air)

There are several types of cooling systems, including central station systems, split systems, packaged units, and through wall systems.

Large buildings commonly use a central station system. The unit itself can be placed in the basement, on the roof, or split between these two locations.

A split system is more commonly used in smaller buildings, including some residential applications. In this type of application, the compressor and condenser coil are located outside in a unit whereas the evaporator coil and air handler is indoors.

A packaged unit is generally placed on the roof with one unit for each zone. Air is provided to interior spaces through a series of ducts.

A through wall unit has the evaporator coil and fan on the inside, and a condenser coil, fan, and compressor on the outside. These are frequently found in residential and hotel applications, and tend to service a single room.

Many interior spaces require air treatment in the form of either humidifying or dehumidifying. In humid parts of the country, dehumidification will reduce the perceived temperature during the summer months. Similarly, more humidity might be introduced during the winter for temperature increase and to reduce static electricity that is generated by really dry air conditions.

COMMISSIONING

The best and most efficient systems can be specified and installed, yet if they are not working the way they are intended to, energy can be wasted and the benefits of these systems nullified. **Commissioning** refers to the process by which all new equipment is checked to make sure it is working according to manufacturer recommendations. Quality assurance activities include checking shop drawings, demonstrating the equipment, training owner personnel, testing, adjusting and balancing HVAC, and commissioning. All of these cost money and an owner might question why such activities are required. Basic commissioning is now a prerequisite in the LEED Green Building Rating System. Points are awarded for commissioning under both the Green Globes Rating System and the LEED Green Building Rating System (McClendon, 2008).

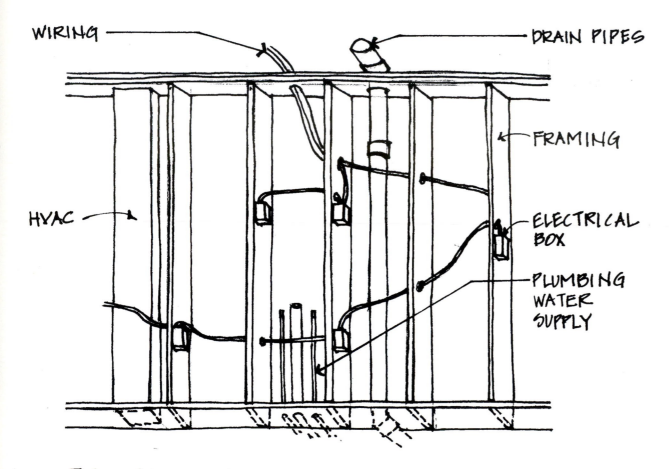

WIRING — DRAIN PIPES

FRAMING

HVAC

ELECTRICAL BOX

PLUMBING WATER SUPPLY

TYPICAL MECHANICAL SYSTEMS

Figure 4.16
Typical mechanical system integration in a wall.

IMPACTS TO INTERIOR DESIGN

Generally speaking, an interior designer does not get involved with the design of the mechanical systems; however, the placement of ducts, registers, and returns are an integrated part of the design of interior space. Coordination of these items with light fixtures, sprinkler heads, ceiling mounted equipment such as projectors and screens, smoke detectors, and ceiling design details ensure that the design intent and functional properties of the space will be realized. The designer might also be involved in locating the thermostat for a system. These are generally mounted 44 to 48 inches above the finished floor. Space must also be allotted for mechanical equipment and HVAC mixing boxes that are used to adjust the amount of air and temperature going into the space from the main supply source. These are connected to the thermostat.

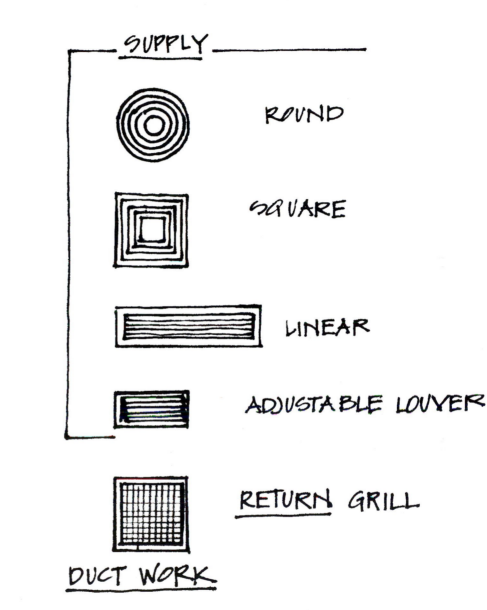

Figure 4.17
HVAC symbols for reflected ceiling plans.

KEY TERMS

bioenergy	hydrogen
boilers	hydronic
central station system	hydropower
coal	oil
commissioning	natural gas
conduction	nuclear energy
convection	passive cooling
dehumidifying	packaged unit
electric power	pellet stove
electric resistance	psychrometric chart
evaporation	radiant heat
forced air	radiation
fossil fuel	radiators
furnace	renewables
fusion	solar
geothermal	split system
heat pump	thermal mass
humidifying	through wall unit
HVAC	wind

ASSIGNMENTS/EXERCISES

1. Go to the Architecture 2030 website (www.architecture2030.org) and view each of the videos. What did you learn? What surprised you? What can you do?

2. The power of one: Assume a new practice in your life today that will make a difference in the world. Examples: lower your heat five degrees, or raise your air conditioning five degrees. Consider opening the windows instead of using AC. Walk to class.

3. Go to www.carbonfootprint.com and calculate your carbon footprint.

4. Go to www.earthday.net/footprint/ and reflect on your ecological footprint.

RESOURCES

U.S. Department of Energy (DOE) website, www.energy.gov/

Liu, X. (2007). "Providing 'Green' Solutions with Geothermal Applications." *Architech*, September 2007, 1–6.

McClendon, S. (2008)." What Architects Need to Know About HVAC Commissioning, Retrocommissioning, and Recommissioning." *Archi-Tech*, September 2008, 51–55.

Excellent video clips on the environmental impacts of fossil fuel use can be found at the Architecture 2030 website (www.architecture2030.org).

CHAPTER 5

Electrical Systems and Lighting

⊖— SINGLE RECEPTACLE OUTLET

⊖— DUPLEX OUTLET

⊕— DOUBLE DUPLEX OUTLET

WP ⊖— WATERPROOF OUTLET

GFCI ⊖— GROUND FAULT CIRCUIT

⊕≡ TRIPLEX OUTLET

D ⊖≡ DRYER OUTLET

R ⊖≡ RANGE OUTLET

DW △ SPECIAL PURPOSE OUTLET

◉ FLOOR OUTLET

ⓒ CLOCK OUTLET

ⓕ FAN OUTLET

⊡ FLOOR DUPLEX OUTLET

↦ BRANCH CIRCUIT

╫ THREE-WIRE RACEWAY

╫ FOUR-WIRE RACEWAY

—— CONCEALED WIRING (WALL/CEILING)

- - - - " " (FLOOR)

- - - - EXPOSED WIRING

—• WIRING TURNED UP

—○ WIRING TURNED DOWN

⌒ SWITCH LEG

ⓣ THERMOSTAT

Ⓣⱽ TV OUTLET

For example, the fully informed consumer, armed with least-cost reasoning, would certainly choose to buy compact fluorescent lightbulbs that have lower lifetime costs than incandescent bulbs. But the same narrow economic rationality would cause that consumer to refuse to pay higher utility costs to clean up nuclear wastes and decommission reactors used to generate that electricity that is used with greater efficiency.

David Orr, Earth in Mind

OBJECTIVES

- Design an effective lighting solution
- Compare lamp types and their appropriate uses in an interior
- Identify lamps and fixture types
- Draw a reflected ceiling plan

INTRODUCTION

Power companies provide electricity for most buildings. This electricity can be generated by several sources, as mentioned in the previous chapter in the discussion of fuel sources. The single biggest source of energy use in a building is for electric lighting. Thus this chapter presents basic principles of electricity and electric lighting.

ELECTRICITY

Electricity travels from the utility company to the user through a combination of overhead and underground electrical lines. Transformers are used to step down the electrical current to specific locations and for specific uses. Most residences in the United States use a single phase, three-wire system with 120 volt and 240 volt service. The majority of outlets use 120 volts, although some appliances and air conditioning units require the higher voltage, 240 volts. A 120/208 volt, three-phase, four-wire system is what is used by the majority of commercial buildings.

Electrical power travels across electrical lines to a point of entry at each building it serves. A service drop is used to connect overhead electrical lines to a building. A metal conduit runs the electrical line through a meter that reports power usage to the utility company. The entire system must be grounded to avoid electrical shock and fire. From the meter, electrical lines are run directly to a panel board in residential projects. In larger projects, the electrical lines will first pass through a service switch that can be used to disconnect service to the entire building.

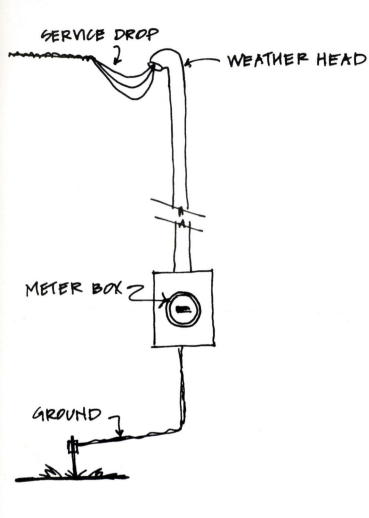

SERVICE DROP

WEATHER HEAD

METER BOX

GROUND

COMPONENTS OF ELECTRICAL SYSTEMS

Connection to Building

Electrical power is typically connected to a building using a drop head. The power line is then run through an exterior meter (which must be grounded) and then into the interior electrical panel.

◀ Figure 5.1 Residential electric.

Cable Types

Several types of cable are available depending on the use. Commercial electrical power requires hard conduit, whereas romex flexible cable can be used residentially as long as it is enclosed.

▼ Figure 5.2 Small commercial electric.

INSULATED SHEATH

HIGH CAPACITY TELEPHONE DATA

COPPER CORE

COAXIAL CABLE

GLASS-LINED

FIBER OPTIC CABLE

METAL   GROUND

ARMORED BX CABLE

PVC
COPPER GROUND

ROMEX

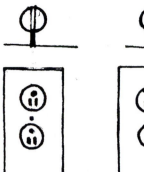

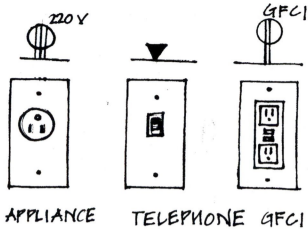
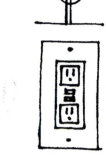

**15 AMP
DUPLEX**

**20 AMP
DUPLEX**

APPLIANCE

TELEPHONE GFCI

120 V

120 V

240 V

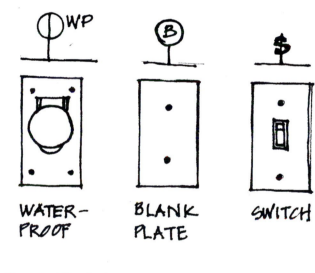
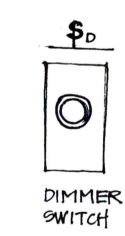

**WATER-
PROOF**

**BLANK
PLATE**

SWITCH

**DIMMER
SWITCH**

Electrical Symbols

Designers use common electrical symbols on
electrical plans, and need to understand them
to read plans from subcontractors.

Figure 5.3a Large commercial electric.

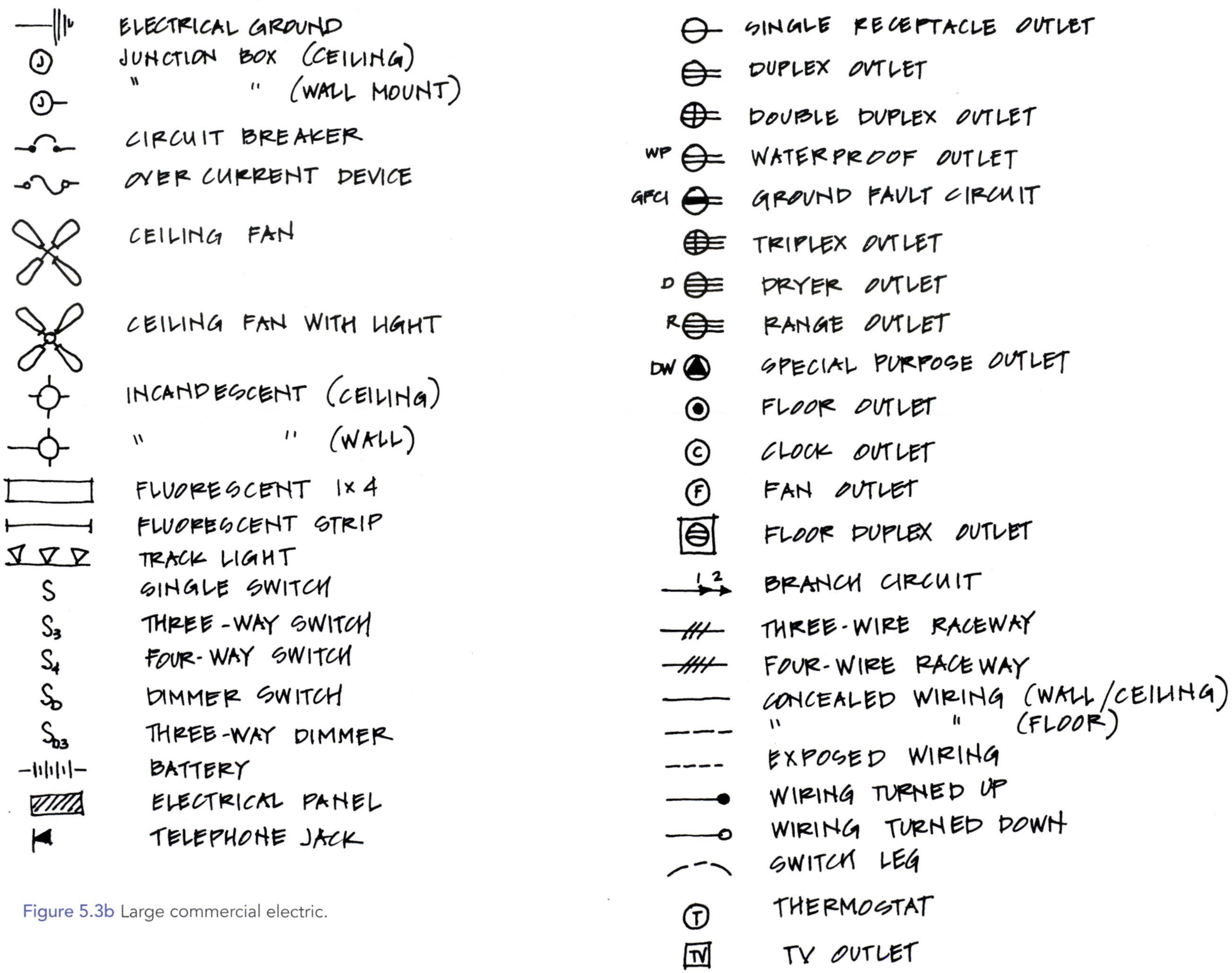

—‖‖‖	ELECTRICAL GROUND
J	JUNCTION BOX (CEILING)
J	" " (WALL MOUNT)
⌣	CIRCUIT BREAKER
⌣	OVER CURRENT DEVICE
✕	CEILING FAN
✕	CEILING FAN WITH LIGHT
⊕	INCANDESCENT (CEILING)
⊕	" " (WALL)
▭	FLUORESCENT 1×4
▭	FLUORESCENT STRIP
▽▽▽	TRACK LIGHT
S	SINGLE SWITCH
S₃	THREE-WAY SWITCH
S₄	FOUR-WAY SWITCH
S_D	DIMMER SWITCH
S_D3	THREE-WAY DIMMER
—‖‖‖—	BATTERY
▨	ELECTRICAL PANEL
◄	TELEPHONE JACK

⊖	SINGLE RECEPTACLE OUTLET
⊖	DUPLEX OUTLET
⊕	DOUBLE DUPLEX OUTLET
WP ⊖	WATERPROOF OUTLET
GFCI ⊖	GROUND FAULT CIRCUIT
⊕	TRIPLEX OUTLET
D ⊜	DRYER OUTLET
R ⊜	RANGE OUTLET
DW ▲	SPECIAL PURPOSE OUTLET
⊙	FLOOR OUTLET
C	CLOCK OUTLET
F	FAN OUTLET
⊟	FLOOR DUPLEX OUTLET
→1 2	BRANCH CIRCUIT
—⫽⫽—	THREE-WIRE RACEWAY
—⫽⫽—	FOUR-WIRE RACEWAY
———	CONCEALED WIRING (WALL/CEILING)
- - - -	" " (FLOOR)
- - - -	EXPOSED WIRING
—●	WIRING TURNED UP
—○	WIRING TURNED DOWN
⌒	SWITCH LEG
T	THERMOSTAT
TV	TV OUTLET

Figure 5.3b Large commercial electric.

ENERGY MANAGEMENT DEVICES

The use of energy can be managed in several ways. Current estimates indicate that the United States uses about 2 trillion kWh of electricity per year. Of this, approximately 25 percent goes to building energy systems (primarily lighting, heating, and air). According to the Energy Administration, 86 percent of our energy in the United States is generated by fossil fuels (natural gas, coal, and petroleum). Approximately 47 percent of all energy in a residence goes to heating. In a commercial application, 32 percent is used for heating and an additional 23 percent is used in artificial lighting. The most basic way to control energy use is to keep buildings well-insulated and lower the thermostat temperature. Lighting control devices also contribute significantly to energy use reduction. Motion sensors and daylight sensors are commonly used to provide artificial lighting only when a space is occupied or when day lighting is insufficient. Dual switching options for rooms are another way to reduce energy towards artificial lighting. Allowing **fixtures** closest to the windows to be switched off during peak daylight hours reduces reliance on artificial lighting. Operable windows can allow for reduced use of heating and air conditioning in some parts of the country during moderate weather.

INTERIOR DESIGN IMPLICATIONS

The single most potent impact an interior designer can have on the energy efficiency and the ultimate sustainability of a building is through good lighting design. One of the most common mistakes made in a space is to over light. By calculating the actual number of fixtures needed, the number of fixtures can usually be reduced. By accounting for day lighting within a space through the use of separately switched fixtures, energy use can be significantly reduced. The use of day-light enhancing devices such as light shelves can also reduce the overall energy load of the building. The less lighting used, the less air conditioning needed because lighting creates one of the biggest heat loads in an interior.

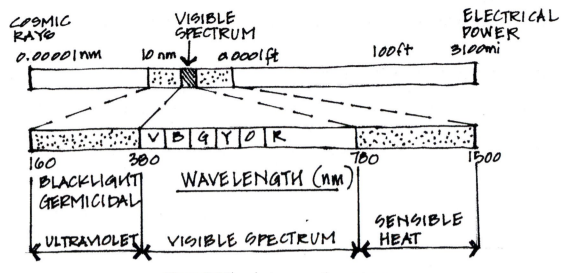

Figure 5.4 The electromagnetic spectrum.

LIGHTING

What is light? Light is defined as the visible part of the electromagnetic spectrum. It is a form of energy that is visible to the human eye. Light does not contain color; rather, the color is a function of the light energy being reflected off of different surfaces.

Man has sought to produce artificial light since fire was first used within a man-made environment. Firelight was first supplemented with candlelight. Gas and oil lamps were invented, and finally electrical lamps became readily available in the early twentieth century. It is interesting to note that all artificial light sources—incandescent, fluorescent, and high-intensity discharge (HID)—were originally used as outdoor sources and were only later brought into the interior environment.

Why is the study of artificial lighting important to interior design? There are two primary reasons why an interior designer needs to understand and master artificial lighting. The first is that lighting affects the health and welfare of people. The second is because bad lighting can ruin even the best interior design. Lighting is a critical element of the design process. Mastery over how it works is crucial for creating a good design. To be a competent interior design professional, knowledge of lighting is required.

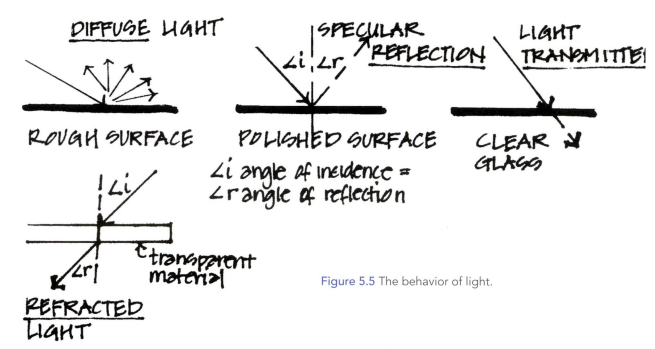

Figure 5.5 The behavior of light.

BEHAVIOR OF LIGHTING

As electromagnetic waves, lighting reacts in various ways when it meets a solid surface. Depending on the material of the surface, the light may be reflected, refracted, transmitted, diffused, or some combination of these outcomes.

PSYCHOLOGY OF LIGHTING

John Flynn, a noted environmental psychologist, completed some of the earliest studies of the effects of lighting on people. His research demonstrated how people perceive different levels and types of lighting. Specifically, he sought to explain what types of lighting levels result in the perception of public space versus private space. Similarly, he tried to explain perceptions of warmth and coolness based on color temperature of the artificial lighting in a space.

Perceptions of Public/Private

How lighting is distributed within a space affects how people view that space. Shadows in the corners combined with high contrast tends to create a space that is perceived as private or intimate, whereas an overly lit room with little to no contrast in light level creates a public and open feeling.

Cool versus Warm

The color temperature of light and the colors used within a space affect whether the space feels cool or warm. People tend to perceive warmer light sources (incandescent) and warmer color palettes as warmer. By contrast, the use of cool light sources (fluorescent) combined with blue, for example, will be perceived as cooler though the actual temperature of the rooms may be identical.

Health and Lighting

Several research studies have been conducted to assess the impact of lighting on humans. Good lighting has been associated with increased worker performance. Control over light levels correlates with higher employee satisfaction. Research demonstrates that daylight within classrooms increased test performance among children. Other studies have indicated that shift workers are at an increased risk of serious diseases such as cancer. The apparent cause of this is disruption to the natural circadian rhythm within the human body. The human body responded to light levels in the environment through a complex series of chemical changes within the body. People who work all night and do not have "normal" exposure to sunlight can suffer the consequences of an upset circadian rhythm. Studies show that all living things—plants and animals—have some form of circadian rhythm and are impacted by light. Although all of the impacts of natural and artificial lighting have not been studied, several causes of discomfort can be identified and avoided through proper lighting design.

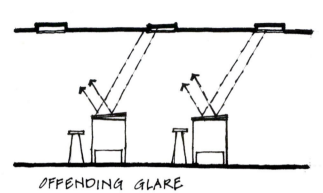

OFFENDING GLARE

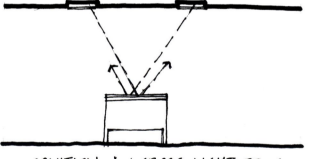

SOLUTION A : CROSS LIGHT FROM SIDES

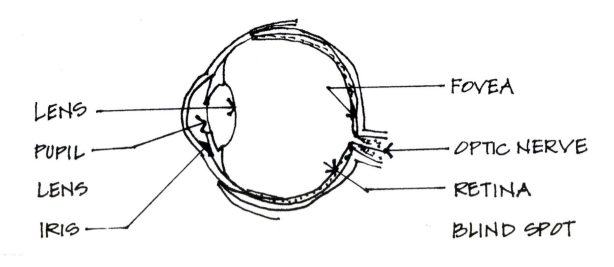

◄ Figure 5.6 Glare diagrams.

▲ Figure 5.7 The human eye.

Glare

Glare is created by an excessive amount of light coming from the wrong direction into people's eyes. For example, when an overhead fixture has a visible **lamp** that is within the line of sight, this is perceived as glare. This is termed *direct glare*. Indirect glare also causes visual discomfort. This problem frequently arises when a light source reflects on a computer screen or visual display terminal. Glare can be avoided through the careful placement of luminaires or by using diffusers.

The eye functions much like a camera. Images are transmitted via the parts of the eye to the optic nerve and then are perceived in the brain. The lens allows the eye to focus, and the iris expands and contracts much like the aperture on a camera, allowing more or less light in as needed. Because of the location of the optic nerve slightly off center at the back of the eyes, a blind spot is created. The brain compensates for this by filling in the information. This phenomenon also results in our ability to perceive depth.

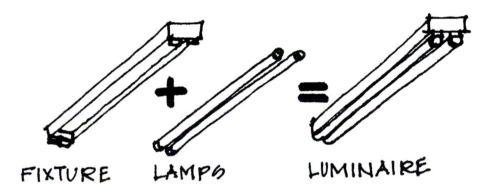

FIXTURE   LAMPS   LUMINAIRE

Figure 5.8 Fixture + Lamp(s) = Luminaire.

Proper Terminology

One of the first things to clarify when learning about lighting is that what is often called a light **bulb** is actually a lamp, and what is often called a lamp is in reality a fixture that holds a lamp. Together the lamp and fixture (plus a ballast and other items required to make a functioning light source) form a **luminaire**.

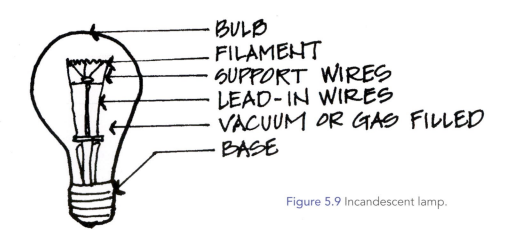

Figure 5.9 Incandescent lamp.

LAMPS AND THEIR APPROPRIATE APPLICATIONS/ENERGY IMPLICATIONS

Incandescent

The **incandescent** light source provides lighting for most homes in the western hemisphere, particularly in the United States. Only recently has this source come under severe scrutiny. Incandescent lighting is warm in appearance and is perceived by most westerners as a flattering source of artificial lighting. It is easily dimmed to create a variety of moods within a space. Although inexpensive to purchase, the incandescent lamp is very inefficient and gives off more heat than light. As a result, entire countries, such as Australia, have vowed to replace the incandescent lamp with compact fluorescent sources that are considerably more energy efficient. States, such as California, have introduced legislation to limit the use of the incandescent and require fluorescent lighting in some rooms of the house. The primary use of the incandescent lamps outside of residential applications is retail. The halogen lamp, a form of incandescent originally developed for slide projectors, is now commonly used in some restaurants and certain types of retail space—especially jewelry stores, boutiques, and other locations—to highlight specific merchandise or to create a specific mood.

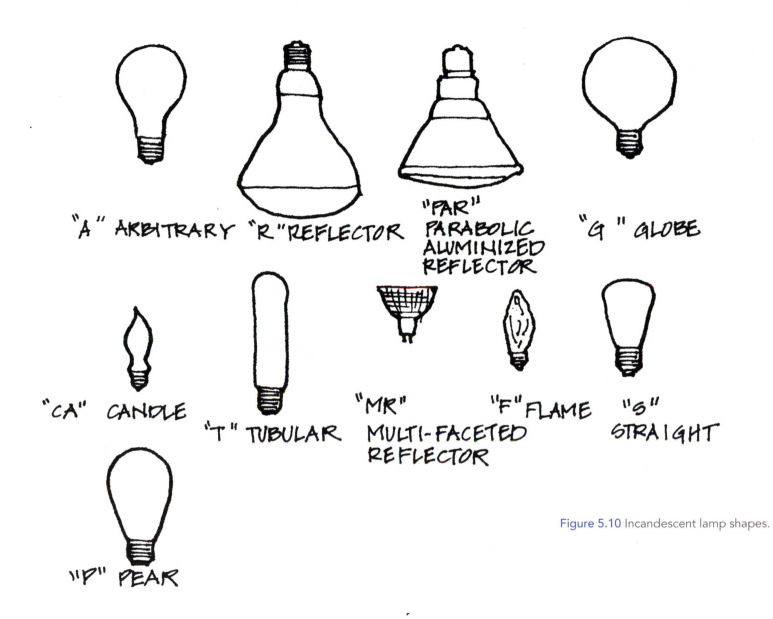

"A" ARBITRARY "R" REFLECTOR "PAR" PARABOLIC ALUMINIZED REFLECTOR "G" GLOBE

"CA" CANDLE "T" TUBULAR "MR" MULTI-FACETED REFLECTOR "F" FLAME "S" STRAIGHT

"P" PEAR

INCANDESCENT BULB SHAPES

Figure 5.10 Incandescent lamp shapes.

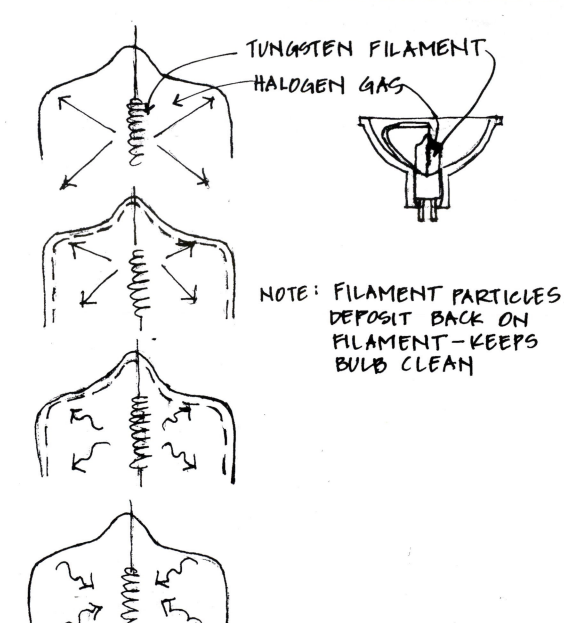

TUNGSTEN FILAMENT

HALOGEN GAS

NOTE: FILAMENT PARTICLES DEPOSIT BACK ON FILAMENT — KEEPS BULB CLEAN

Halogen

The **halogen** lamp is a form of incandescent. The first halogen lamp introduced into interior design was the MR-16 (multi-reflector $^{16}/_8$ inch, or 2 inches in diameter). The original purpose of the MR-16 consisted of projection. Its value to interiors derived from its ability to provide a strong focused beam of light particularly effective in illuminating display items and art work. Halogen light is much whiter than regular incandescent, though is still a warmer light than most fluorescent sources.

Figure 5.11 Halogen lamp.

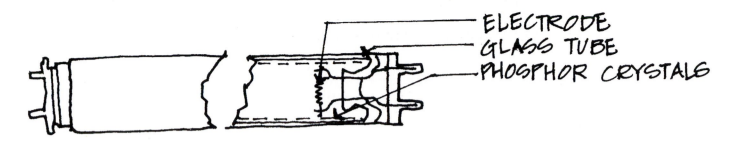

ELECTRODE
GLASS TUBE
PHOSPHOR CRYSTALS

FLUORESCENT

▲ Figure 5.12 Fluorescent lamp.

▼ Figure 5.13 Fluorescent lamp shapes.

Fluorescent

The majority of commercial spaces in the United States and Canada use **fluorescent** lighting sources. Fluorescent lamps provide an energy efficient, long-lasting, and economical choice for this type of application. Recent strides have been made in reducing the amount of mercury contained within fluorescent lamps as well as to improve the color temperature of the light source when a warmer light is preferred. High color temperatures and high color rendering indexes are possible with fluorescent sources, although the cost is also higher. Fluorescent lamps do introduce a couple of sustainability challenges. First, the disposal of the lamps introduces mercury into the landfill. Secondly, compact fluorescents include integrated ballasts within the lamp to allow for use within standard incandescent type fixtures. As a result, each time one is thrown away, the entire lamp and ballast enter into the waste stream.

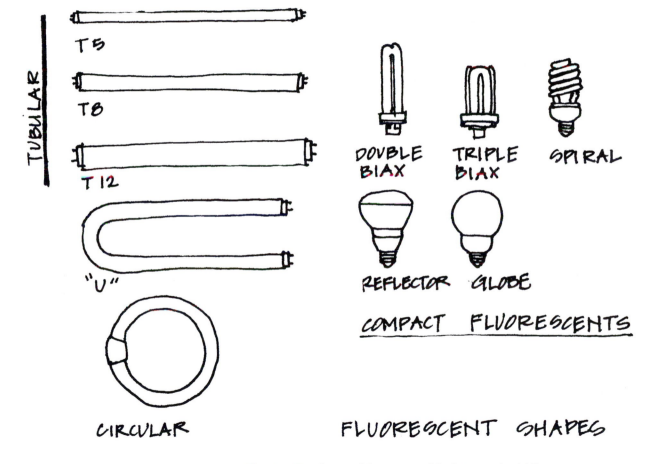

TUBULAR

T5

T8

T12

"U"

CIRCULAR

DOUBLE BIAX

TRIPLE BIAX

SPIRAL

REFLECTOR   GLOBE

COMPACT FLUORESCENTS

FLUORESCENT SHAPES

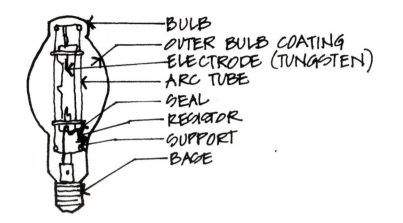

MERCURY

Figure 5.14a–b High-intensity discharge lamp.

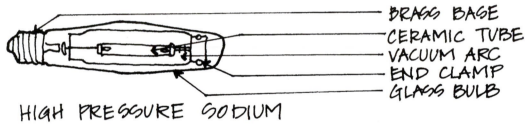

HIGH PRESSURE SODIUM

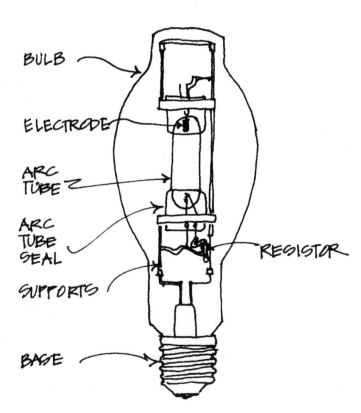

High Intensity Discharge (HID)

Traditionally, most types of **high intensity discharge (HID)** lamps have been used in outdoor applications such as street lighting, roadway lighting, and landscape lighting. Parking garages and factories exemplify the only interior applications of these sources, with the exception of metal halide. As the whitest of the HID lamp sources, metal halide lamps are often used in recreational facilities, warehouses, and big box stores. In the past decade, metal halide sources have been developed with high color rendering indices and a whiter light, making them a suitable choice for retail lighting particularly in hard to reach locations. As these lamps age, the color of light provided can vary and the difference is visible. The majority of the other HID lamps still operate in the yellow range of the color spectrum, making color rendering difficult.

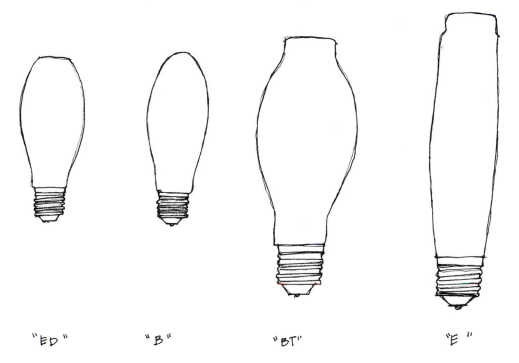

"ED"   "B"   "BT"   "E"

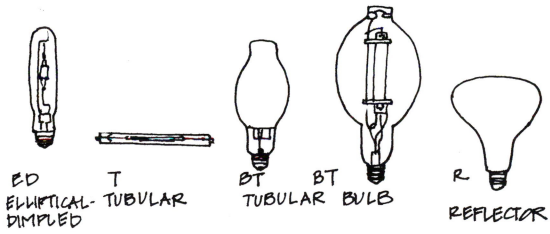

ED
ELLIPTICAL-   T   BT   BT
DIMPLED   TUBULAR   TUBULAR BULB   R
                                                  REFLECTOR

HIGH INTENSITY DISCHARGE SHAPES

Figure 5.15 HID shapes.

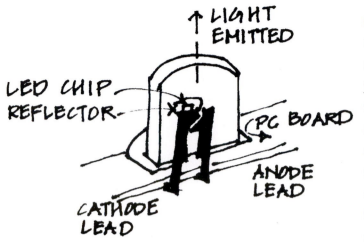

LOW FLUX LED

Light Emitting Diodes (LED)

Light emitting diodes (LED) are being introduced into the marketplace as the energy efficient answer to interior lighting. It should be noted that this technology is still relatively new. The subject of whether this is the fourth interior light source and ready for use as ambient light has been the subject of many recent articles by both lighting designers and architects (DiLouie and Willmorth, 2008; Broderick, 2008; and Sullivan, 2007). Concerns over this exciting new light source seem to center on the lack of photometric data available from manufacturers and actual lumen output of LEDs. In recent CALiPER testing, 4-foot linear LED replacement lamps used in place of standard T8s or T12s were found to fall short of manufacturer claims (Broderick, 2008). None of the LEDs tested provided even half the light output of the fluorescents. New LED standards are currently being produced by the *Illuminating Engineering Society of North America* (IESNA).

To produce white light from LEDs, one of two things is done: Red, blue, and green diodes are combined to create white light, or white is produced through the addition of a phosphor coating. Despite the concerns over LEDs for general illumination, many designers are incorporating them into interiors at a rate that is faster than manufacturer data is produced. The primary benefit of the LED is energy efficiency.

Figure 5.16 LED.

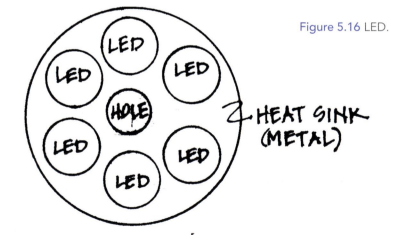

LED CLUSTER

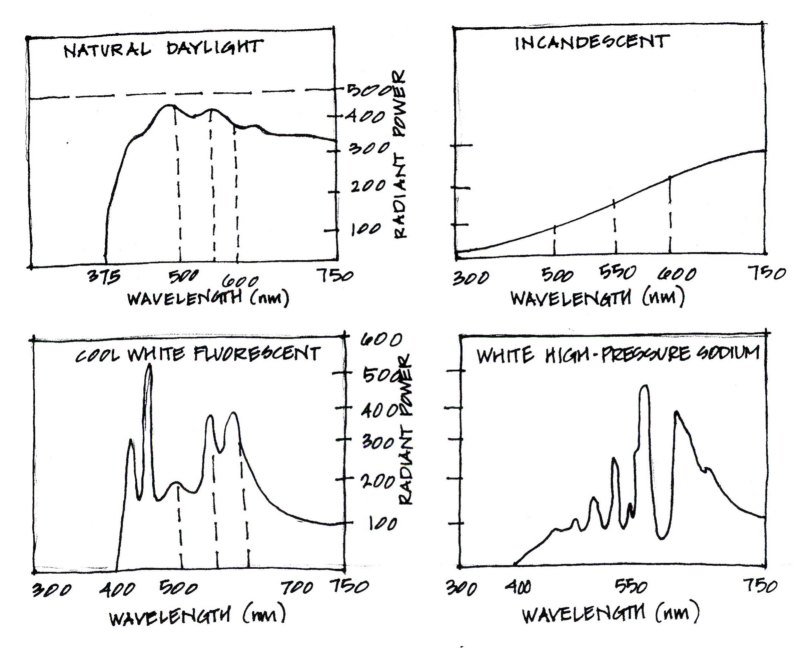

Figure 5.17 Spectral distributions for various lamp types.

CORRELATED COLOR TEMPERATURE (CCT)

Each lamp has a **correlated color temperature (CCT)** that is provided in degrees **Kelvin**. The CCT indicates how white the light is compared to daylight. A higher CCT equates to a cooler light source.

COLOR RENDERING INDEX

All lamps have a **color rendering index (CRI)**. The CRI of a lamp measures its ability to render color. This ability to render color is rated on a 100-point scale with 100 being the best and 0 being the worst. The measurement is based on a standard reference comparison of eight colors. It is important to remember that the CRI is the average of how the light source renders the eight colors. In other words, two different lamp types with a CRI of 80 may not look the same when used.

Most everyone has experienced the phenomenon of **metamerism**. When selecting two socks under incandescent lighting, both appear to be black. However, as soon as one steps outside to find one of the socks is actually navy blue—this is metamerism. The color of the light source will actually determine the color we see when we view an object. Things that appear to match when viewed beneath one light source, may not match under another. Consequently, it is extremely important to select colors, textiles, materials, and all other interior finishes under the actual light source that will be used in the finished space. It is also important to specify both the CRI and color temperature of the lamps to be used to ensure that no metamerism occurs within the design product.

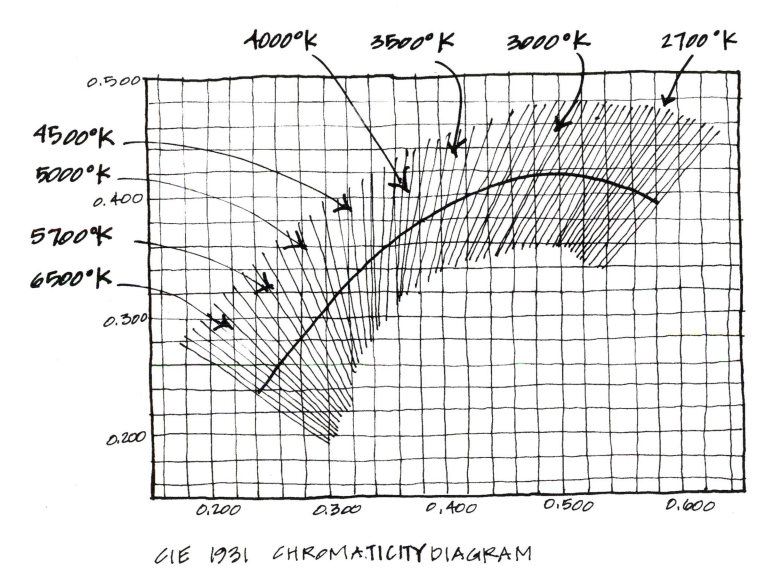

4000°K   3500°K   3000°K   2700°K

4500°K
5000°K
5700°K
6500°K

0.500
0.400
0.300
0.200

0.200   0.300   0.400   0.500   0.600

CIE 1931 CHROMATICITY DIAGRAM

Figure 5.18 CIE 1931 Chromaticity diagram.

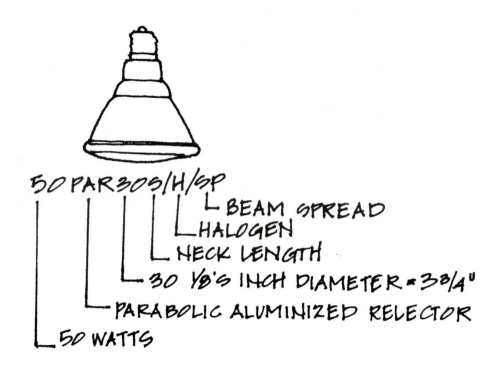

50 PAR30S/H/SP

L BEAM SPREAD
L HALOGEN
L NECK LENGTH
L 30 ⅛'s INCH DIAMETER = 3¾"
L PARABOLIC ALUMINIZED RELECTOR
L 50 WATTS

▲ Figure 5.19 How to read a lamp—incandescent.

A-21

L 2⅛" = 2⅝" DIAMETER
L ARBITRARY SHAPE

▲ Figure 5.21 How to read a lamp—arbitrary incandescent.

▼ Figure 5.20 How to read a lamp—fluorescent.

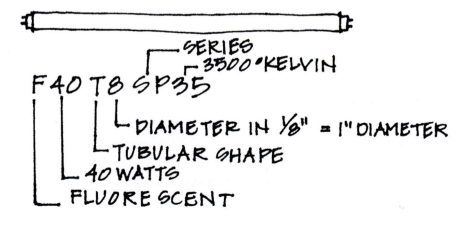

SERIES
3500° KELVIN

F40 T8 SP35

L DIAMETER IN ⅛" = 1" DIAMETER
L TUBULAR SHAPE
L 40 WATTS
L FLUORESCENT

Together color temperature and CRI impact how an interior space will feel and look. Figure 5.18 captures the range which most people find comfortable.

Figures 5.19 to 5.21 indicate how to read lamp designations for various types of lamps including incandescent, fluorescent, and high intensity discharge.

Fixtures

There are several types of light fixtures for a variety of different uses. Some of the most common light fixtures include: wall sconces, pendants, wallwashers, uplight fixtures, downlight fixtures, uplight/downlight fixtures, suspended fixtures, recessed fixtures, and surface mounted fixtures. Each fixture type provides a slightly different light distribution. When selecting an actual fixture for a project, it is critical to obtain the specification sheet to determine the actual light pattern provided by the specific fixture.

Figure 5.22 Fixture types and their symbols.

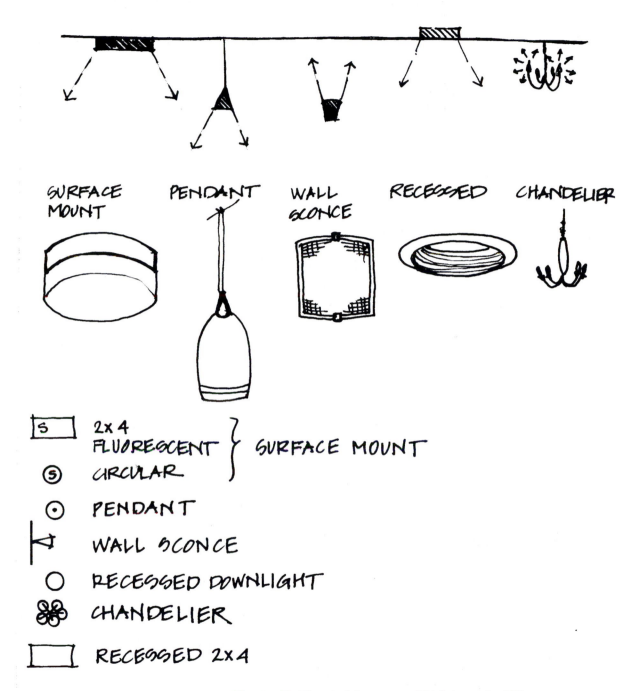

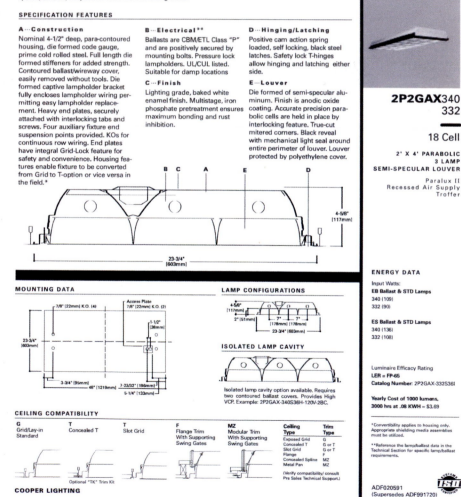

Fixture manufacturers produce cuts sheets for their light fixtures. These include information about the construction of the fixture, the electrical requirements, available finishes, lamp requirements, size, and operation.

Figure 5.23a–b (*this page and opposite*)
Typical cut sheets. Source: Cooper Lighting.

PHOTOMETRICS

2P2GAX-332S36I
Electronic Ballast
F32T8/35K lamps
2900 lumens

Spacing criterion:
(II) 1.2 x mounting
height, (⊥) 1.6 x
mounting height

Efficiency = 74.7%

Test Report:
2P2GX332S36I.IES

LER = FP-65

Yearly Cost of 1000
lumens, 3000 hrs at
.08 KWH = $3.69

Coefficients of Utilization

rc	80%				70%				50%			30%			10%			0%
rw	70	50	30	10	70	50	30	10	50	30	10	50	30	10	50	30	10	0
RCR																		
0	89	89	89	89	87	87	87	87	83	83	83	80	80	80	76	76	76	75
1	83	80	78	76	81	79	77	75	76	74	72	73	71	70	70	69	68	67
2	77	72	68	65	76	71	67	64	69	65	63	66	64	61	64	62	60	59
3	72	65	60	56	70	64	59	56	62	58	55	60	57	54	58	55	53	51
4	66	58	53	48	64	57	52	48	56	51	48	54	50	47	52	49	46	45
5	61	52	46	42	59	51	46	41	50	45	41	48	44	41	47	43	40	39
6	56	47	41	36	54	46	40	36	45	40	36	44	39	35	42	38	35	34
7	51	42	36	31	50	41	35	31	40	35	31	39	34	31	38	34	31	29
8	47	37	31	27	46	37	31	27	36	31	27	35	30	27	34	30	27	25
9	43	33	27	23	42	33	27	23	32	27	23	31	26	23	30	26	23	21
10	40	30	24	20	39	30	24	20	29	24	20	28	23	20	28	23	20	19

Effective floor cavity reflectance 20%

Zonal Lumen Summary

Zone	Lumens	%Lamp	%Fixture
0-30	1892	22.5	30.1
0-40	3281	39.1	52.3
0-60	5730	68.2	91.3
0-90	6279	74.7	100.0
0-180	6279	74.7	100

Typical VCP Percentages

Room Size (Ft.)	Height Along		Height Across	
	8.5'	10.0'	8.5'	10.0'
20 x 20	69	66	77	75
30 x 30	77	72	83	78
30 x 60	81	76	86	83
60 x 30	79	76	85	83
60 x 60	83	80	87	86

Candela

Angle	Along II	45°	Across ⊥
0	2288	2288	2288
5	2277	2284	2297
10	2244	2282	2325
15	2191	2273	2359
20	2118	2256	2381
25	2028	2223	2434
30	1921	2179	2599
35	1797	2171	2707
40	1655	2177	2546
45	1494	2081	2025
50	1309	1786	1350
55	1096	1294	808
60	856	764	532
65	581	378	320
70	290	189	150
75	77	60	26
80	27	15	12
85	8	5	5
90	0	0	0

ORDERING INFORMATION

SAMPLE NUMBER: 2P2GAX-332S36I-120V-EB81-U

HR=Heat Removal [1]
HRDO=Heat Removal Damper Open
HRDC=Heat Removal Damper Closed

Width
2=2' Width

P=Paralux Louver

2=2' Louver Depth

Trim Type
G=Grid/Lay-in (Standard)
G or **T**=Concealed T
G or **T**=Slot Grid [3]
F=Flange Trim
MZ=Modular Trim
Convertible Fixture Standard G (Grid) Type-Fixtures can be field converted to T-option or vice-versa. [3] Fixture also adaptable with flanged or modular trims.

AX=Air Supply Floating Louver
X=Blank Side/Floating Louver - Non-Air Supply (Omit A)
AVX=Air Supply Floating Louver with Directional Air Vane (Add V)

Number of Lamps [4]
3 lamps
(Not included)

Wattage (Length)
40=40W T12 (48")
32=32W T8 (48")

Louver Color
S=Silver
G=Gold
W=White

Cell Configuration
36=3 Rows of 6, 18 Cell

Louver Finish
H=Semi-Specular/Haze (Gold only)
I=Semi-Specular/Haze (Low Iridescent Standard (Silver Only)
MI=Specular/Mirrored (Low Iridescent) (Silver Only)
P=Painted (White only)

Voltage [5]
120V=120 Volt
277V=277 Volt
347V=347 Volt
UNV=Universal Voltage 120-277 [6]

Options
GL=Single Element Fuse
GM=Double Element Fuse
WTR=White Reveal
Lamps=Lamps Installed
Flex=Flex Installed
Emergency=EM Installed

Ballast Type [5]
LE3=T12 Magnetic Energy Saving
LEOC8=T8 Magnetic Energy Saving
EB8_=T8 Electronic Instant Start. Total Harmonic Distortion < 20%
No. of Ballast
1, 2 or 3
EB8_/PLUS=T8 Electronic Instant Start. High Ballast Factor >1.13. Total Harmonic Distortion < 20%
No. of Ballast
1, 2 or 3
ER8_=T8 Electronic Program Rapid Start. Total Harmonic Distortion < 10%
No. of Ballast
1, 2 or 3
TEB8_=T8 Electronic Instant Start. Total Harmonic Distortion < 10%
No. of Ballast
1, 2 or 3
EB2_=T12 Electronic Rapid Start.
No. of Ballast
1 or 2
DLS=Digital Lighting System Dimming

Options
PAF=Painted After Fabrication
2BC=2nd Ballast Cover
RIF1=Radio Interference Suppressor
FR=Suitable for Fire Rated Applications
EQ=T-BAR Safety Earthquake Clips [2]
MEP=Modified End Plate/
For End Filler Applications (See Accessory Section)
20GA/REP=20 Gauge Riveted Endplates. For use in New York City.
RLS=Rotor-Lock Socket (T8 Lamps Only)
(Additional options available. See Accessory Section)

Packaging
U=Unit Pack
PAL=Job Pack, out of carton
PALC=Job Pack, in carton

NOTES: [1] Integral end plate grid lock feature not available in heat removal. [2] An EQ Grid Clip is recommended for all 9/16" ceiling systems. [3] Convertibility applies to housing only, appropriate shielding media assemblies must be utilized. [4] Standard off-center ballast on 3-lamp fixtures. [5] Products also available in non-US voltages and frequencies for international markets. [6] Not available when specifying emergencies, voltage must be specific.

For complete product data, reference the Fluorescent Specification binder. Specifications & dimensions subject to change without notice. Consult your Cooper Lighting Representative for availability and ordering information.

SHIPPING INFORMATION

Catalog No.	Wt.
2P2GAX-332S36I	42 lbs.

COOPER Lighting

Visit our web site at www.cooperlighting.com
Customer First Center 1121 Highway 74 South Peachtree City, GA 30269 770.486.4800 FAX 770.486.4801 7/04 ADF020591

SUSTAINABILITY AND LIGHTING DESIGN

Lighting accounts for the single largest percentage of energy use in buildings. As such, it is critical to understand issues of sustainability as they relate to lighting design and fixture and lamp selections. Simply put, energy efficiency of a light source can be determined based on the amount of energy needed to produce the light output in lumens and is expressed as **lumens per watt (LPW)**.

A second measure to consider is the effectiveness of the fixture in putting light where light is needed. Correctly controlling the distribution of light can reduce or eliminate glare, **light trespass**, and **light pollution**. Light trespass occurs when light from one building spreads to an adjacent building. Light pollution occurs when light is directed into the night sky or other areas disrupting wildlife. Examples include disruption of the sea turtle mating process through light pollution along coastal areas and the impact of migratory birds from light levels in the sky. The **International Dark Sky Association (IDA)** seeks to halt environmental light pollution.

Manufacturers are now working on lamp and ballast recycling programs to divert these from the landfill, and in the case of fluorescent lamps, recapture the mercury before if is released into the environment. The 1995 U.S. Environmental Protection Agency **Universal Waste Rule** requires companies handling and consuming fluorescent and HID lamps to recycle them. To date, Litecontrol, based in Hanson, Massachusetts, is the only lighting manufacturer to have one of its products meet cradle to cradle protocol. It has had its entire product line certified (Casey, 2008).

GREEN SEAL'S LIGHTING RECOMMENDATIONS

Compact Fluorescent

- Not for use in spaces with extremely high ceilings, where a tight beam of light is required, where the temperatures are extreme, on a dimming circuit for some lamps (there are some dimmable fluorescent lamps on the market), or where electromagnetic interference is likely.

High Intensity Discharge

- For open office, hallways, atriums, meeting areas, and other general lighting: metal halide with a CRI of 60 or more.
- For general assembly, manufacturing or retail: metal halide with CRI of 70 or more.
- For warehouse and loading areas: high pressure sodium.
- For sport/gymnasium and specialty retail: metal halide with CRI of 70 or more.

Linear Fluorescent

- Choose T-8 lamps and electronic ballasts.
- Choose lamps with the lowest mercury content for your application as is possible.
- Consider a 2-lamp or 3-lamp two-by-four fixture.
- Consider 2-foot long T-8 lamps with two-by-two fixtures.
- Polished aluminum in troffers can create glare.

SENSORS

Automatic Sensors

One of the best ways to reduce energy is to harvest the available daylight. A variety of sensors are available for use in conjunction with daylight harvest. These include **open loop** and **closed loop** systems. In the open loop system, solar sensors measure the daylight and control the electric lighting to maintain a uniform lighting level. These must be set up and are not subject to changes within the space and lumen sensors. Closed loop systems measure the illuminance on the work surfaces, and are quick to set up.

Vacancy Sensors

Vacancy sensors automatically turn off the lights when a space is not occupied. The energy savings resulting from the use of vacancy sensors is estimated between 30 and 50 percent. Three types of vacancy sensors are available: passive infrared, passive acoustic, and ultrasonic. Passive infrared sensors sense body heat; ultrasonic sensors send out sound waves to detect changes in the space; and passive acoustical controls rely on microphones to detect human sounds.

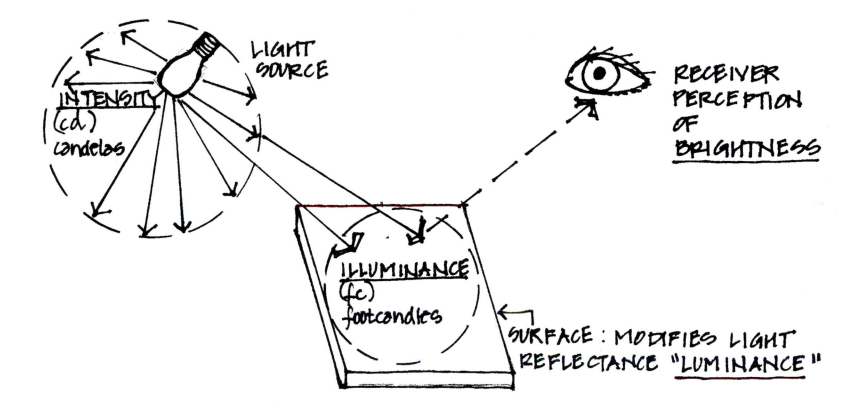

Figure 5.24 Lighting metric illustrated.

LIGHTING METRICS

Five lighting metrics are used to quantify lighting. The science of light is called **photometry**. Photometrics describes the recorded measures of light as described by the lighting metrics.

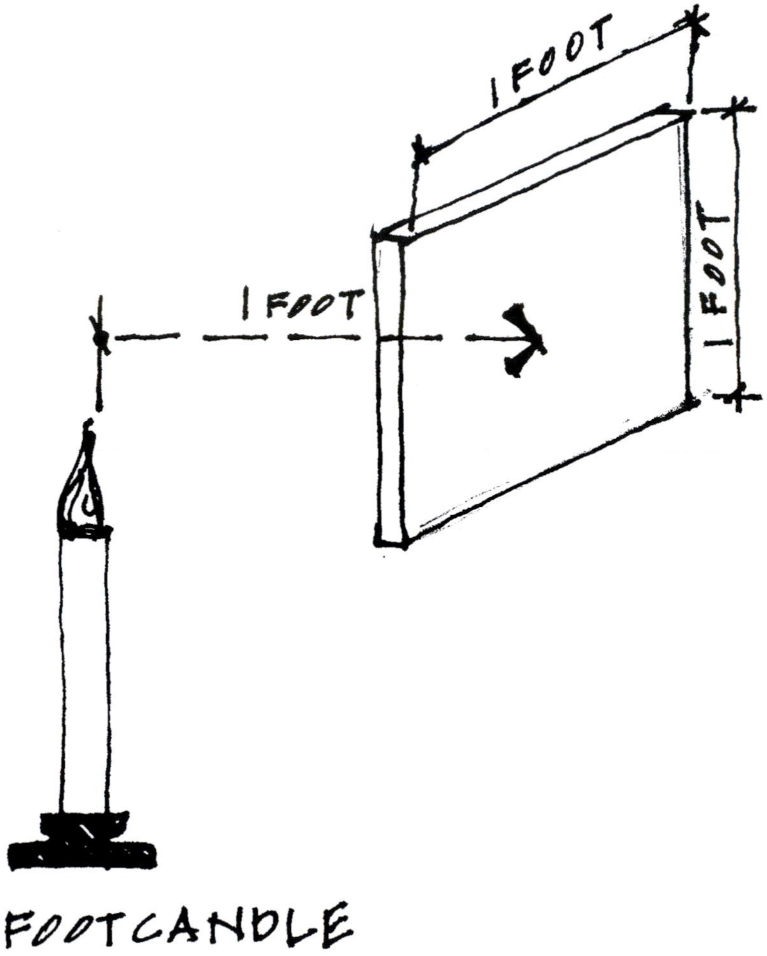

FOOTCANDLE

Figure 5.25 Footcandle illustrated.

LUMINOUS FLUX

Luminous flux is the time rate flow of light.

LUMINOUS INTENSITY

Luminous intensity is the directional force causing luminous flux to be emitted. It is measured in candelas.

ILLUMINANCE

Illuminance is defined as the density of luminous flux incident at a point on a surface. The unit of measurement is the footcandle.

LUMINANCE

Luminance refers to the luminous intensity of a source in a particular direction divided by the area of the source.

LUMINOUS EXITANCE

Luminous exitance describes the density of luminous flux leaving a surface in all directions at a point.

CALCULATIONS

SIMPLE LUMEN METHOD

The simple lumen method is a rule of thumb, quick method for calculating the number of fixtures you might need in a space. This is a preliminary calculation to assist you in the early phases of a lighting design project. Actual calculations should always be completed.

Process of Calculation

Step 1: Determine desired footcandle level for the space. You can find this in the IESNA guidelines of recommended footcandle levels. These can also be found in *Graphic Standards* (Ramsey and Sleeper) and *Interior Graphic Standards* (Kruse). This table provides the number of footcandles needed to perform specific tasks within differing types of spaces.

Step 2: Multiply the number found in Step 1 by two.

Step 3: Find the area of the room.

Step 4: Multiply the number in Step 2 by the area (Step 3).

Step 5: Using any lamp manufacturer's catalogue, find the number of lumens for the type of lamp you plan to use (see Table 5.1 for some common lamps).

Step 6: Divide the number from Step 4 by the number of lumens found in Step 5. This gives you the number of lamps you need. Remember to then divide this by the number of lamps per fixture if your fixture uses more than one lamp.

TABLE 5.1

LAMP LUMENS OUTPUT

OBTAINED FROM GE LAMP PRODUCTS CATALOG, 2006

LAMP	NUMBER OF LUMENS
A-19 60-watt incandescent	840
F14.5 60-watt incandescent	900
G25 40-watt incandescent	510
MR 16 standard 35-watt halogen	2900
MR 11 standard 35-watt halogen	2900
T5 14-watt, 21.6" fluorescent	1240
T8 32-watt, 4' fluorescent	2660
T12 32-watt, 4' fluorescent	2650

WATTS PER SQUARE FEET METHOD (CHART OF WATTS PER LAMP TYPE)

The watts per square foot method is another rule of thumb, quick method for calculating the number of fixtures you might need in a space. This is a preliminary calculation to assist you in the early phases of a lighting design project. Actual calculations should always be completed.

Step 1: Calculate the area of the space you are lighting.

Step 2: Look up the recommended watts per square foot for the space you are designing from the applicable energy code (see Table 5.2 for examples).

Step 3: Multiply area (Step 1) by watts per square foot from the energy code based on the foot-candle levels you need to achieve (Step 2) to get total number of watts for the space.

Step 4: Divide the result of Step 3 by the number of watts per lamp you plan to use. Remember this gives you the number of lamps you will need not the number of fixtures. Divide this number by the number of lamps per fixture.

TABLE 5.2
WATTS PER SQUARE FOOT GUIDELINES
ADAPTED FROM THE *ADVANCED LIGHTING GUIDELINES*, 2001

CODE	OFFICE SPACES	RETAIL SPACES	ASSEMBLY SPACES	SCHOOLS
California 1995	1.5	2.00	2.00	1.80
California 2001	1.20	1.70	1.80	1.40
ASHRAE 1999	1.3	1.90	1.60	1.50

Source: *Advanced Lighting Guidelines*, 2001.

LUMEN METHOD

The most accurate method for calculating lighting levels and the number of fixtures required to achieve a specific level of light is the lumen method. The formula for the lumen method is as follows:

$$fc = \frac{\text{number of lamps} \times \text{initial lamp lumens} \times \text{LLF} \times \text{CU}}{\text{Area}}$$

This formula can be manipulated if you are trying to discover the number of lamps (and, therefore, fixtures) you will need for a specific space to achieve a particular lighting level.

$$\text{Number of lamps} = \frac{\text{Area} \times \text{fc}}{\text{Initial lamp lumens} \times \text{LLF} \times \text{CU}}$$

To use this formula, follow these steps.

Step 1: Calculate the area of the room/space.

Step 2: Look up the required footcandle level for the given space from IESNA tables.

Step 3: Look up the lamp you plan to use within the manufacturer's catalog to find the initial lamp lumens.

Step 4: Find the Light Loss Factor (LLF). The LLF is composed of all those variables that will reduce the number of lumens provided by a lamp. These include luminaire dirt depreciation (LDD) and lamp lumen depreciation (LLD). To calculate the LLF simply multiply the LLD times the LDD. Specific LLD factors can be found for each lamp type. Approximate averages are provided in Table 5.3.

TABLE 5.3 LAMP LUMEN DEPRECIATION FACTORS (LLD)

LAMP TYPE	LLD
Incandescent	0.85
Fluorescent	0.87
HID	0.70

TABLE 5.4
LEVEL OF SPACE, CLEANLINESS, AND
LUMINAIRE DIRT DEPRECIATION (LDD) GUIDELINES

LEVEL OF CLEANLINESS OF THE SPACE	LDD
Very Clean	0.90
Clean	0.85
Medium	0.80
Dirty	0.75
Very Dirty	0.60

LDD quantifies the amount of lumens lost as a function of dirt in the space and in the light fixture as a result.

Although very specific determinations can be made by using the IESNA guidelines to obtain exact information for the specific fixture type, the general guidelines shown in Table 5.4 can be used.

To look up the coefficient of utilization (CU), a simple calculation must first be performed. The room cavity ratio (RCR) calculated the volume of space that will be lit as a ratio. The RCR is then used in conjunction with the **reflectance** value of the ceiling and walls to determine the CU.

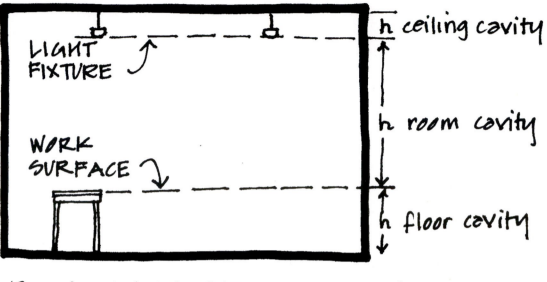

ROOM CAVITY RATIO DIAGRAM

Figure 5.26 Room cavity ratio illustrated.

Calculating the RCR

$$RCR = \frac{5 \times h\,(L + W)}{(L \times W)}$$

Note: use room cavity "h"

Coefficent of Utilization (CU) charts are located within the manufacturer's literature. See Figure 5.23. To find the CU, simply use the RCR on the left column and scroll across the appropriate reflectances along the top rc=ceiling reflectance value and rw= wall reflectance. The intersection of the x and y axis equals the CU.

You now have all the numbers to calculate the number of lamps you need to light the space to your footcandle level. Remember to divide this by the number of lamps per fixture to find the actual number of fixtures.

EXPLANATION OF COMPUTER CALCULATIONS

Several lighting manufacturers provide free online software programs for doing photometric calculations; however, it is critical that you understand how these programs work to know whether the data you enter is correct. Mastering the manual calculation methods allow you to quickly check yourself on the computer outputs. In addition to freeware programs, there are also professional lighting designer software programs available for purchase.

TABLE 5.5 REFLECTANCE VALUES*

COLOR	REFLECTANCE
White	90%
Gray	80%
Light blue	70%
Medium yellow	60%
Medium gray	40%
Medium brown	30%
Dark blue	5%
Dark wood	10%

* Typical reflectance values for surfaces. (Actual values can be obtained from manufacturers such as paint companies.)

DESIGNING WITH LIGHT (DESIGN PROCESS)

The following brief list provides an overview of the steps taken in the design of the lighting system:

- Identify the spaces and the tasks within the space.
- Verify the number of footcandles required for the task.
- Select the best lamp type for this application (color temperature, CRI, energy efficiency, cost).
- Select luminaire consistent with design concept for the space.
- Do lumen calculations to determine the number of lamps required and the number of luminaires required.
- Analyze daylight in the space and how this will impact the need for artificial lighting.
- Create solutions for handling and managing the daylight.
- Do lighting layout.
- Create a three-dimensional model of lighting to study distribution.
- Design special lighting effects to emphasize architectural elements of the space and provide sketches of your design ideas

THE LIGHTING DESIGN PACKET FOR EACH PHASE

- **Programming**—information identifying spaces, tasks and required illumination
- **Schematic Design**—sketches of desired lighting effects; how it coordinates with design concept and architecture
- **Design Development**—selection of lamps and luminaires, lighting calculations
- **Construction Documents**—specification sheets for lamps and luminaires, final drawings reflecting ceiling plans including dimensions, notes and details, lighting fixture schedule

LIGHTING PLANS

The critical pieces of documentation used to convey lighting design intent to a contractor are the lighting plan, specifications, and any design details for specialty lighting installations. These documents must be clear and complete, and must include all information needed to create a finished solution while leaving no design decisions to chance. Fixtures and lamps should be specified, including information on color temperature and color rendering index. Failure to include all of this information may result in unintended results, metamerism of colors, and other design failures.

CONVENTIONS FOR LIGHTING PLANS

For easy understanding by electricians, contractors, and other trades people in the field, it is customary to use a **reflected ceiling plan**, which is a layer added to the floor plan. In a computer-aided drawing (CAD) program, this would be a separate layer to show lighting. By hand, the floor plan is traced onto a separate drawing for lighting. Standard symbols are used for reflected ceiling plans, but may vary slightly from office to office; therefore, always provide a legend or key explaining what the drawing symbols being used indicate. The best resources for standard designations are *Graphic Standards* and other commonly used resources.

In addition to a lighting plan, reflected ceiling plans and electrical plans are also commonly used.

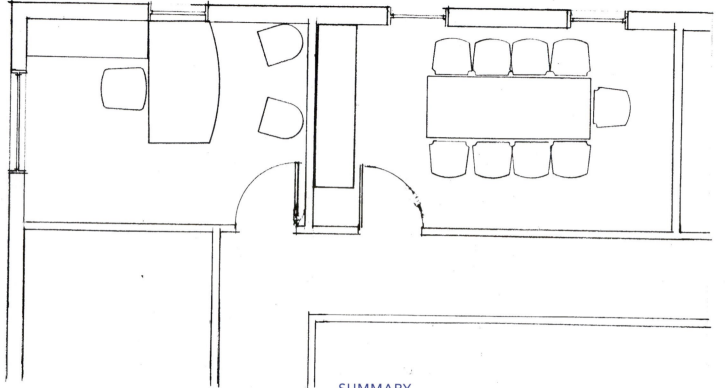

FLOOR PLAN
1/4" = 1'-0"

SUMMARY

Lighting is an integral part of the designed interior. Designers should be knowledgeable about lighting sources, color, and temperature to ensure their design intent is realized. One of the single best ways to ruin a well-designed interior space is with bad lighting design. The following case studies demonstrate the effective integration of lighting.

▲ Figure 5.27 Partial floor plan.

▶ Figure 5.28 Partial reflected ceiling plan.

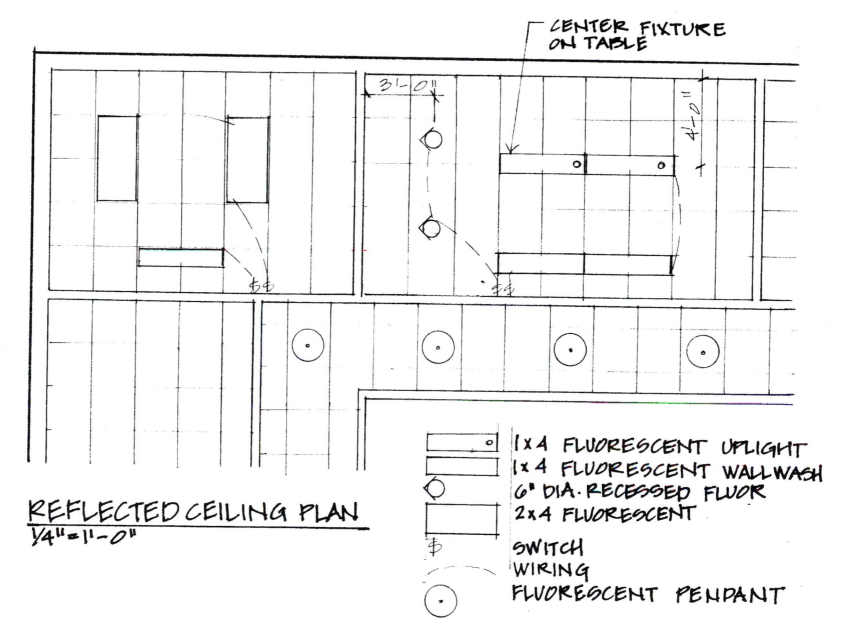

CENTER FIXTURE ON TABLE

3'-0"

4'-0"

REFLECTED CEILING PLAN
1/4" = 1'-0"

1x4 FLUORESCENT UPLIGHT
1x4 FLUORESCENT WALLWASH
6" DIA. RECESSED FLUOR
2x4 FLUORESCENT
SWITCH
WIRING
FLUORESCENT PENDANT

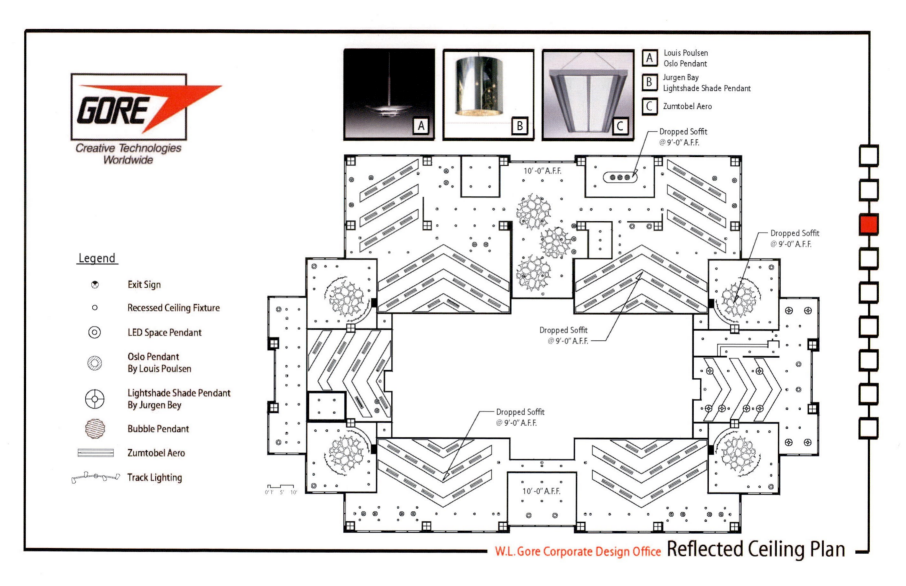

Figure 5.29 Reflected ceiling plan.

Figure 5.30 Perkins + Will, Haworth Showroom, NYC.
Photo Credit: Steve Hall, Hedrich Blessing Photography.

PERKINS + WILL—HAWORTH SHOWROOM, HOLLAND, MICHIGAN

Figures 5.32 through 5.35 illustrate a different Haworth showroom with a different approach to the lighting scenario. Square suspended tracks provide the lighting in the main two-story entry space while the one-story spaces feature square recessed fluorescent fixtures. Globes are suspended over the table in Figure 5.35.

◀ Figure 5.31 Perkins + Will, Haworth Showroom, NYC. Photo Credit: Steve Hall, Hedrich Blessing Photography.

▶ Figure 5.32 Perkins + Will, Haworth Showroom, Holland, Michigan. Photo Credit: Steve Hall, Hedrich Blessing Photography.

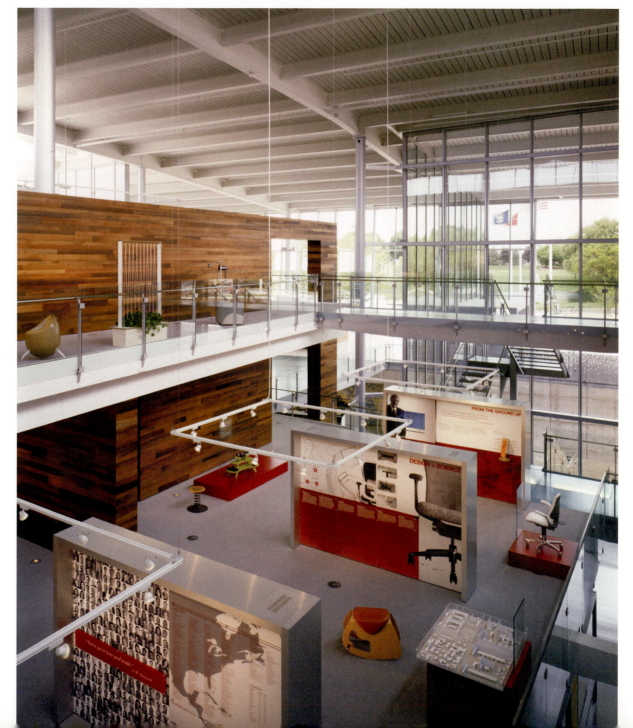

Figure 5.33 Perkins + Will, Haworth Showroom, Holland, Michigan.
Photo Credit: Craig Dugan, Hedrich Blessing Photography.

Figure 5.34 Perkins + Will, Haworth Showroom, Holland, Michigan.
Photo Credit: Craig Dugan, Hedrich Blessing Photography.

STUDIO27ARCHITECTURE—
WU AND BURNETT RESIDENCE

Daylighting and electric lighting combine to form the lighting strategy in the Wu and Burnett residence. A skylight provides lighting through the center of the space and is supplemented by electric lighting. Tubular fluorescents situated vertically alongside the mirror provide lighting for the bathroom.

◄ Figure 5.35 Perkins + Will, Haworth Showroom, Holland, Michigan. Photo Credit: Steve Hall, Hedrich Blessing Photography.

▶ Figure 5.36 studio27architecture, Wu and Burnett residence. Photo Credit: Anice Hoachlander, Hoachlander Davis Photography, LLC.

151

▲ Figure 5.37 studio27architecture, Wu and Burnett residence. Photo Credit: Anice Hoachlander, Hoachlander Davis Photography, LLC.

▶ Figure 5.38 studio27architecture, Wu and Burnett residence. Photo Credit: Anice Hoachlander, Hoachlander Davis Photography, LLC.

Figure 5.39 studio27architecture, Wu and Burnett residence. Photo Credit: Anice Hoachlander, Hoachlander Davis Photography, LLC.

Figure 5.40 studio27architecture, Wu and Burnett residence. **Photo Credit:** Anice Hoachlander, Hoachlander Davis Photography, LLC.

KEY TERMS

bulb	light trespass
closed loop	light pollution
coefficient of utilization (CU)	luminaire
color rendering index (CRI)	luminaire dirt depreciation (LDD)
correlated color temperature (CCT)	luminance
fixture	luminous flux
fluorescent	luminous intensity
glare	luminous exitance
halogen	lumen per watt (LPW)
high intensity discharge (HID)	metamerism
International Dark Sky Association (IDA)	open loop
illuminance	photometry
incandescent	reflectance
Kelvin	reflected ceiling plan
lamp	Universal Waste Rule
light emitting diode (LED)	vacancy sensors
lighting plan	

ASSIGNMENTS/EXERCISES

The following is a list of possible assignments which can be used to reinforce the lighting design concepts outlined in this chapter.

EXPERIMENT 1: PERCEPTION

This experiment is designed to demonstrate many of the principles of perception discussed in this chapter.

Equipment

Leftover cardboard, matt board, or other supplies from previous projects (minimum size 24 × 24)—two sheets

X-acto and blades

Plain white paper

Markers (at least ten or so)

Straight edge (metal)

Architect's scale

Pencil and other drafting tools

Project

The following steps are used to complete the project:

1. Build two identical corridors at ½" = 1'-0". Provide a few small openings for light. Use the same exact openings on both models.
2. Each corridor shall be 6 feet wide with an 8 foot ceiling, and should be 20 feet long
3. Using white paper, create inserts that make the hallway change. Try different patterns and colors on the ceilings and walls that help to change your perception of the length and/or the height of the corridor.

Note: The success of your project will be measured on how different the two hallways appear in the completed models. Try several options before permanently affixing your papers.

EXPERIMENT 2: SEEING LIGHT

1. Select two images from a magazine that show a variety of lighting conditions. The best images for this lab will be those with multiple shadows and shading.
2. On a piece of 10-inch by 10-inch trace, render the entire image using only a #2 pencil and different levels of pressure. Do not outline objects—use only shading with the pencil as your method.

EXPERIMENT 3: LIGHTING LAB: COLOR DEMO

The third experiment invloves mixing colored light. Using red, blue, and green light, make observations about the following:

Fabric/Textile 1

Under red light

Under blue light

Under green light

Under all three lights together

Fabric/Textile 2

Under red light

Under blue light

Under green light

Under all three lights together

EXPERIMENT 4: LIGHTING MODEL

The model created for this assignment will be used several times. Please do a good job. <u>Craftsmanship and design count!</u>

Overall

Create a two-room vignette (minimum of two rooms). Recommendation—use a previous design project completed in an earlier studio course. The rooms should have visual connections from one room to the next. These can be in the form of door openings and/or pass-throughs, or other similar openings.

The scale for the model is 1" = 1'- 0". Models must be sturdy and built to last the semester. Please use balsa wood, matt board, task board, and other materials to ensure a well-built model.

Details

Three of the walls and floor of the model will be *fixed.* Build a ledge along the top of the walls to support several different ceiling solutions. The ledge should not be a big design feature, but rather a functional requirement of the model—do not make it any bigger than it needs to be to have a ceiling plane rest upon it! Make *one* wall hinge open so that photos can be taken inside your model. Only *one wall of one room* needs to swing open; however, make sure it is one that allows you to see into the other room.

Exterior walls should have windows and doors as needed to make the spaces realistic.

For this assignment leave all walls that might normally lead to other rooms blank—i.e., no openings.

Be creative with this assignment. The ceiling height must be a minimum of eight feet, but may be taller. Look to achieve different lighting effects using the model. Select and design spaces carefully.

EXPERIMENT 5: LIGHTING MODEL—CEILING OVERLAYS

Overall

For this lab, create two different lighting scenarios for the model.

The scale for the model is 1" = 1' - 0".

Details

Create one flat ceiling plane with basic incandescent lighting options. Cut the circles from the ceiling plane to mimic the effect of recessed downlights.

For the second ceiling option, create an interesting ceiling. This may include soffits, trayed ceilings, bulkheads, and other architectural features that help define the space and the lighting solutions. Be creative.

EXPERIMENT 6: LIGHTING MODEL—DAYLIGHT

Use the model and a solid flat ceiling plane for this lab.

Overall

For this lab, create a ceiling plane with no artificial light openings. The ceiling may include skylights, monitors, and clerestory lighting.

Details

For this lab, create a series of devices that change the effect of daylighting in your model. These may include, but are not limited to, louvers, light shelves, monitors, clerestories, skylights, and other sun shading devices. Please do not add curtains or blinds. Use architectural design features to manipulate the light. These should be removable so before and after photos of each device can be taken.

Create a minimum of four different lighting conditions within a space using only these devices and actual sunlight. Take as many photos as are needed to demonstrate the different effects created by each device.

EXPERIMENT 7: FIELD OBSERVATION

For this lab, select two spaces in which to observe the lighting. These may be any two of the following list: retail, healthcare, hospitality, institutional, office, corporate.

Visit the spaces and record the following information for each one:

OBSERVATIONS JOURNAL FORMAT

Name of installation:

Location:

Date visited:

Time of day:

Weather conditions (sunny, overcast, etc.):

1. Type of lighting:
2. Description of luminaire(s) (fixture and lamp):   SKETCH LUMINAIRE(s)
   (Describe and sketch ALL)

3. Lighting plan (sketch)
4. What works well about the lighting:
5. Suggestions for improvement:
6. Include any details, photographs, or sketches
   that help illustrate the lighting scenario.

RESOURCES

Illuminating Engineering Society of North America (IESNA)

International Association of Lighting Designers (IALD)

National Council on Qualifications for the Lighting Professions (NCQLP) www.ncqlp.org

Manufacturer websites such as Lightolier (www.lightolier.com), Cooper Lighting (www.cooperlighting.com), and others

Lamp manufacturer websites for Philips(www.philips.com), GE (www.ge.com), Sylvania (www.sylvania.com), and others

Broderick, J. "Are LED replacement lamps ready?" *LD + A*, October 2008, 20–23.

Casey, M. "Going green: Lighting manufacturers tackle sustainable business practices." *Architectural Lighting*, June 2008, 23-24.

DiLouie, C. "Additive color mixing." *Architectural SSL*, October 2008, 42.

Greene, K. "Sustainability: Lighting the way to a greener planet." *Archi-Tech*, April 2008, 43–47.

Murdoch, J. (1999). *Lighting Metrics*. IESNA #TM-1-99.

Sullivan, C.C. (2007). The Fourth source: Light emitting diodes (LEDs) for general illumination. Retrieved from http://continuingeducation.construction.com on 10/6/08.

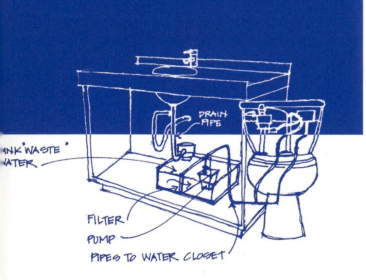

NK WASTE
ATER

FILTER
PUMP
PIPES TO WATER CLOSET

DRAIN
PIPE

CHAPTER 6

Plumbing Systems

In 1990 the World Health Organization estimated that 1230 million people did not have access to adequate drinking water. By 2000 this figure was estimated to have risen by 900 million people. Add to this already chronic problem the devastating impacts of climate change and the results can be catastrophic, even in the most developed countries of the world.

Sue Roaf, Ecohouse

OBJECTIVES

- Design efficient bathrooms and kitchens by stacking and grouping plumbing on common walls
- Prepare plans with adequate clearances for plumbing

INTRODUCTION

Human beings require clean water to live. For the first time in history, the water supply and its future ability to maintain human kind is in question. Contemporaneously, with the decline in the availability of clean water, we continue to use massive quantities of potable water to flush toilets in the United States. While some die of thirst, we waste the very thing other needs to survive.

The way we use and process water in the United States is undergoing some fairly significant changes. The traditional method of providing indoor plumbing comes from one of two sources: a municipal water plant or a private on-site well. Like water supply, the waste stream is also handled in a similar fashion either using an on site septic system or a municipal waste management facility. Our water supplies are prone to pollution by a variety of man-made interventions, including the use of fertilizers that get into local streams and lakes as well as the water table, factory by-products pumped into local water sources, and the introduction of raw sewage in some instances.

A relatively new wastewater processing system is being introduced into some areas of the country. Through the use of wetlands, some biologicals can be reintroduced into the local ecology that, in turn, can be used to purify the water naturally.

- **Potable water**—Water that is suitable for drinking is called **potable water**.
- **Black water**—Waste water that contains sewage is called **black water.**
- **Gray water**—Waste water from sinks, bathtubs, and washing machines is called **gray water**.

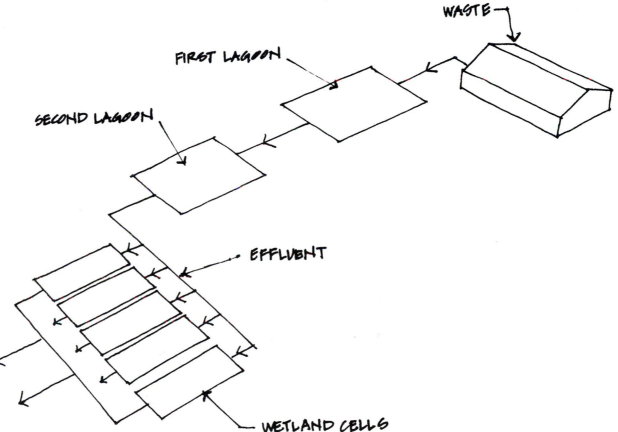

Figure 6.1 Wetlands diagram.

Figure 6.2 Typical sewer treatment plant diagram.

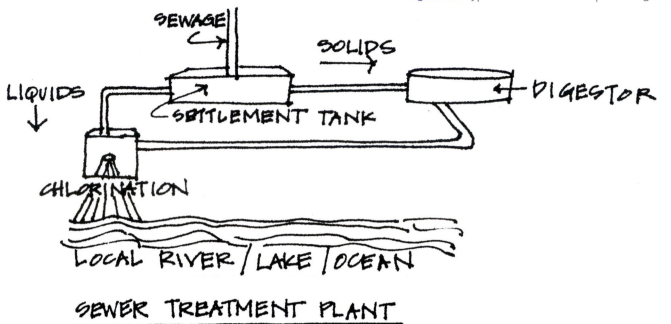

SEWER TREATMENT PLANT

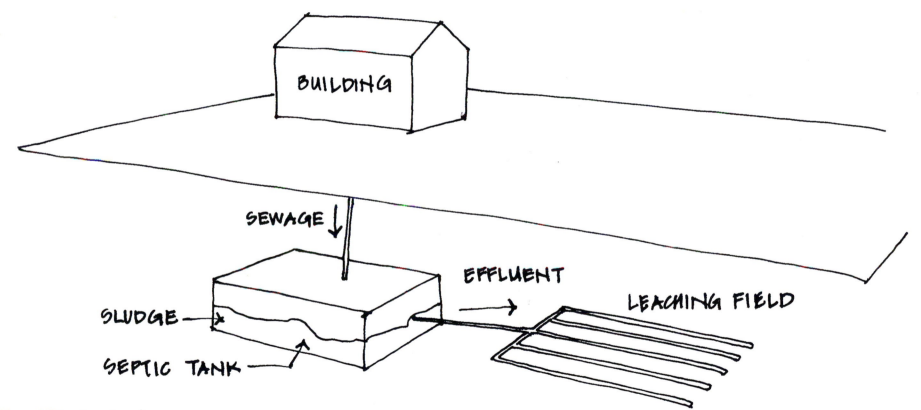

Figure 6.3 Septic system diagram.

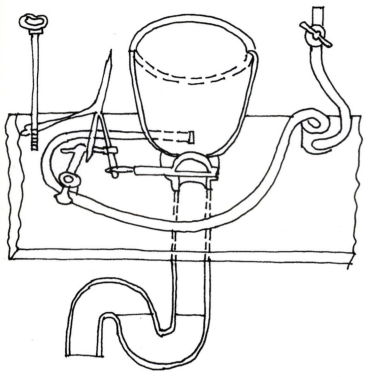

Figure 6.4 Historic toilets.

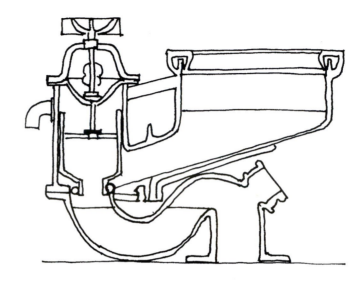

PLUMBING SYSTEMS

Plumbing refers to the introduction and elimination of water and human byproducts to and from a building. Indoor plumbing is a relatively new phenomenon in the history of buildings. Whereas some residences featured indoor privies, outhouses were common well into the nineteenth century and, in some parts of the country, into the twentieth century. In some rural locations outhouses are still in use today in the United States. Although Leonardo da Vinci envisioned indoor water, the first patent for a flushing toilet was granted to Alexander Cummings, a watchmaker, in 1775. This English invention did not travel to the United States, and in 1870 American John Randolph Mann received a patent for a three-pipe siphonic closet. Between 1900 and 1932, 350 patents were issued for indoor plumbing related fixtures.

Plumbing systems are divided into water supply and waste water. The water supply systems operate under pressure, and the waste systems operate by gravity, thus requiring a slope in waste pipes.

FIXTURES AND WATER CONSERVATION

In an effort to reduce the amount of potable water being discharged into the waste stream, several items have been introduced into the market for use in buildings.

HIGH EFFICIENCY TOILETS

EPA's WaterSense program means that certified toilets are 20 percent more efficient than other products.

LOW FLOW TOILETS

Recent legislation has required that new **water closets** use less water than those of the past. All major manufacturers now provide low flow toilets.

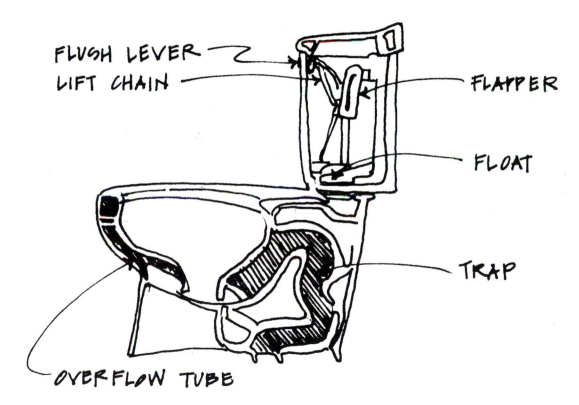

FLUSH LEVER
LIFT CHAIN
FLAPPER
FLOAT
TRAP
OVERFLOW TUBE

Figure 6.5 Low flow toilet.

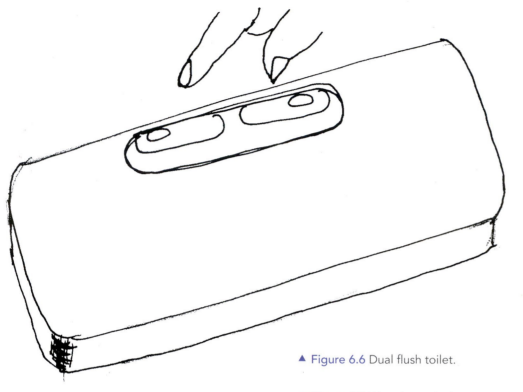

▲ Figure 6.6 Dual flush toilet.

▼ Figure 6.7 Waterless urinal.

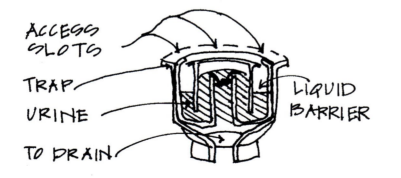

DUAL FLUSHING TOILETS

Some toilets are equipped with a dual flushing mechanism that allows the toilet to be flushed according to its usage. When less water is required, one flush is used, versus two flushes when more water is required.

WATERLESS URINALS

Waterless **urinals** do not require water to operate and thus provide extensive water savings.

LOW WATER URINALS

These urinals are designed to reduce water usage by 85 percent.

AUTOMATIC FAUCETS

Automatic faucets are commonly used in commercial projects. A motion sensor turns the water on when hands are sensed beneath it. Following a specific period of time, the faucet then shuts off water flow.

GRAY WATER REUSE

Water from the sink, shower, and bathtub can be reused to flush the water closet (toilet).

LIGHT POWERED FAUCETS

Several manufacturers have developed faucets that use light to power the automatic sensors with no electricity required.

LOW FLOW SHOWER HEADS

Low flow shower heads reduce the amount of water used during a shower.

▼ Figure 6.10 Low flow showerhead.

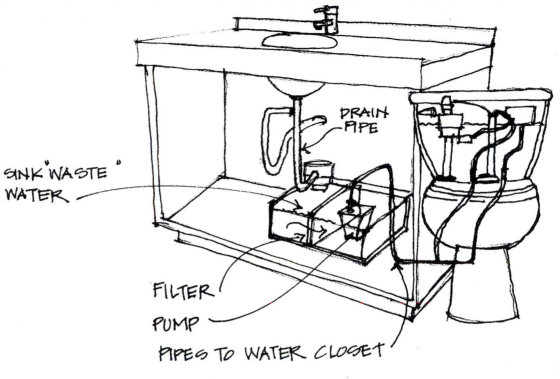

DRAIN PIPE

SINK "WASTE" WATER

FILTER

PUMP

PIPES TO WATER CLOSET

▲ Figure 6.8 Gray water toilet diagram.

▼ Figure 6.9 Light-powered faucet.

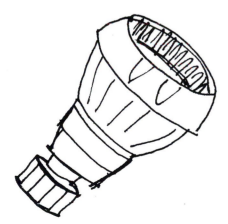

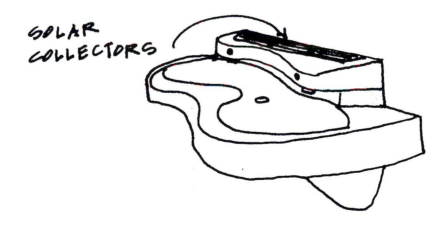

SOLAR COLLECTORS

▼ Figure 6.11 Tankless hot water heater.

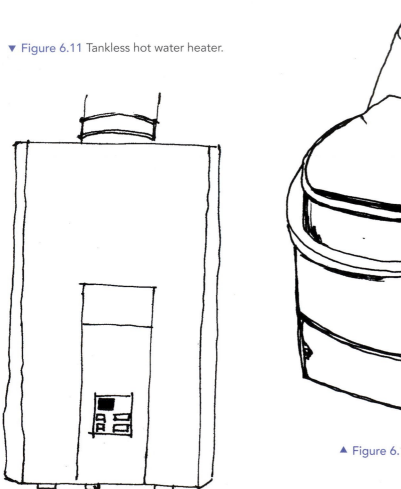

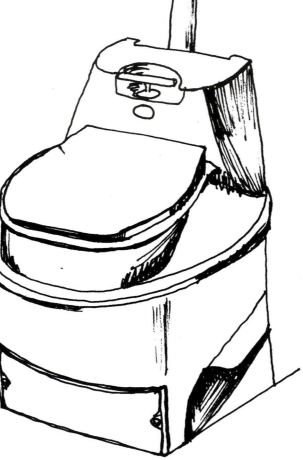

▲ Figure 6.12 Composting toilet.

TANKLESS HOT WATER HEATER

A tankless hot water heater heats water on demand and does not store water.

COMPOSTING TOILET

In rural locations where municipal water supply and sewer facility is not available, composting toilets can be used. The composting toilet does not use water to operate. Waste is treated and over time decomposes into usable compost.

IMPACTS ON INTERIOR DESIGN

The location of plumbing lines within a building have an impact on the space planning and interior design of a space. Although just about anything can be done, good design requires that an interior designer understands the limitations of what is practical and economical.

HOW TO PLACE PLUMBING FIXTURES

Generally speaking, the fewer plumbing walls, the better the solution. A shared chase wall lessens the need for multiple 6-inch or thicker walls. Additionally, this saves on the amount of supply pipe and waste pipe, and multiple fixtures can then share the vent pipe to the roof. For all of these reasons, shared plumbing walls contribute to good design.

◄ Figure 6.13 Recommended spacing of bathroom fixtures based on NKBA suggested guidelines

► Figure 6.14 Bathroom layouts meeting minimum code requirements.

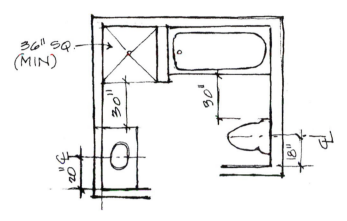

RECOMMENDED CLEARANCES

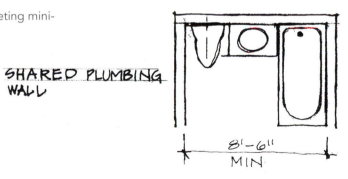

CODE CLEARANCES

SHARED PLUMBING WALL

8'-10" MIN

SHARED PLUMBING WALL

8'-6" MIN

CLEARANCES REQUIRED AND RECOMMENDED

The building code provides minimum clearances for water closets and urinals. It is important to keep in mind that minimum clearances may not equate to comfort. As Americans get larger, a wider spacing from adjacent walls is preferable to provide a more comfortable experience. The building code also requires the number of fixtures within a space, depending on the use and occupancy (Table 6.1).

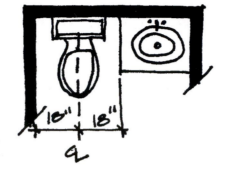

▲ Figure 6.15 Recommended water closet placement.

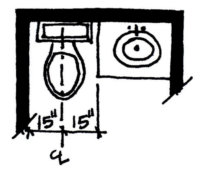

◄ Figure 6.16 Minimum clearances around water closet.

TABLE 6.1 PLUMBING REQUIREMENTS, ADAPTED FROM TABLE IBC, 2006

CLASSIFICATION	OCCUPANCY	DESCRIPTION	WATER CLOSETS Male	WATER CLOSETS Female	LAVATORIES Male	LAVATORIES Female	BATHTUBS OR SHOWERS	DRINKING FOUNTAINS	OTHER
Assembly	A-1	Theaters	1 per 125	1 per 65	1 per 200		—	1 per 500	1 service sink
	A-2	Nightclubs/bars	1 per 40	1 per 40	1 per 75		—	1 per 500	1 service sink
		Restaurants	1 per 75	1 per 75	1 per 200		—	1 per 500	1 service sink
	A-3	Auditoriums without permanent seating	1 per 125	1 per 65	1 per 200		—	1 per 500	1 service sink
		Passenger terminals	1 per 500	1 per 500	1 per 750		—	1 per 1000	1 service sink
		Places of worship	1 per 150	1 per 75	1 per 200		—	1 per 1000	1 service sink
	A-4	Coliseums, arenas, skating rinks	1 per 75 for the first 1,500; 1 per 120 remaining	1 per 40 for the first 1,500; 1 per 60 remaining	1 per 200	1 per 150	—	1 per 1000	1 service sink
	A-5	Stadiums, amusement parks, bleachers	1 per 75 for the first 1,500; 1 per 120 remaining	1 per 40 for the first 1,500; 1 per 60 remaining	1 per 200	1 per 150	—	1 per 1000	1 service sink
Business	B	Business	1 per 25 for the first 50 and 1 for the remainder exceeding 50		1 per 40 for the first 80 and 1 per 80 for the remainder exceeding 80		—	1 per 100	1 service sink
Educational	E	Educational facilities	1 per 50		1 per 50		—	1 per 100	1 service sink
Institutional	I-1	Residential care	1 per 10		1 per 10		1 per 8	1 per 100	1 service sink
	I-2	Hospitals, ambulatory nursing home patients	1 per room		1 per room		1 per 15	1 per 100	1 service sink
		Employees	1 per 25		1 per 35		—	1 per 100	—
		Visitors (other than residential care)	1 per 75		1 per 100		—	1 per 500	—
	I-3	Prisons	1 per cell		1 per cell		1 per 15	1 per 100	1 service sink
	I-3	Reformatories	1 per 15		1 per 15		1 per 15	1 per 100	1 service sink
	I-4	Adult day care and child care	1 per 15		1 per 15		—	1 per 100	1 service sink
Mercantile	M	Retail stores, service stations, shops	1 per 500		1 per 750		—	1 per 1000	1 service sink
Storage	S-1 S-2	Structures for storage	1 per 100		1 per 100		See plumbing code	1 per 1000	1 service sink

Note: Always consult the actual building code.

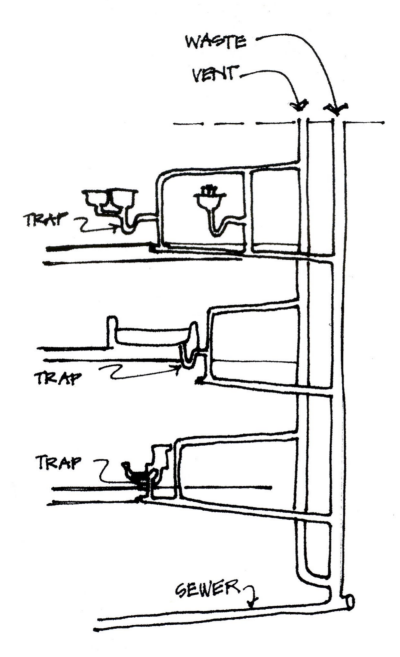

WASTE

VENT

TRAP

TRAP

TRAP

SEWER

STACKING

STACKING OF PLUMBING

In addition to placing all plumbing close together within a floor level, it is also preferable to **stack** plumbing from floor to floor. This way supply pipes, waste pipes, and vents can all be shared from floor to floor.

Figure 6.17 Diagram showing stacked plumbing fixtures.

CHASE WALLS

When a wall is thickened to accommodate plumbing, it is called a **chase wall**. Chase walls often run from floor to floor in large buildings, and can be shared by stacked fixtures.

Figure 6.18a–b Typical plumbing in wall a) plan view; b) perspective view

SLOPE OF WASTE PIPES

When placing bathroom fixtures, it is important to keep in mind the required slope of waste pipes which must fit within the floor thickness.

Figure 6.19 Diagram showing waste pipe network.

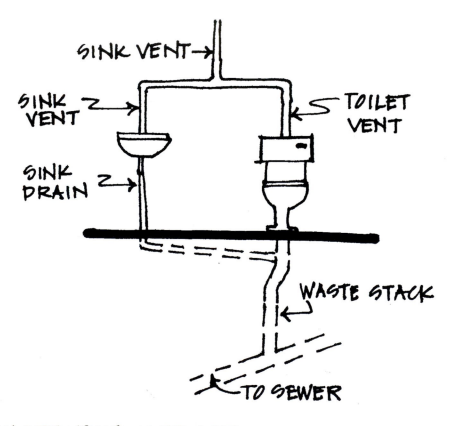

WASTE PIPE NETWORK

TRAPS

All bathroom fixtures must include a trap. The trap prevents sewer gases from backing up into the occupied interior space.

BATHROOM ACCESSORIES—HAND DRYERS VERSUS PAPER TOWELS

Energy-efficient hand dryers reduce the need for paper towels for hand drying in the bathroom.

Figure 6.20a–c Diagrams showing traps in a) lavatory; b) trap detail; and c) water closet section.

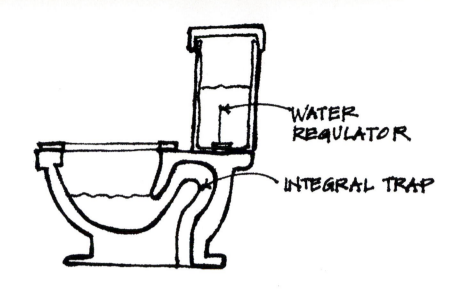

WATER CLOSET

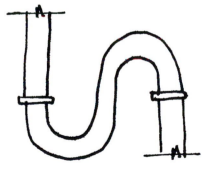

TRAP DETAIL

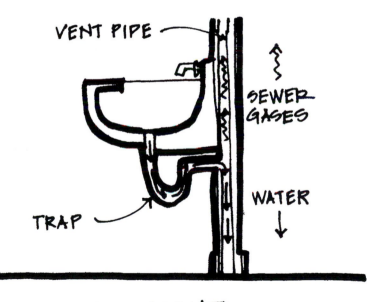

LAVATORY WITH VENT

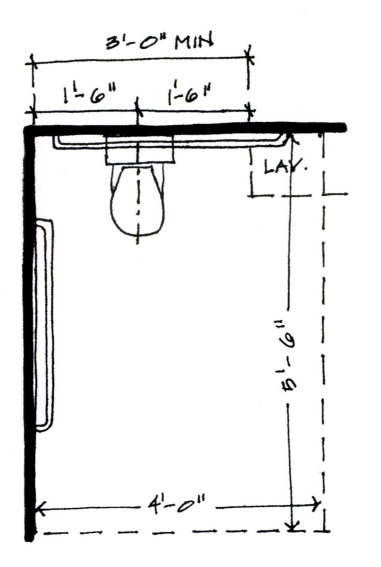

ACCESSIBLE - FRONT
APPROACH

VENTILATION

An important consideration in bathroom design is ventilation. This can be achieved in one of two ways—through the use of a window to allow for natural ventilation, or mechanically using a ceiling or wall mounted ventilation fan. Introducing air movement into the space helps to remove odors as well as reduce the likelihood of mold.

ACCESSIBLE BATHROOMS

In public projects, a certain percentage of the bathroom fixtures must be Americans with Disabilities Act (ADA) compliant. This law impacts the height of water closets and lavatories, the inclusion of grab bars, the size of some bathroom stalls, and the type of faucets and accessories used within a bathroom (and kitchen.)

Figure 6.21a–c ADA compliant bathroom fixture layouts. Always check the Code of Federal Regulations, 28 CFR Part 36 for actual layouts.

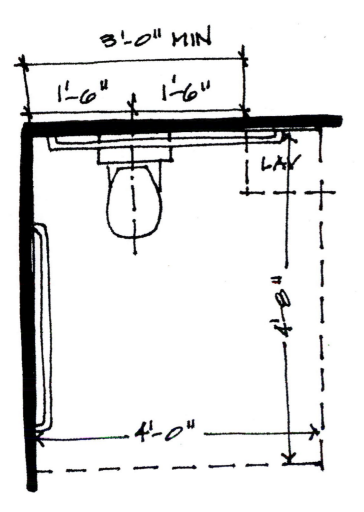

3'-0" MIN

1'-6" 1'-6"

LAV

4'-8"

4'-0"

ACCESSIBLE-SIDE
APPROACH

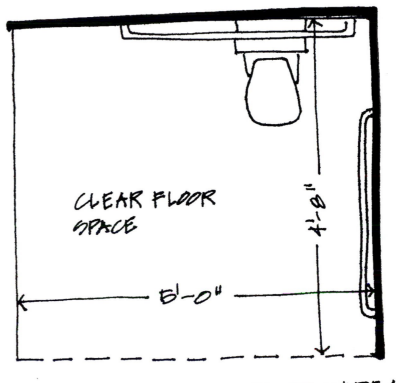

CLEAR FLOOR
SPACE

5'-0"

4'-8"

SHORTER STALL· WIDER WIDTH

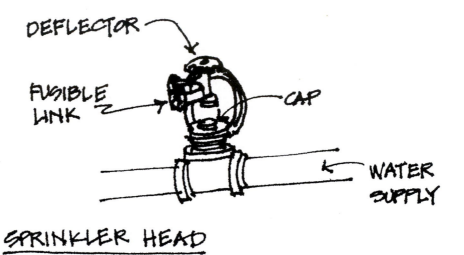

Figure 6.22 Typical sprinkler head.

OTHER PLUMBING CONCERNS

In addition to plumbing fixtures, designers must also be aware of sprinkler heads within the interior space. While specialists design the sprinkler systems for buildings, designers must integrate the placement of sprinkler heads with lighting and other ceiling mounted items. Access to sprinkler plumbing must also be provided.

KEY TERMS

black water

chase wall

gray water

lavatory

plumbing

potable water

stack

urinal

water closet

ASSIGNMENTS/EXERCISES

1. Using old (or current) design projects, assess whether you have optimized the location of the plumbing. Have you reduced the number of plumbing walls as much as possible? Is all of the plumbing located in a common location? Is the plumbing stacked from floor to floor?

2. Visit your local plumbing showroom and find the WaterSense compliant fixtures.

3. Assess your actions with regard to water usage. What can you do to reduce water use in your day-to-day life? Adopt one new water-reduction habit.

4. Identify a series of four or five case study interiors that use sustainable materials and maximize eco-efficient plumbing solutions. Include these in your course notebook for future reference.

RESOURCES

American Standard: www.americanstandard-us.com/

Kohler: www.kohler.com/

Comprehensive list of plumbing manufacturers: www.plumbingnet.com/

www.aiasdrg.org/sdrg.aspx?Page=26

www.edcmag.com

WaterSense toilet list from the EPA: www.epa.gov/watersense/pp/find_het.htm

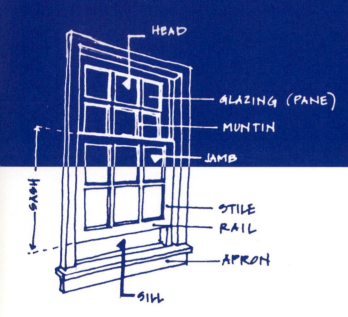

HEAD

GLAZING (PANE)

MUNTIN

JAMB

STILE

RAIL

APRON

SILL

6 OVER 6 DOUBLE-HUNG

CHAPTER 7

Walls

Sustainable designs are system designs. They help solve the economic, social, and environmental issues simultaneously and as a single system.

Daniel E. Williams, Sustainable Design: Ecology, Architecture, and Planning

OBJECTIVES

- Choose interior wall finishes that are sustainable and appropriate
- Identify wall types
- Design interior walls appropriate to their use
- Specify interior wall finishes in finish schedules and finishes plan

INTRODUCTION

Structural systems and various materials for walls, floors, and roofs were discussed in Chapter 3. This chapter on walls will discuss wall systems, how the wall assembly works as a unit, and the finish materials for them.

FRAMING SYSTEMS

As mentioned in Chapter 3, there are several different ways a wall can be framed. As a review, the three main systems are stud walls, masonry or concrete bearing walls, and column and beam structural frame walls with infill. A new type of wall being used is the structural panel wall.

STUD WALLS

Stud wall can be built from either wood or light gauge steel. These come in industry-standard sizes, with the most common being 2 inches by 4 inches or 2 inches by 6 inches. It is important to note that these are nominal dimensions and not the actual dimensions. Table 7.1 shows the relationship when using light frame wood construction.

The standard spacing for wall studs is 12 inches on center, 16 inches on center, or 24 inches on center. The stud wall starts with a two-by-four or four-by-six laid horizontally to which the individual studs are nailed. A top plate is added after all the verticals are in place. Window and door openings are then framed as needed with sills and headers spanning between studs that are doubled at the sides, sills, and headers. Partial studs known as cripples are used to space the remainder of the distance both above and below the opening.

TABLE 7.1 WOOD FRAMING MEMBERS

WOOD FRAMING MEMBER	NOMINAL DIMENSIONS	ACTUAL DIMENSIONS
2 × 4	2 × 4	$1\frac{3}{4}$" × $3\frac{1}{2}$"
2 × 6	2 × 6	$1\frac{3}{4}$" × $5\frac{1}{2}$"

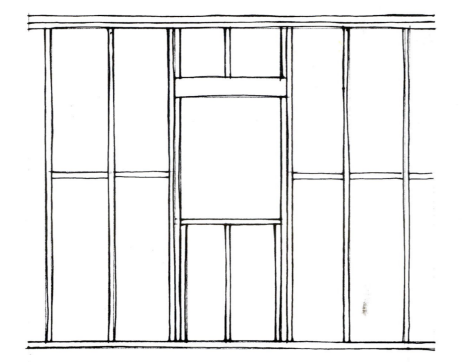

After stud walls are framed, they are sheathed to make them stable against wind loads. Sheathing can be either plywood or oriented strand board (OSB). OSB is far less expensive than plywood. Both plywood and OSB contain adhesives and often formaldehyde that are toxic chemicals. A sustainable choice would avoid both of these. Use formaldehyde free in order to reduce volatile organic compounds (VOCs) in the indoor air (see Chapter 10).

◄ Figure 7.1 Typical 2 × stud wall construction. Use FSC-certified wood products.

▼ Figure 7.2
Typical light gauge steel stud construction.

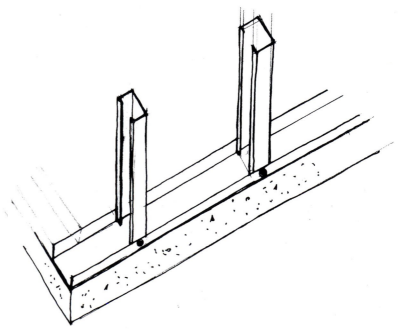

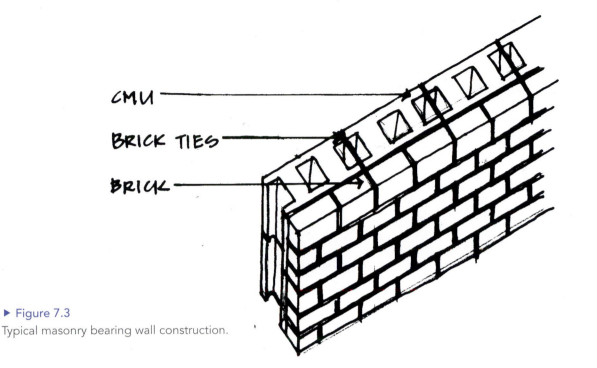

CMU

BRICK TIES

BRICK

▶ Figure 7.3
Typical masonry bearing wall construction.

CONCRETE AND MASONRY BEARING WALLS

As mentioned in Chapter 3, masonry and concrete bearing walls are monolithic and made from either concrete masonry units (CMU), brick or stone bearing walls, or reinforced concrete. In some cases the CMU walls will be faced with a veneer of brick held to the CMU with brick ties. The challenges with this type of wall system include placement of electrical wiring, boxes, and switching; penetrations for plumbing and HVAC; and attachment of interior finish materials and artwork.

STRUCTURAL FRAME WALLS

The structural frame, column and beam systems can be in-filled in a variety of ways including stud wall infill, insulation panel in-fill, and other materials. Structural insulation panels (SIPs) can be made from wood or steel framing and differing forms of insulation with the most common type being rigid insulation.

In some cases, walls need to be insulated. Exterior walls are insulated in most parts of the country. Interior walls may also contain insulation for acoustical purposes.

▼ Figure 7.4 Typical structural frame construction.

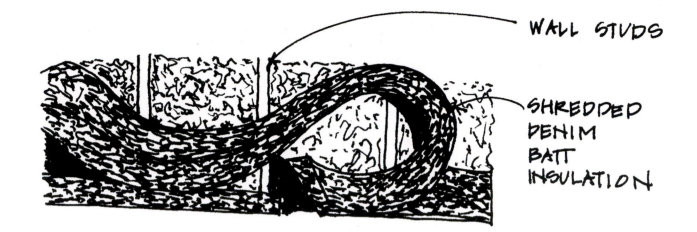

▲ **Figure 7.5** Batt insulation composed of recycled shredded denim.

▼ **Figure 7.6**
Cellulose insulation made from wood pulp.

▼ **Figure 7.7** Rigid insulation.

INSULATION

There are several forms of insulation traditionally used within exterior walls and interior acoustical partitions. The three main types include batt insulation, cellulose insulation, and rigid board insulation. Recent developments in sustainable construction have led to variations on these three types. Insulation can be made from recycled paper pulp or recycled blue jeans and other natural fibers to reduce its environmental impact.

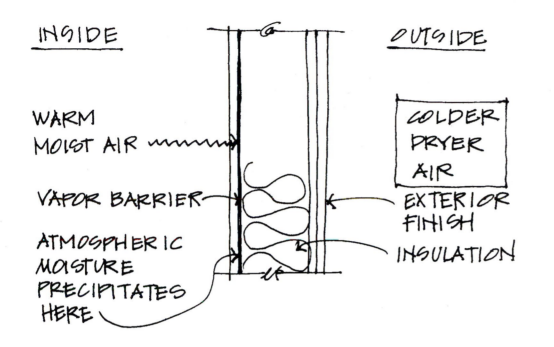

INSIDE   OUTSIDE

WARM
MOIST AIR

VAPOR BARRIER

ATMOSPHERIC
MOISTURE
PRECIPITATES
HERE

COLDER
DRYER
AIR

EXTERIOR
FINISH

INSULATION

VAPOR RETARDERS

Condensation within the wall cavity occurs when there is a substantial difference in temperature between the inside and the outside. The vapor retarder is installed in the wall towards the warmer side. This can vary depending on the climate zone. In cold climates, the vapor retarder is installed towards the inside; in hot and humid climates, towards the outside.

▲ Figure 7.8 Typical location of vapor barrier within a wall section.

▶ Figure 7.9 Condensation diagram.

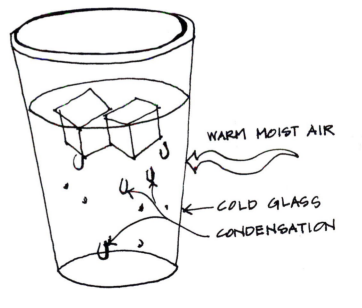

WARM MOIST AIR

COLD GLASS

CONDENSATION

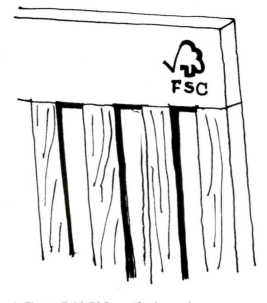

▲ Figure 7.10 FSC certified wood.

EXTERIOR MATERIALS

With stud walls, structural frame walls, and structural insulated panel walls, a variety of exterior cladding materials are used. Sustainable siding options include Forest Stewardship Council (FSC) certified wood shingles or boards, concrete panels and concrete board siding, and stucco.

Concrete is composed of portland cement, aggregate, and water. When mixed, these components undergo a chemical reaction through which they harden over a period of approximately 28 days. The Romans were the first to use portland cement as a building material, such as the dome of the Pantheon. A variety of admixtures make concrete a versatile material that can cure faster or slower as needed, can be used in a variety of temperature ranges, and can be colored as desired.

Stucco is similar to plaster and is used for exterior applications usually over wood.

Oftentimes, siding options are painted or stained, and stucco exteriors are painted. In addition to the sustainable characteristics of the cladding material, the coating must also meet environmental criteria. A wide variety of low VOC or no VOC coatings are now available for this use.

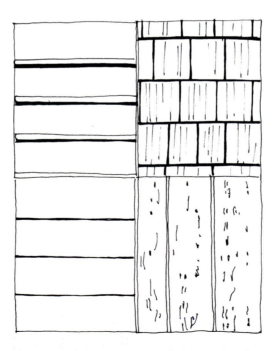

◄ Figure 7.11 Concrete board siding.

Figure 7.12 Concrete panels as exterior material.

Figure 7.13 Exterior stucco.

INTERIOR SUBSTRATE MATERIALS

The final component of the sustainable wall assembly consists of the interior finish material. By far, gypsum wallboard (also called dry wall or sheet rock) is the most commonly used interior wall substrate. Whereas some manufacturers offer recycled gypsum and recycled paper facing for their products, a more sustainable option is plaster finished walls. Unfortunately, plaster work is time intensive and few trades people today have this knowledge.

Gypsum wallboard consists of gypsum sandwiched between two layers of heavy paper. Manufacturers produce several types of wallboard for various uses. Type X is fire-rated. There are also wallboards that are water resistant, abuse resistant, foil backed (which provides a vapor barrier), and pre-finished. Sheets come in a 4-foot by 8-foot standard size and thicknesses of $\frac{1}{2}$ inch and $\frac{5}{8}$ inch.

Plaster work is applied in a three-coat system. Lath (either wood strips or metal wire) provides the base for the first coat, referred to as the brown coat. A scratch coat covers the brown coat and the three-layer system is completed by a finish coat. Several types of texturing options can be done to the finish coat ranging from smooth to heavily textured. Like concrete, plaster work cures as the lime, gypsum, and water undergo a chemical reaction.

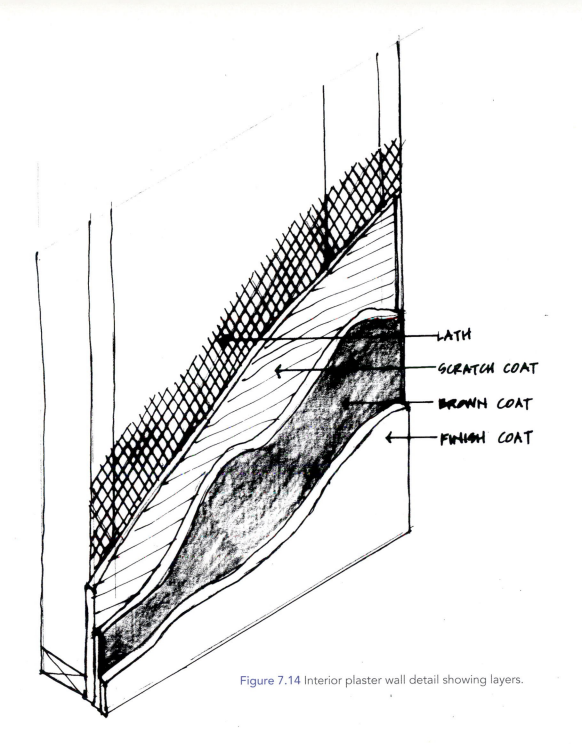

LATH

SCRATCH COAT

BROWN COAT

FINISH COAT

Figure 7.14 Interior plaster wall detail showing layers.

WALL FINISH (INTERIOR)

How the space will be used helps to determine the appropriate wall finish that a designer chooses. In addition to painted plaster or wallboard, several other wall finishes adorn interior spaces, including tile, wood panels, stone, brick, fabric, paper, carpet, wire mesh, metal slats, 3-Form/acrylic panels, and various types of glass.

TILE

In a wet location, tile must be installed over cement board to avoid water penetration into the framing materials and insulation of the wall. Wall tiles can be made from many different materials, including concrete, clay, glass, metal, porcelain, and stone. In addition, they can come in several different shapes.

WOOD

Traditionally, wood paneling was applied directly to the wall studs. With the advent of manufactured paneling—which is much thinner than traditional wood paneling in thickness—these panels were more often applied over a gypsum wallboard substrate. Today, many forms of wood are used as a wall finish, including full wall panels, wainscots, and in conjunction with other materials. To meet sustainability objectives of a project, the use of FSC-certified wood is recommended.

THICK SET
1¼" MORTAR BED

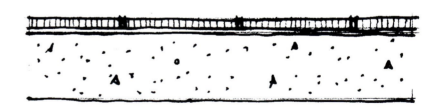

THIN SET

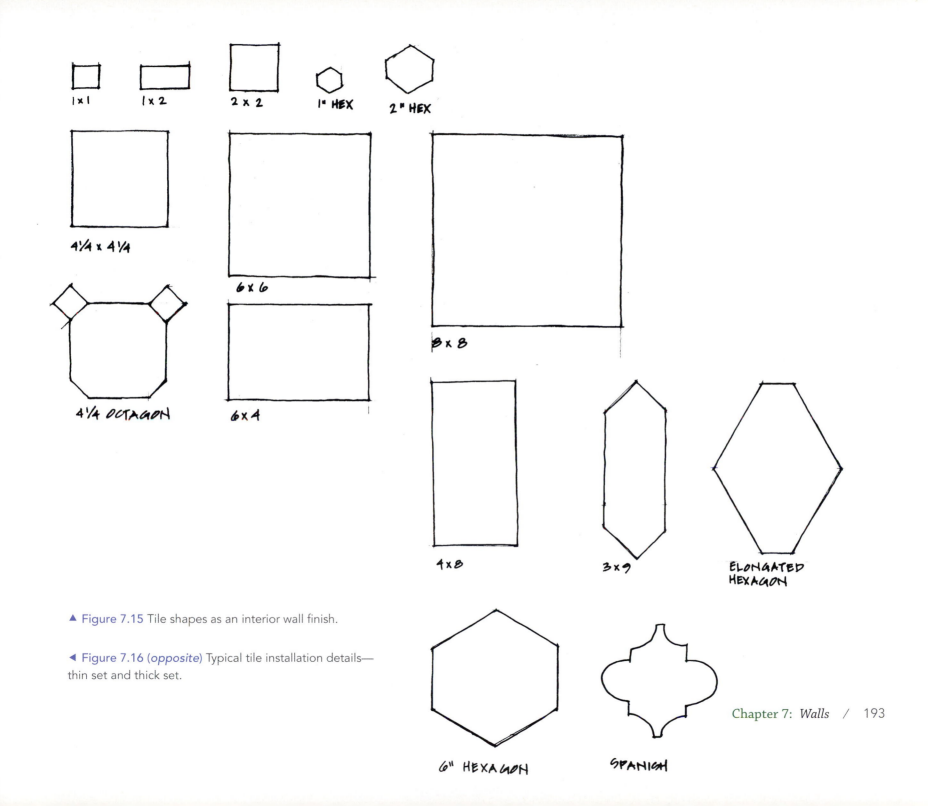

1 x 1 1 x 2 2 x 2 1" HEX 2" HEX

4¼ x 4¼

6 x 6

4¼ OCTAGON

6 x 4

8 x 8

4 x 8

3 x 9

ELONGATED HEXAGON

6" HEXAGON

SPANISH

▲ Figure 7.15 Tile shapes as an interior wall finish.

◄ Figure 7.16 (*opposite*) Typical tile installation details—thin set and thick set.

BRICK/STONE

Brick and stone can be used as in an interior wall finish in one of two ways: as a continuation of the exterior wall, or as a decorative applied finish. In historic construction, it was not uncommon for the masonry bearing wall to be exposed on the interior, especially in basements and service areas. Generally, in the more finished spaces, these surfaces would have been plastered or white washed. Today these would be **furred** out as is commonly done with concrete block. Furring uses thin strips of wood or metal channels screwed into the masonry that provide a surface to which the drywall can be attached.

WALL TEXTILES

For acoustical purposes, fabric, paper, or carpeting may be used on a wall surface. Several points must be considered prior to using such a material. The building code will determine the fire rating required for all surfaces within a given occupancy use. Also, the designer needs to be aware of the multitude of green ratings used within the textile and carpet industries. By far, the most stringent of these is to meet the cradle to cradle protocol.

INTERIOR DETAILING

Where two surfaces meet, **trim** work is used to make a clean joint. At the floor level, a base molding covers the joint between the floor and the base of the wall. Crown molding obscures the joint between the top of the wall and the ceiling plane. Because the walls and ceiling materials are often the same, crown molding is not always needed, although it is still commonly used in traditional interiors. A chair molding is used to divide the lower third of the wall from the upper two-thirds. Its functional purpose is to protect the wall from chair backs, particularly in a dining room or someplace with heavy traffic circulation. If wood panels are used below the chair rail, these panels are known as wainscoting.

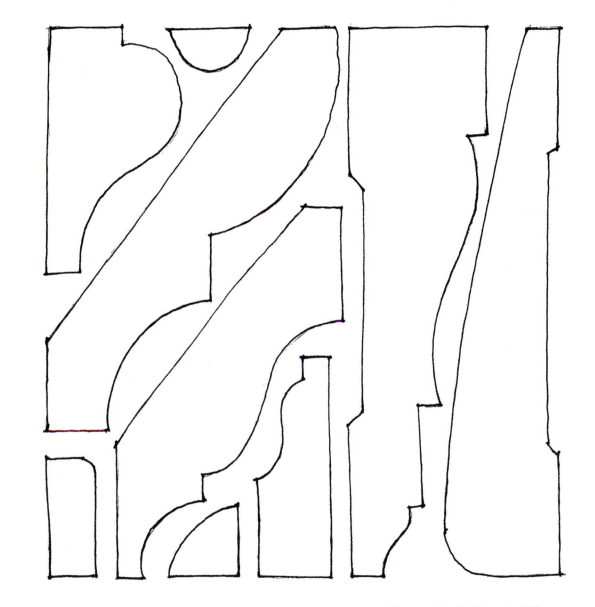

Figure 7.17 Standard wood molding profiles.

TRIM WORK

Sustainable trim options include FSC-certified wood products, reclaimed lumber that can be milled into trim, and plaster cast moldings.

CASEWORK (BUILT-IN FURNITURE)

Oftentimes, a designer will provide built-in furniture pieces such as bookcases, cabinets, and other storage solutions. These built-in units are called **casework**. Designers should be aware of joinery types, wood and other materials most often used for casework, as well as operational and decorative hardware options in order to design these items consistent with the design intent of the overall project.

The most commonly used green options for casework include: plyboo (a plywood made from bamboo), medium-density fiberboard (MDF) without formaldehyde or other off-gassing toxins, and FSC-certified wood products. Consideration should be given to obtaining materials within an immediate radius of the building site. Casework is commonly built from solid wood, plywood, or MDF. Until recently, the adhesives used in plywood and some fiberboards emitted volatile organic compounds (VOCs) into the air. As sustainability initiatives have helped change the manufacturing process, new low or no VOC options are now available. MDF provides paint-grade casework. Both plywood with a veneer finish and solid wood can be used for either paint grade or stain grade casework depending on the quality of the wood and the desires of the designer.

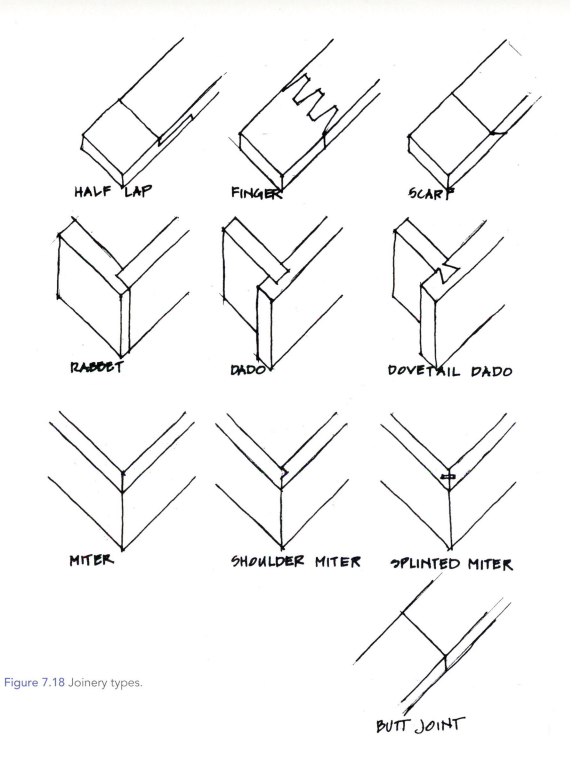

HALF LAP   FINGER   SCARF

RABBET   DADO   DOVETAIL DADO

MITER   SHOULDER MITER   SPLINTED MITER

BUTT JOINT

Figure 7.18 Joinery types.

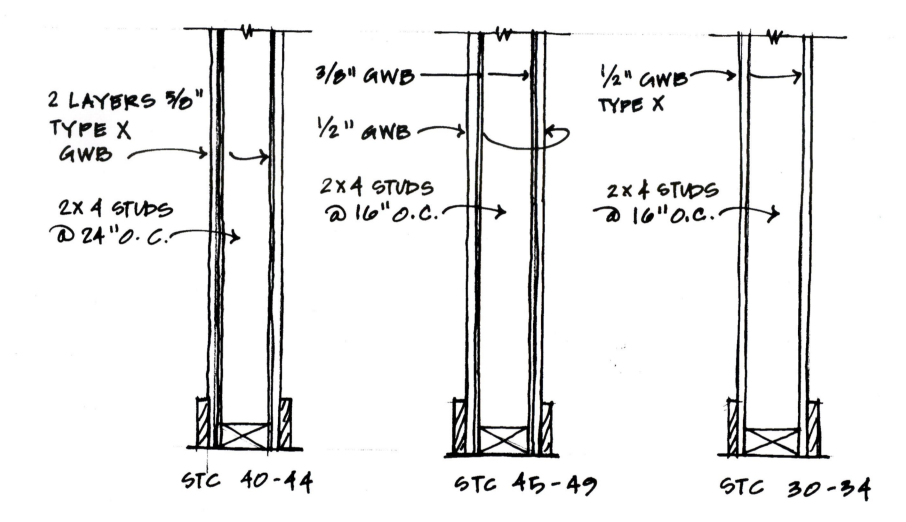

2 LAYERS 5/8"
TYPE X
GWB

2×4 STUDS
@ 24" O.C.

STC 40-44

3/8" GWB

1/2" GWB

2×4 STUDS
@ 16" O.C.

STC 45-49

1/2" GWB
TYPE X

2×4 STUDS
@ 16" O.C.

STC 30-34

Figure 7.19 Typical acoustical partitions.

INTERIOR DESIGN CONSIDERATIONS

ACOUSTICAL PARTITIONS

To control noise and sound transmission from one space to the next, acoustical partitions should be used. This is covered in more detail in Chapter 10.

FIRE WALLS

Another wall type with which an interior designer must be familiar is the fire-rated partition, called a fire wall. Based on the use of the space, specific fire separations are required by the applicable building code. These might be one-hour, two-hour or even three-hour fire-rated partitions.

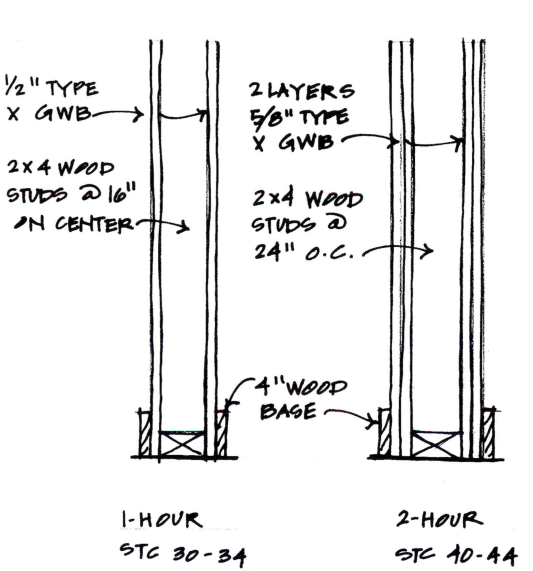

½" TYPE X GWB

2 X 4 WOOD STUDS @ 16" ON CENTER

4" WOOD BASE

2 LAYERS 5/8" TYPE X GWB

2 X 4 WOOD STUDS @ 24" O.C.

1-HOUR STC 30-34

2-HOUR STC 40-44

Figure 7.20
Typical fire-rated partitions, 1-hour and 2-hour.

BEARING WALLS

Interior designers cannot legally change the structure of a building in any way. If a designer believes that a partition is bearing loads or has any doubts about how to tell, they must always consult an architect or structural engineer. Some general rules of thumb can apply:

- Never remove a column.
- In wood construction, generally speaking, the flooring runs perpendicular to the framing; however, when in doubt, consult an expert.

CURVED WALLS

New designers are often quite fond of curved walls. Several points should be considered before creating curved walls for a design. Every material has a maximum curving radius. How tight the radius of a wall can be may be limited by the materials a designer plans to use. It is important to consider the underlying framing and finish material when deciding to use a curve. Also, contractors can easily snap chalk lines to locate orthogonal walls. To construct a curved wall, the radius of the wall must be properly indicated on the design plans and clearly located within the context of the other walls. Think through how you would build this wall in a model. What information do you need to be successful? Chances are that if it is hard for you to build in a model, it is even harder to construct in reality. Anything out of the ordinary will generally cost more. Curved walls can be used to create interest and enrich a design; however, their use should be carefully considered first.

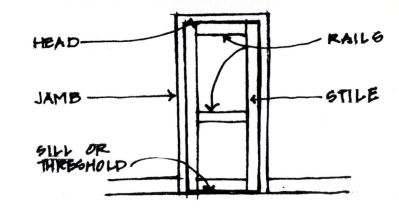

INTERIOR DOORS AND WINDOWS

Interior walls include doors and, in some cases, interior windows. Both doors and windows become part of the fire-rated assembly of the wall and are rated according to their fire-resistant characteristics.

DOORS—MATERIALS

Doors are most commonly made from wood or steel. Depending on the use and location, they may be either solid or hollow core. Solid doors can have mineral cores, particleboard cores, or wood cores. For acoustical separation as well as fire rating, solid core doors are required. Standard door sizes for ADA compliance are 3 feet wide by 6 feet, 8 inches high. They increase in width in increments of 2 inches. Interior doors are usually 1⅜ inches thick whereas exterior doors are 1¾ inches thick. Other heights are available depending on the individual manufacturer.

CONFIGURATION

Doors consist of some standard parts including panels, stiles, and rails. These elements can be assembled in several different configurations to achieve a variety of appearances.

FLUSH

6-PANEL

LOUVER

GLAZED

DUTCH

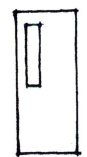

VISION

Figure 7.21 Interior doors—configuration.

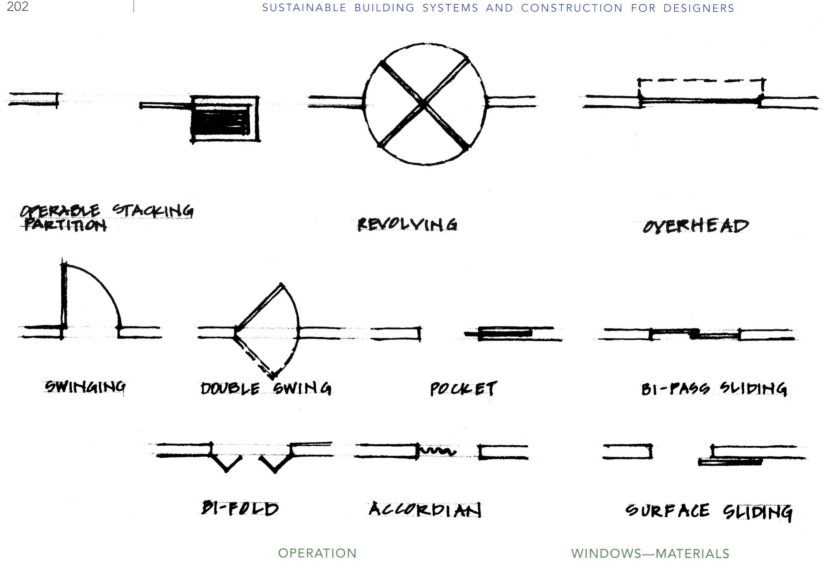

OPERABLE STACKING PARTITION   **REVOLVING**   **OVERHEAD**

SWINGING   **DOUBLE SWING**   **POCKET**   **BI-PASS SLIDING**

BI-FOLD   **ACCORDIAN**   **SURFACE SLIDING**

OPERATION

Figure 7.22 Interior doors—operation.

Doors have several different types of operations including sliding, pocket, swinging, bifold, and overhead.

WINDOWS—MATERIALS

Similar to doors, windows are generally made from wood or metal. Aluminum and steel are both used to make interior windows.

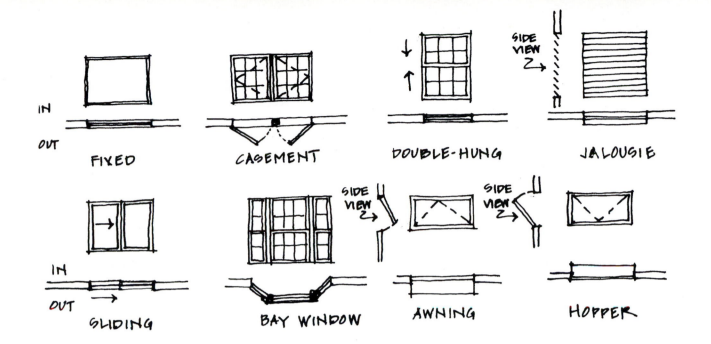

FIXED   CASEMENT   DOUBLE-HUNG   JALOUSIE

SLIDING   BAY WINDOW   AWNING   HOPPER

▲ Figure 7.23 Interior windows—operation.

▶ Figure 7.24 Window parts.

OPERATION

There are several different operational configurations for interior windows.

PARTS OF THE WINDOW

Window terminology is both complex and often misused. While many of these components may not be a part of the interior window, it is still important to understand the terminology associated with window construction.

ENERGY ISSUES

In a sustainable building, windows and doors represent one of the most important components of the building envelope. Most air leakage occurs around window and door openings, making them an integral part of a sustainable design solution.

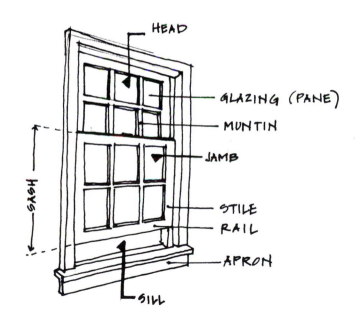

HEAD

GLAZING (PANE)

MUNTIN

JAMB

STILE

RAIL

APRON

SILL

SASH

6 OVER 6 DOUBLE-HUNG

WALL SCHEDULES, FINISH SCHEDULES, AND FINISH PLANS

A variety of construction documents are used to indicate the types of partitions in a building and the finishes they contain.

Wall Schedule/Wall Types/Partition Types

The wall schedule is used to describe the wall types used within a given project. All acoustical partitions, fire-rated partitions, and any other specialty wall types in addition to all standard interior and exterior wall types are included in the wall schedule. Partial sections for each of these variations are also generally included.

Finish Schedule

A **finish schedule** uses a table format to communicate all information about the interior finishes and details of every room within a project. This includes floor finish, base molding, wall finishes, ceiling type and height, paint colors, and casework information.

TABLE 7.2 TYPICAL FINISHES SCHEDULE

NO.	ROOM NAME	FLOOR	BASE	WALLS				CEILING	REMARKS
				N	S	E	W		
101									
102									
103									
104									
105									
106									
107									
108									
109									
110									

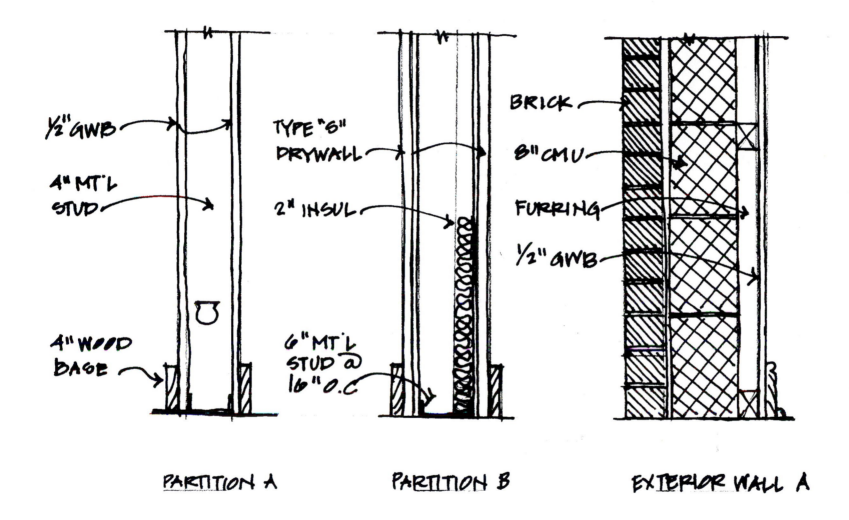

½" GWB

4" MT'L STUD

4" WOOD BASE

TYPE "6" DRYWALL

2" INSUL

6" MT'L STUD @ 16" O.C

BRICK

8" CMU

FURRING

½" GWB

PARTITION A

PARTITION B

EXTERIOR WALL A

Figure 7.25 Wall types as seen in a partition schedule.

finish plan
vintage vines wine bar **+** lounge

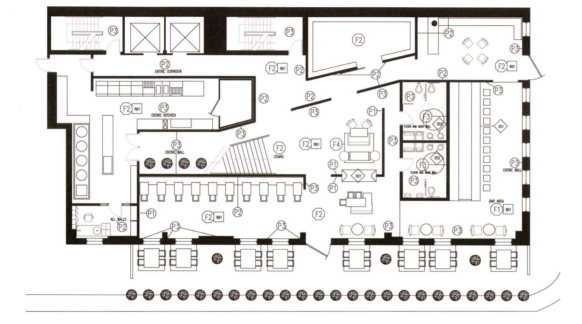

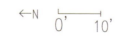

←N 0' 10'

MARK	MANUFACTURER	DESCRIPTION
P1	Benjamin Moore	Chambourde AF645
P2	Benjamin Moore	Granite AF660
P3	Benjamin Moore	Deep in thought AF30
F1	Teregren Bamboo	Synergy Java
F2	Colledani - Materia	Epoxy Resin Cement Floor - White
F3	Daltile	Metal Fusion Ceramic Tile – Zinc Oxide 16x24
F4	Milliken Carpet	Rising Sun Area Rug RF52-75094 Color M12 81"x 83.5"
SS1	Storm Copper Components	.187" Thick Copper Panel 24x48
SS2	VT Industries	Madras Indian Slate Formica 3688-77
RB1	Johnsonite Rubber Wall Base	4x120 4SC Snow White
BB1	Ambient Bamboo Wall Base	Carbonized Strand Woven 5/8" Thick

Finish Plan

A variation on the finishes schedule sometimes used by interior designers is the finish plan. In this method, a plan overlay is used and all of the finish information is included within each of the rooms on the actual plan.

Figure 7.26 Typical finishes plan.

CASE STUDIES

The case study examples included here demonstrate multiple approaches to the wall in interior space.

The Perkins + Will design for the Haworth Showroom in Washington, D.C. integrates wallboard walls (Figure 7.27), glass walls (Figure 7.28), low height acoustical partitions (Figure 7.29a and b), and sliding glass walls (Figure 7.30) to define various parts of the showroom spaces.

Figure 7.27 Perkins + Will, Haworth Showroom, Washington, D.C.
Photo Credit: Nick Merrick, Hedrich Blessing Photography.

Figure 7.28 Perkins + Will, Haworth Showroom, Washington D.C. Photo Credit: Nick Merrick, Hedrich Blessing Photography.

Figure 7.29a–b, Figure 7.30
(*clockwise from bottom left*)
Perkins + Will, Haworth Showroom,
Washington D.C. Photo Credit: Nick
Merrick, Hedrich Blessing Photography.

Figure 7.31 studio27architecture, Design Army, Washington D.C. Photo Credit: Anice Hoachlander, Hoachlander Davis Photography, LLC.

studio27architecture implements openings in wallboard partitions of the Design Army Building (Figure 7.31) to create interest and allow light from a skylight to penetrate deeper into the interior space (Figure 7.32). Half walls composed of wallboard are accented with a wood countertop, which also becomes part of the finished wall surface (Figure 7.33). Translucent panels are used to create the separation between the stair and adjacent space (Figure 7.34). In the Combination 1136 + 1167 space, the designers use a combination of wallboard, metal cable rails, mirrors, and wood wall surfaces to create a series of layered spaces (Figure 7.35). A steel framework with wood shelves is used as a dividing partition between the stair and adjoining space on one side (Figure 7.36) whereas a translucent glass wall is used on the other side of the stair to separate the master bedroom (Figure 7.37). Throughout the space, a consistent vocabulary of maple, steel, and metal cables are used to enhance a drywall interior skin (Figure 7.38a and b).

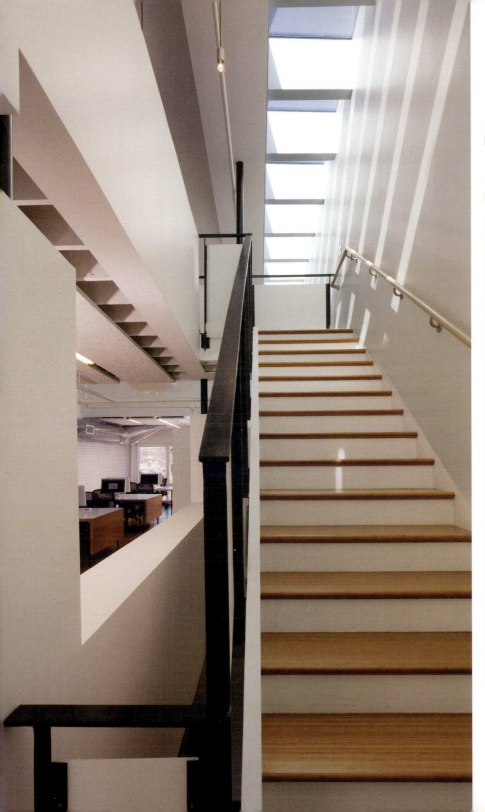

◄ Figure 7.32 studio27architecture, Design Army, Washington D.C.
Photo Credit: Anice Hoachlander, Hoachlander Davis Photography, LLC.

▼ Figure 7.33 studio27architecture, Design Army, Washington D.C.
Photo Credit: Anice Hoachlander, Hoachlander Davis Photography, LLC.

◄ **Figure 7.34** studio27architecture, Design Army, Washington D.C. **Photo Credit:** Anice Hoachlander, Hoachlander Davis Photography, LLC.

▲ **Figure 7.35** studio27architecture, Combination 1136 + 1167, Arlington, VA. **Photo Credit:** Anice Hoachlander, Hoachlander Davis Photography, LLC.

► **Figure 7.36 (*opposite*)** studio27architecture, Combination 1136 + 1167, Arlington, VA. **Photo Credit:** Anice Hoachlander, Hoachlander Davis Photography, LLC.

213

▲ Figure 7.37 studio27architecture, Combination 1136 + 1167, Arlington, VA. Photo Credit: Anice Hoachlander, Hoachlander Davis Photography, LLC.

▶ Figure 7.38a–b (*opposite*) studio27architecture, Combination 1136 + 1167, Arlington, VA. Photo Credit: Anice Hoachlander, Hoachlander Davis Photography, LLC.

In the D.C. Navigator's building, RTKL uses salvaged wood and brick to create texture and juxtaposition in the conference room (Figure 7.39).

The Cofra Building design by Perkins + Will includes a variety of textural wall details. Tile is used to create a rhythmic texture in the elevator lobby (Figure 7.40). Blue glass is contrasted with wooden slats to create interest and dimension in the lobby space (Figure 7.41).

Figure 7.40 Wall texture detail. Perkins + Will, Cofra. Photo Credit: ArchPhoto, Eduard Hueber.

Figure 7.41 Wall texture detail. Perkins + Will, Cofra. Photo Credit: ArchPhoto, Eduard Hueber.

KEY TERMS

admixtures

base board

casework

chair rail

concrete

cornice

crown

finish plan

finish schedule

furred

gypsum wallboard (GWB, sheet rock)

medium density fiberboard (MDF)

plaster

plyboo

stucco

trim

ASSIGNMENTS/EXERCISES

1. Create a list of all the different partition types for a recent design project.

2. Draw typical sections for each partition type identified in the above assignment. Use all sustainable materials for each section and label accordingly.

3. Identify several interior case studies that use sustainable interior finishes. Keep these in your course notebook for future reference.

RESOURCES

Ballast, David Kent. (2005). *Interior Construction and Detailing for Designers and Architects.* Belmont, California: Professional Publications, Inc.

CHAPTER 8

Floors

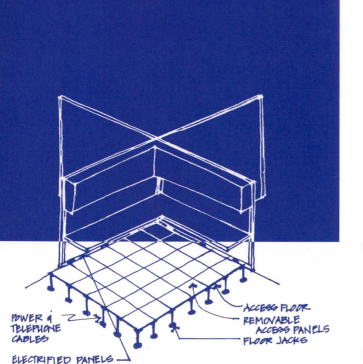

POWER & TELEPHONE CABLES

ACCESS FLOOR
REMOVABLE ACCESS PANELS
FLOOR JACKS

ELECTRIFIED PANELS

SYSTEMS FURNITURE

The mid-course correction I think Earth and humanity need probably depends on, more than any other one thing, changed minds, i.e., new paradigms.

Ray Anderson, Mid-Course Correction

OBJECTIVES

- Identify floor systems (concrete, wood, and steel)
- Select appropriate sustainable floor finishes

INTRODUCTION

This chapter describes the floor system including the framing and finish materials.

FRAMING SYSTEMS

The various types of floor framing systems are presented here based on the material used.

WOOD

Wood floor framing systems can be divided into two basic types: light frame construction (which uses joists) and heavy timber frame construction that uses beams and girders.

Light Frame

Light frame construction uses multiple small wood members to carry a load. In the wall, these are called studs; when they carry a floor load, they are called joists. Most light frame floor framing systems use 2 × 8, 2 × 10, or 2 × 12. These members are spaced either 12, 16, or 24 inches on center—meaning from the center line of one to the center line of the adjacent member. Standard spans and the loads they can carry vary depending on the wood species and the grade of the lumber. Standard variations and typical spans can be found in the building code. The floor joists are then covered with a sub-flooring material—usually plywood or OSB.

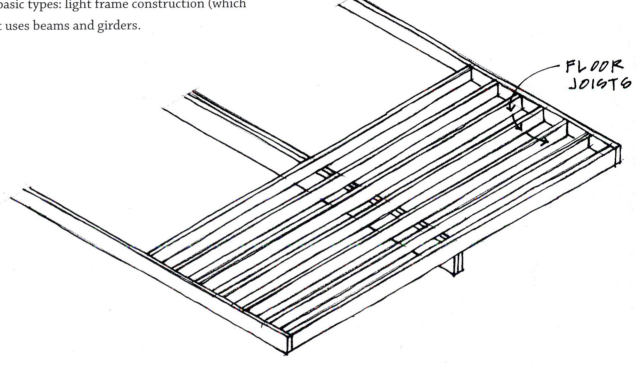

FLOOR JOISTS

Figure 8.1
2 × wood floor framing using FSC framing members.

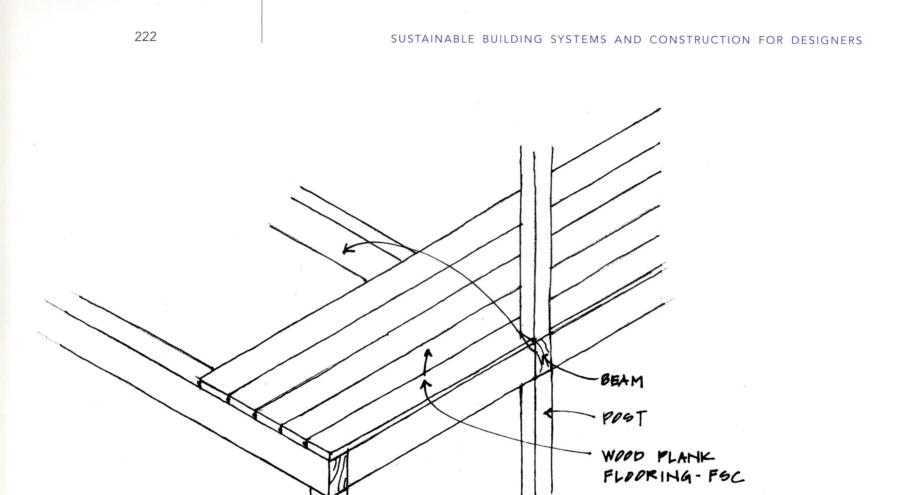

BEAM

POST

WOOD PLANK
FLOORING - FSC

Heavy Timber

Heavy timber framing relies on a structural frame consisting of columns and beams. The horizontal beams are then used to support girders. Girders then carry the weight of floor planks to the beams where the load can be transferred to the columns.

Figure 8.2
Heavy timber floor framing with wood blank floor.

STEEL

Like wood construction, steel floor framing is either light gauge with multiple open web joists or structural steel with beams and girders.

Structural Steel with Concrete in Metal Decking

A structural steel floor framing system relies on regularly placed columns that support steel beams. Girders span these beams and are used to carry a metal decking. Concrete is poured into the metal decking to create a floor system.

Figure 8.3 Structural steel floor system.

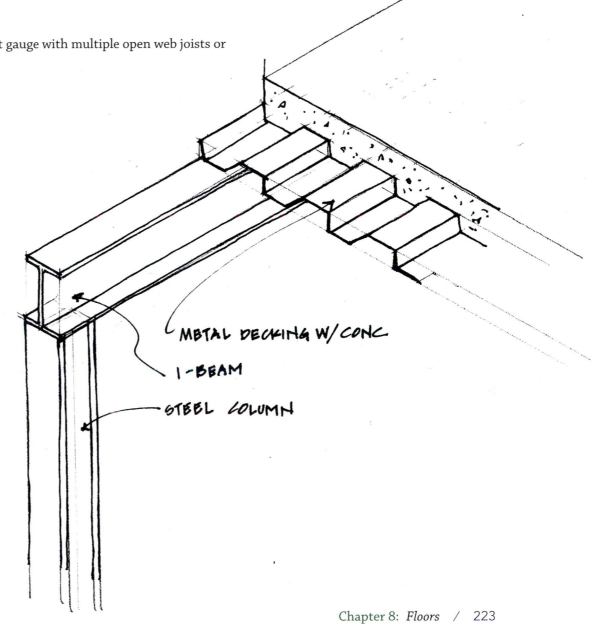

METAL DECKING W/ CONC

I-BEAM

STEEL COLUMN

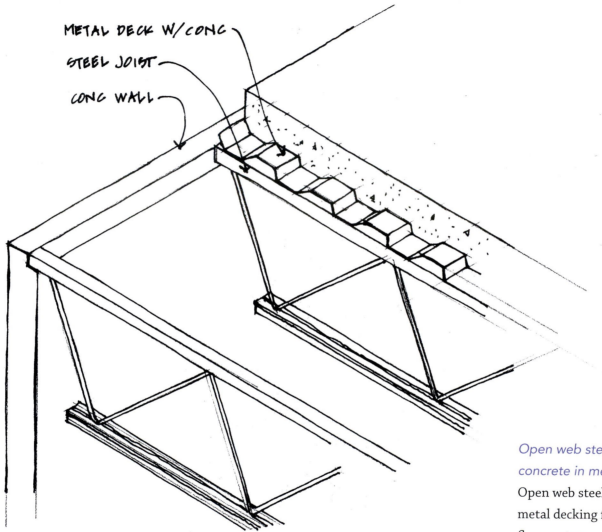

METAL DECK W/CONC

STEEL JOIST

CONC WALL

Open web steel joist with concrete in metal decking

Open web steel joists are also used to carry metal decking for a concrete-metal decking floor system.

Figure 8.4 Open web steel joists.

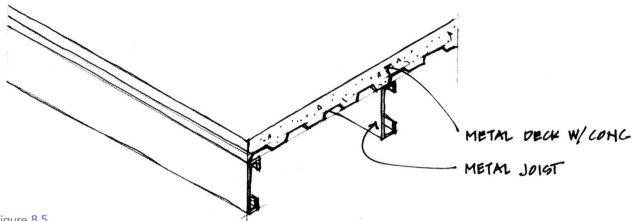

Figure 8.5
Poured in place concrete slab in metal deck.

CONCRETE

Concrete as a flooring system is either poured in place on the site or is cast at a plant and assembled on site.

Slab-poured in Place

Poured-in-place concrete slabs are used in both residential and commercial construction. Woven wire mesh is used to reinforce the concrete, as is steel rebar. Formwork is generally constructed from wood or steel, and is later removed after the slab of concrete has cured. Concrete cures through a chemical reaction that is not complete for twenty-eight days.

Pre-cast Slabs (Single T, Double T, Plank)

Several variations of **pre-cast** concrete floor slabs exist. These are poured in a factory under controlled settings, and are then trucked to the job site where they are assembled.

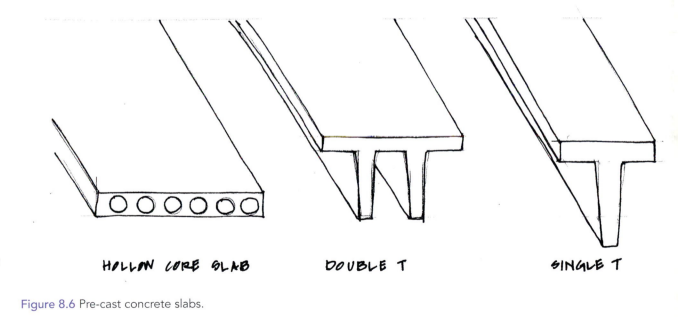

Figure 8.6 Pre-cast concrete slabs.

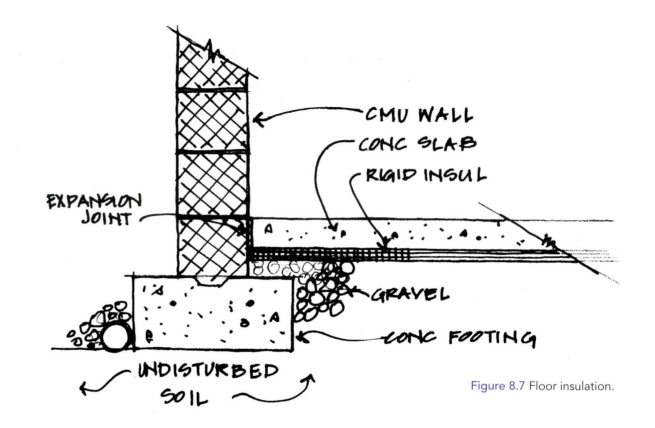

Figure 8.7 Floor insulation.

INSULATION

When a first floor is located above a crawl space, or is directly on the earth (as in a slab on grade), the underside of the floor must be insulated in most areas of the country. This insulation is used to prevent cold air moving from the ground into the finished space above, as well as to keep a stable temperature for the concrete slab.

In some cases insulation may be used under upper floors—between the ceiling and the floor—for sound attenuation.

INTERIOR FLOOR FINISH MATERIALS

Multiple materials are used as floor finishes. The use of the space and building code requirements are generally used to narrow the focus on the type of floor finishes to use. Floor finish materials are usually divided into hard surfaces and soft surfaces. Resilient flooring surfaces are a form of soft surfaces in that they allow some give.

HARD SURFACES

Concrete

Concrete is often used as a sub-floor and can easily be a finished floor surface. Various textures and colors are available, as are surface-applied finishes to seal the concrete.

Brick

Brick pavers, although more commonly used outdoors, can also serve as a finished floor. Several patterns of brick are available. Brick pavers tend to be thinner than actual bricks, although full bricks were sometimes used to finish basement floors in historic houses.

Figure 8.8 Brick flooring patterns.

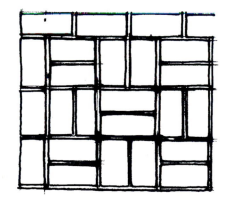
BASKET WEAVE

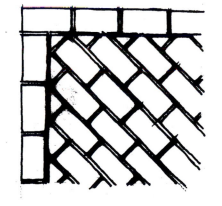
DIAGONAL

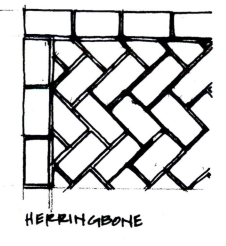
HERRINGBONE

IRREGULAR
(MOSAIC)

RECTANGULAR RANDOM

COURSED

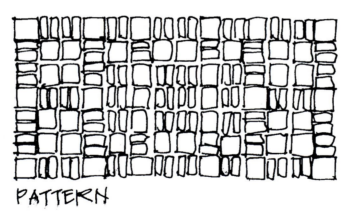

DIAGONAL

PATTERN

Figure 8.9 Stone installation detail.

Stone

A variety of stones can be used as floor finish materials. These include marble, granite, limestone, and slate. All natural stones vary in composition and color, and it is prudent to select actual materials and install them through careful selection of each piece to ensure the best results. Stone is a natural material, but it should be noted that there is a finite amount of stone and it is oftentimes available only in a remote location. Thus, from a sustainability point of view, it is important to keep the entire life-cycle costs of the material in mind. Locally available stone products are preferable to those that come from a great distance.

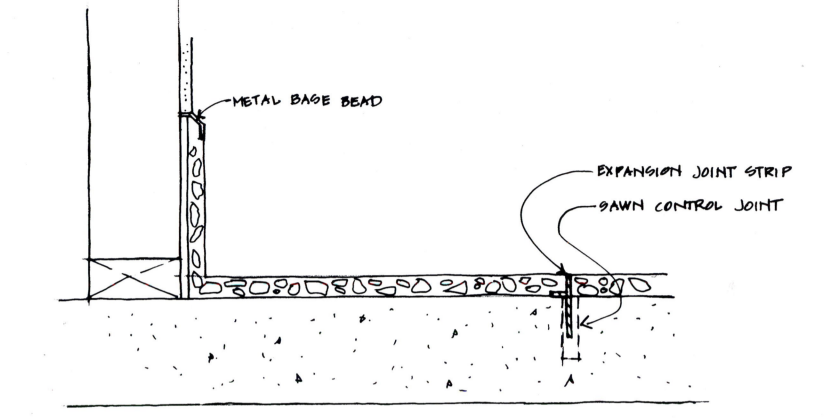

METAL BASE BEAD

EXPANSION JOINT STRIP

SAWN CONTROL JOINT

Terrazzo

Terrazzo has recently regained popularity as a green building material. It is composed of a cement or resin binder with marble or glass chips, which gives it its unique coloring and appearance. The material is poured in place, and like all concrete applications, requires seams to avoid future cracking of the material. Because of its component parts, terrazzo is extremely hard and durable, and is often used in heavily trafficked areas such as lobbies.

Figure 8.10 Terrazzo installation detail.

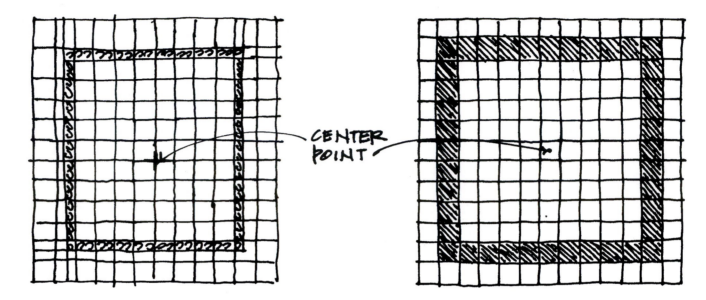

CENTER
POINT

**START AT CENTER
OF ROOM**

Figure 8.11 Tile floor layout.

Ceramic Tile

Ceramic tile can be installed in two ways: on a 1¼-inch thick mortar bed, or as thin set where the tile is adhered to the surface below using a thin layer of adhesive. One of the most important points to consider prior to using tile is if the floor framing is appropriate. Defects in the floor framing can lead to cracking in the grout joints or the tiles themselves. Thus, the floor framing needs to have very little movement to allow for a tile finished floor.

Thin set.   Using a thin layer of wet mortar $\frac{1}{4}$–$\frac{3}{8}$ inch that is troweled on to create a grooved surface, tiles are then set into the mortar. The grooves allow the tile multiple points of contact with the mortar that will create a better bond. When the mortar bed has hardened, the joints between the tiles are then grouted.

Thick set (full mortar bed).   A thicker application involves the use of a $1\frac{1}{4}$-inch mortar bed with reinforcing in some cases. This method is used when the substrate is uneven and must be smoothed out for proper application of the tile. Similar to thin set, the tile must adhere to the mortar and then be grouted after the mortar bed has hardened. When tiles of different thicknesses are desired in a single flooring installation, the thick set method will accommodate this difference to create a uniform finished surface.

Installation.   Tile should be started in the center of the room and then installed towards the edges. The first design consideration is whether the designer prefers grout at the centerlines or a tile at the center of the room. Oftentimes this may relate to any pattern or flooring design that the designer has created. With tile work involving any pattern or diagonal layout, it is important that the designer create an accurate floor pattern drawing for the installer, accounting for actual tile size and grout joints. This will provide a map for the installer as well as assist the designer and contractor in doing proper material takeoffs for ordering the tiles.

SOFT SURFACES

Carpet

Traditionally, carpet has been widely used in a variety of residential and commercial applications. Only recently has carpet come under increased scrutiny as a contributor to poor indoor air quality. Some of the issues to consider when using carpet are as follows: Is there a routine maintenance plan in place to make sure the carpet is vacuumed daily and cleaned per manufacturer recommendations? Does the carpet comply with Carpet and Rug Institute (CRI) Green Label Plus Guidelines? If you cannot answer yes to both of these questions, chances are that carpet is not a suitable material for the application.

Carpet does contribute significantly to noise control, and has excellent acoustical absorption characteristics. Anti-static and anti-microbial agents can also be added to carpeting for specific application types. Recently, many manufacturers have addressed the sustainability of their products. Although some debate exists over the use of polymers in carpet, many manufacturers are working to recycle these petro-based fibers infinitely within the carpet market. Reclamation programs are now being established to reclaim carpeting after it has met its useful life to divert these products from the landfill. It should be noted, however, that these programs do not exist everywhere. Prior to specifying carpet, a designer must research these issues to create a truly sustainable project.

Explanation of Carpet and Rug Institute Ratings

The Carpet and Rug Institute's Green Label Plus program monitors indoor air quality, and is the industry standard for carpet manufacturers interested in sustainability. It should be noted that it is a second-party certification process.

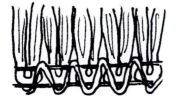
AXMINSTER

WILTON

LEVEL LOOP

TEXTURED LOOP

MULTI LEVEL LOOP

Figure 8.12 Typical carpet weaves.

TUFT
PRIMARY BACK
SECONDARY BACK

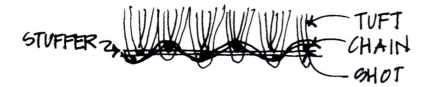
STUFFER
TUFT
CHAIN
SHOT

WOOD

Wood has been used as a floor finish for thousands of year. Traditionally, wood floor finishes are strips, planks, or blocks. Several species of wood can be used for wood flooring: oak, walnut, cherry, maple, teak, and mahogany. The most important consideration from a sustainability position is whether the product comes from a sustainably managed source. A second issue to address is the type of finish used. Wood floors can be finished using low-VOC water-based products or wax, and do not need to include volatile organic compounds in the finish.

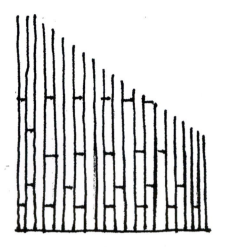

STRIP

▲ Figure 8.13 Strip flooring.

▼ Figure 8.14 Plank flooring.

Strip

Strip flooring is the terminology used when the width of an individual wood piece is less than 3 inches.

Plank

When wider widths are used, such as 3 inches or more, these pieces of wood are known as **planks**. Flooring in many historic buildings are composed of planks, in many cases random width planks. This means that the planks vary in width from 3 inches up to as wide as 10 to 12 inches.

Block

Individual small pieces of wood can be assembled to create a specific design. This is known as **block** flooring when these are then assembled into squares for installation. A common term used by some is *parquet* flooring, although this refers to a specific pattern.

▼ Figure 8.15 Block flooring.

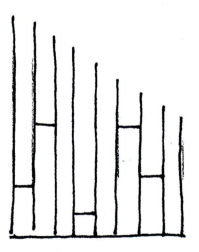

PLANK

BLOCK

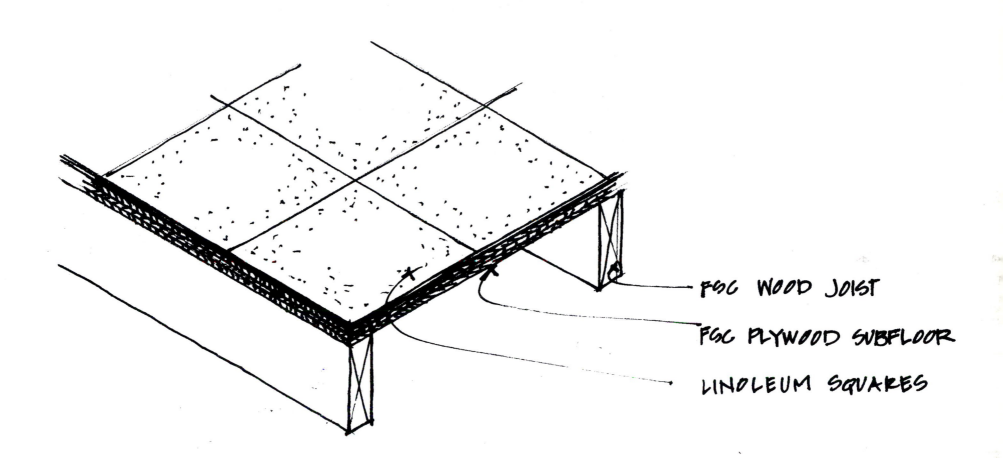

FSC WOOD JOIST

FSC PLYWOOD SUBFLOOR

LINOLEUM SQUARES

RESILIENT FLOORING

Resilient flooring covers a variety of materials, including all forms of vinyl flooring, rubber, and linoleum. By far, the most sustainable choices are natural rubber, cork, and linoleum.

Figure 8.16 Linoleum flooring installation detail.

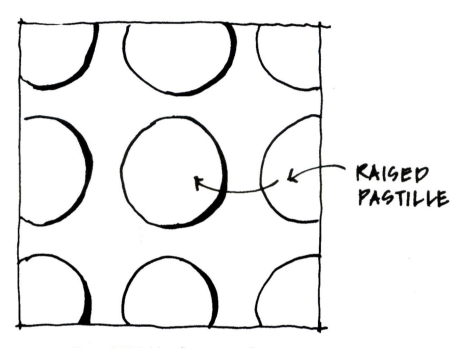

RAISED
PASTILLE

Figure 8.17 Rubber flooring pastilles.

Rubber

Rubber flooring is composed of either a natural or synthetic rubber. Natural rubber is derived from the sap of the rubber plant, which is a tropical plant. It is important when selecting rubber flooring to check all of the materials from which the rubber flooring is constructed. Floorings that include PVC and plasticizers are not likely to meet sustainability criteria, nor would those that off-gas harmful toxins into the air upon installation. The adhesive used to install the rubber is as important as the materials themselves. Low VOC adhesives should meet Green Guard Indoor Air Quality standards.

As a material, rubber is naturally slip resistant but will degrade when exposed to oil. Traditionally, rubber was commonly used on stair treads and in other areas where slip-resistance was a primary concern. This type of rubber flooring comes in tile squares with raised circular pastilles.

With sustainability as a driving concern in many recent design projects, rubber is being used much more extensively in interior spaces. Rubber flooring is available both as a tile and as sheet good. Rubber can be easily cut into patterns and is often used to create floor designs.

Linoleum

Historically, linoleum was used quite extensively prior to the availability of vinyl flooring. As such, some uneducated people may use the term linoleum to refer to all sheet flooring. In reality, linoleum consists of very specific ingredients that are environmentally safe and it is therefore, like rubber, a good resilient flooring choice for sustainable projects. These ingredients include linseed oil, pine resin, wood flour, limestone dust, and jute backing. Linoleum is naturally anti-microbial and resists static build up.

Cork

Cork flooring has also been used since the beginning of the twentieth century. One of its earliest proponents was Frank Lloyd Wright, who used it extensively in the bathrooms and kitchens he designed. Cork was also used in many churches because of its good acoustical properties. Cork is made from the bark of the cork oak tree. It inhibits fire and has good acoustical and insulation properties. Suberin, a substance found in cork bark, is anti-microbial, mold and mildew resistant, and insect resistant.

Bamboo

Bamboo has become a popular sustainable flooring alternative. Bamboo is a grass that can grow as much as three inches in a day. It is important to note that although bamboo is a rapidly renewable resource, one must take into account where the bamboo is coming from and how the flooring is made. Bamboo does not absorb water as easily as wood, and provides a very stable flooring material.

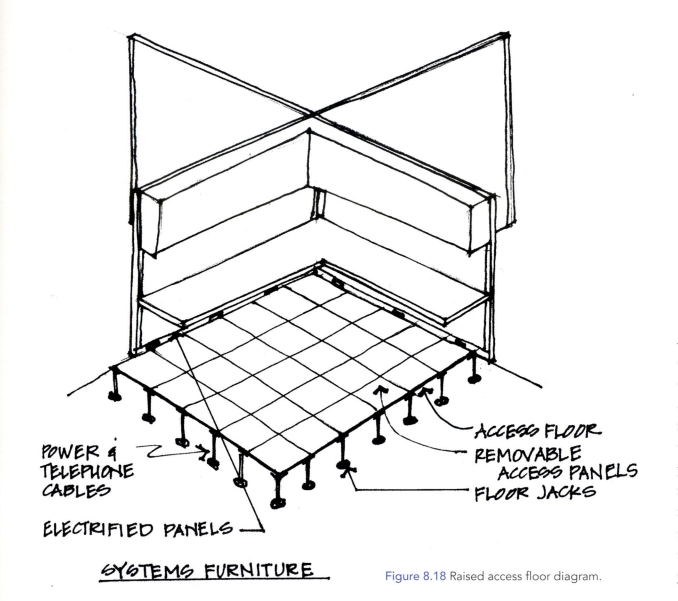

POWER &
TELEPHONE
CABLES

ACCESS FLOOR
REMOVABLE
ACCESS PANELS
FLOOR JACKS

ELECTRIFIED PANELS

SYSTEMS FURNITURE

Figure 8.18 Raised access floor diagram.

ACCESS FLOORING

Access flooring refers to a system, not a specific material. Access flooring is a second level of flooring installed on jacks over a concrete sub-floor. The flooring system is raised on a series of jacks to allow for wires to run between the two floors. This space can also be used as a plenum for the HVAC system. Access floors are installed in 2 foot by 2 foot grids with flooring inlays. These can include carpet tiles or resilient tile squares. Access flooring allows for maximum flexibility and is often used in conjunction with open office systems furniture.

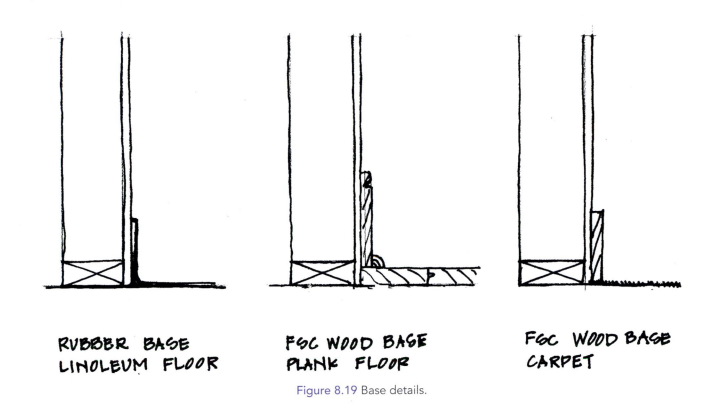

RUBBER BASE
LINOLEUM FLOOR

FSC WOOD BASE
PLANK FLOOR

FSC WOOD BASE
CARPET

Figure 8.19 Base details.

INTERIOR DETAILING

As mentioned previously, the most common way to deal with the joint at the floor and wall is by covering it with a baseboard to hide any imperfections.

BASE BOARDS/BASE MOLDING

Base board trim or base moldings are made from several materials including wood, vinyl and rubber. The most sustainable choices are FSC-certified wood trim and natural rubber trim—both of which are widely available. Stone and tile are also often used as trim in conjunction with stone or tile floors; wood is also often used with these flooring choices.

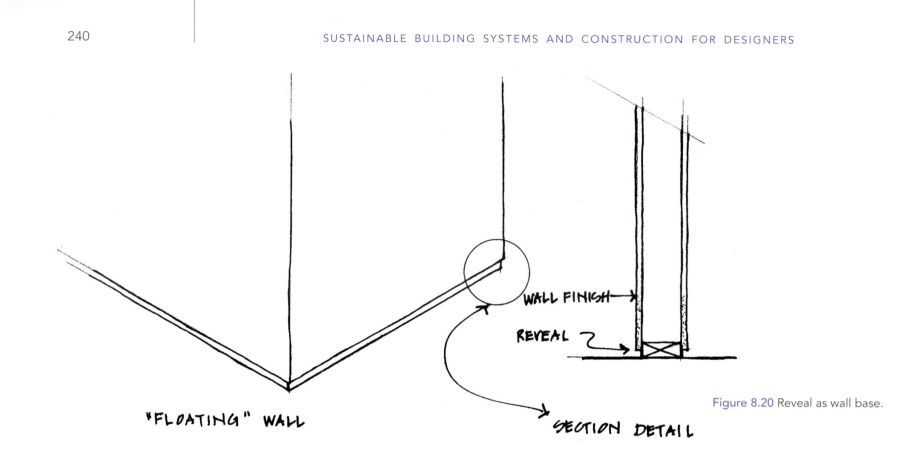

"FLOATING" WALL

SECTION DETAIL

WALL FINISH

REVEAL

Figure 8.20 Reveal as wall base.

Designers may not always want to use a base mold. Other ways of dealing with this joint are to make it a clean connection or to create a reveal.

Reveal

A **reveal** joint is created when the wall surface does not meet the floor. Generally, this reveal will create a sense that the wall is floating, and this may be a desirable design detail.

Clean Joint

A clean joint relies on careful craftsmanship to create a precise connection between the floor material and the wall material. This is extremely hard to accomplish and will result in more time and expense as the reveal joint.

INTERIOR DESIGN CONSIDERATIONS

Interior designers are primarily concerned with the floor finish materials and the furniture, fixtures, and equipment placed on top of the floor framing. The most common problems related to floor framing involve space reuse. Because this is extremely common, it is important to outline some of the issues a designer will eventually face. When a space is renovated and the use is changed, it is important to remember the following basic considerations:

- Type of framing: Can the deflection in the framing support the new finish material (ceramic tile, stone, etc.)?
- Before adding stone, granite, or concrete countertops, was the floor system designed to support this load?
- Was the space originally designed for heavy loads, such as libraries and files?

CASE STUDIES

The following case studies illustrate the use of various flooring materials. Figure 8.21 shows the linoleum floor pattern designed by OTJ Architects for the American Legacy Foundation Building. Similarly, Figure 8.22 features the linoleum floor transition to carpet squares in the same building. A transition detail is illustrated in Figure 8.23.

◀ Figure 8.21 OTJ Architects, American Legacy Foundation Building, linoleum floor pattern. Photo Credit: Copyright 2008 Chris Spielmann, Spielmann Photography.

▲ Figure 8.22 OTJ Architects, American Legacy Foundation Building, linoleum floor transition to carpet squares. Photo Credit: Copyright 2008 Chris Spielmann, Spielmann Photography.

PERKINS + WILL, HAWORTH SANTA MONICA SHOWROOM

Multilevel flooring detail showing raised flooring and tile is included in Figure 8.25 of the Haworth Santa Monica Showroom by Perkins + Will. A detail of the raised flooring is revealed in Figure 8.26.

◀ Figure 8.23 OTJ Architects, American Legacy Foundation Building, floor transition detail. Photo Credit: Copyright 2008 Chris Spielmann, Spielmann Photography.

▶ Figure 8.24 Perkins + Will, Haworth Santa Monica Showroom, multilevel flooring detail showing raised flooring and tile. Photo Credit: Marvin Rand, Marvin Rand Photography.

Figure 8.25 Perkins + Will, Haworth Santa Monica Showroom, multilevel flooring detail showing raised flooring, tile, and air supply vent. Photo Credit: Marvin Rand, Marvin Rand Photography.

Figure 8.26 Perkins + Will, Haworth Santa Monica Showroom, detail raised flooring revealed. Photo Credit: Marvin Rand, Marvin Rand Photography.

Figure 8.27 RTKL, DC Navigators, salvaged wood flooring. Copyright 2008 by RTKL Architects Inc.

RTKL, DC NAVIGATORS BUILDING

RTKL's use of salvaged wood flooring for the DC Navigators project is shown in Figure 8.27.

KEY TERMS

block

cast in place

heavy timber

light frame

planks

pre-cast

reveal

strip

ASSIGNMENTS/EXERCISES

1. In your class sketchbook, sketch examples of four different floor framing systems by visiting a variety of construction sites. (Always get permission to visit the construction site.)

2. Sketch at least ten different flooring installations in your sketchbook. How are transitions between floor finishes handled? What types of patterns can you find?

3. Visit several of the following flooring websites. What makes the product sustainable? Are the manufacturers' claims certified by a third party?

RESOURCES

For an overall sense of the common spans for various types of materials, the building codes books provide excellent tables that a designer can consult.

Sustainable flooring manufacturer websites:

Armstrong Flooring www.Armstrong.com

Nora Rubber www.norarubber.com

Forbo ww.forbo.com

Natural Cork www.Naturalcork.com

Milliken Carpet www.sustainablecarpet.com

Mohawk Carpet www.themohawkgroup.com

Mannington Commercial

　www.manningtoncommercial.com

Johnsonite www.johnsonite.com

Interface Flooring www.interfaceflor.com

Antron Fiber www.antron.net

Crossville Tile www.crossvilleinc.com

Bentley Prince Street www

　.bentleyprincestreet.com

Amtico www.amtico.com

CHAPTER 9

Roofs/Ceilings

In a sense, evolution is nature's design process. The wonderful thing about this process is that it is happening continuously throughout the biosphere. A typical organism has undergone at least a million years of intensive research and development.

Sim van der Ryn, Ecological Design

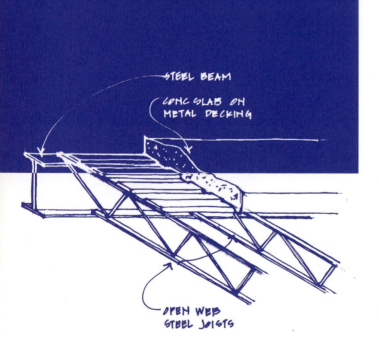

STEEL BEAM

CONC SLAB ON METAL DECKING

OPEN WEB STEEL JOISTS

OBJECTIVES

- Identify the roof framing system and roof shape of a building
- Design ceilings for projects
- Select appropriate ceiling systems

INTRODUCTION

Interior designers do not deal with roof framing specifically because this is a structural issue. They do, however, have to respond to the shape of the roof as it shapes interior space. The ceiling finish also falls under the realm of the designer.

ROOFS

ROOF SHAPES

Many different shapes of roofs exist. Figure 9.1 illustrates some of the more common shapes found in North America.

Figure 9.1 Roof shapes.

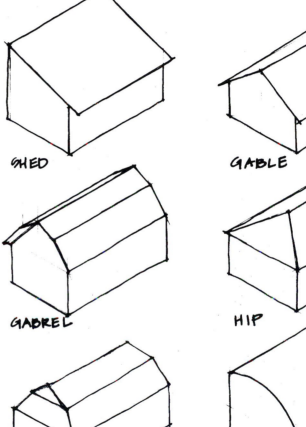

SHED

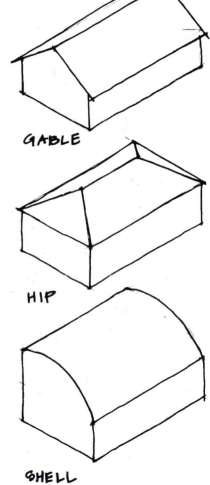

GABLE

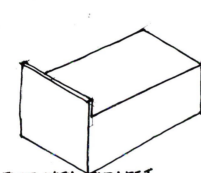

FOLDED PLATE

FLAT WITH PARAPET

GABREL

HIP

TENT-INFLATED

DOME

MANSARD

SHELL

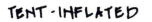

ROOF FRAMING MATERIALS

As discussed in previous chapters on floor and wall framing, the three primary materials used for roof framing are metal, concrete, and wood.

Wood

Wood roof framing is either stick built on-site or prefabricated into trusses and shipped to the site. Stick built roof framing uses light frame construction techniques with rafters and ceiling joists whereas trusses are factory made and delivered to the building site.

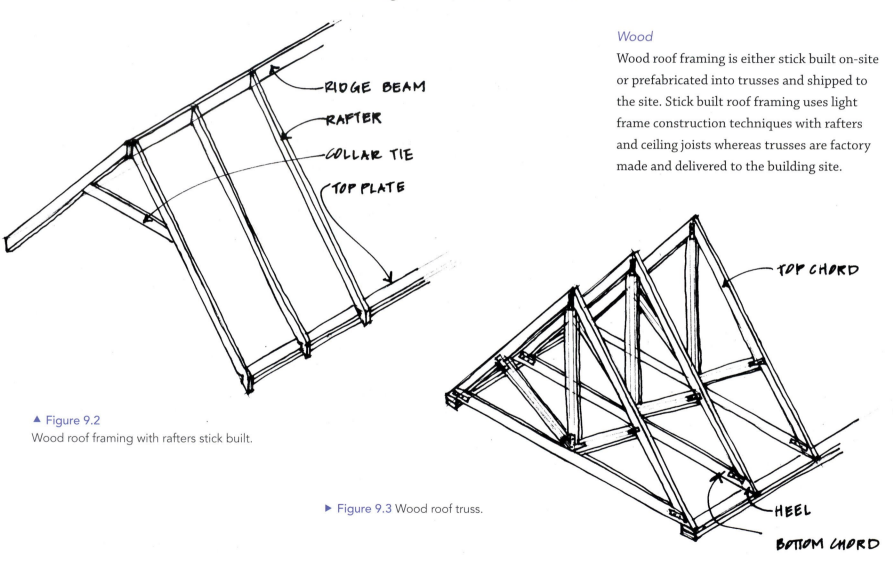

RIDGE BEAM
RAFTER
COLLAR TIE
TOP PLATE

TOP CHORD

HEEL

BOTTOM CHORD

▲ Figure 9.2
Wood roof framing with rafters stick built.

▶ Figure 9.3 Wood roof truss.

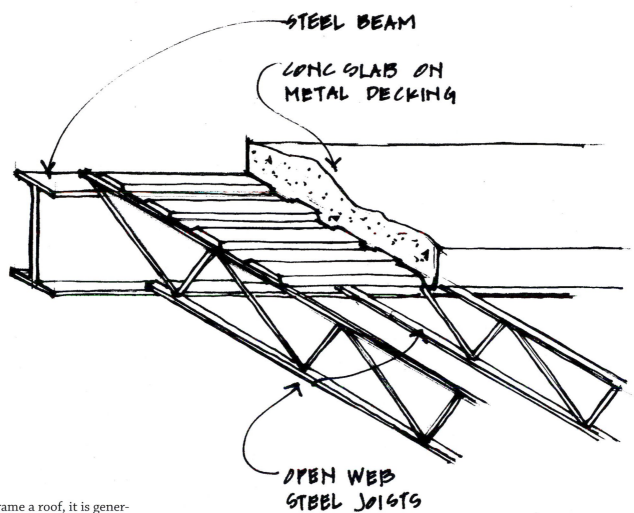

STEEL BEAM

CONC SLAB ON
METAL DECKING

OPEN WEB
STEEL JOISTS

Metal

When metal is used to frame a roof, it is generally composed of open web steel joists that support metal decking filled with concrete. The combination of concrete and steel enables the roof to work in both tension and compression.

Figure 9.4
Metal decking on open web steel joists.

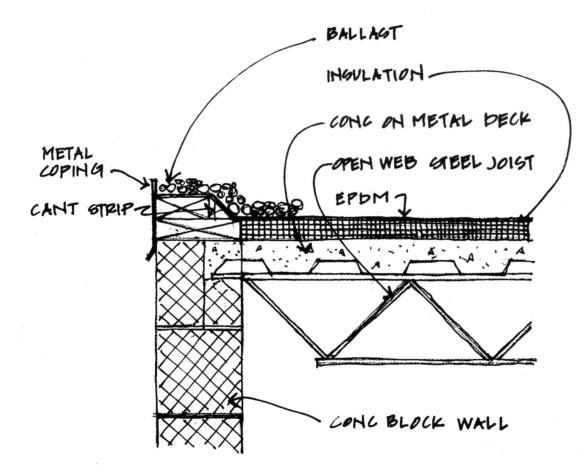

BALLAST

INSULATION

CONC ON METAL DECK

OPEN WEB STEEL JOIST

EPDM

METAL COPING

CANT STRIP

CONC BLOCK WALL

Figure 9.5
Concrete roof deck with EPDM and ballast.

Concrete

Concrete beams may be used to support the roof structure. The panels are similar to those discussed in concrete flooring. These concrete members are either poured in place, or precast and then transported to the site. Concrete requires steel reinforcing to resist cracking.

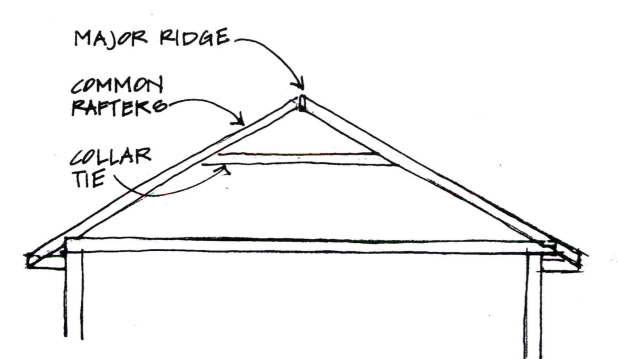

MAJOR RIDGE

COMMON RAFTERS

COLLAR TIE

BELGIAN

BOWSTRING

FINK

SCISSOR

OTHER FRAMING FEATURES

After the roof is framed, it is covered with a finish material. Oftentimes, insulation and sheathing are used between the framing and the finished roofing material.

Figure 9.6 Typical wood roofing systems.

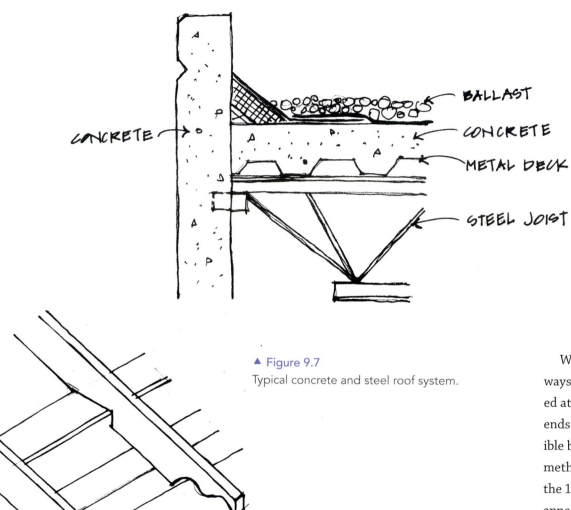

CONCRETE →

BALLAST
CONCRETE
METAL DECK
STEEL JOIST

▲ Figure 9.7
Typical concrete and steel roof system.

◀ Figure 9.8
Wood roof framing with exposed rafter ends.

EXPOSED RAFTER ENDS

SIDING

With wood framing, there are a couple of ways in which the roof rafters can be terminated at the exterior of the wall. Exposed rafter ends are when the rafters themselves are visible beyond the plane of the exterior wall. This method was commonly used on bungalows in the 1920s and 1930s. A more finished-looking appearance is achieved when the rafters are boxed in using a soffit (horizontal) and fascia board (vertical). In this case, the soffit must be vented to prevent moisture buildup.

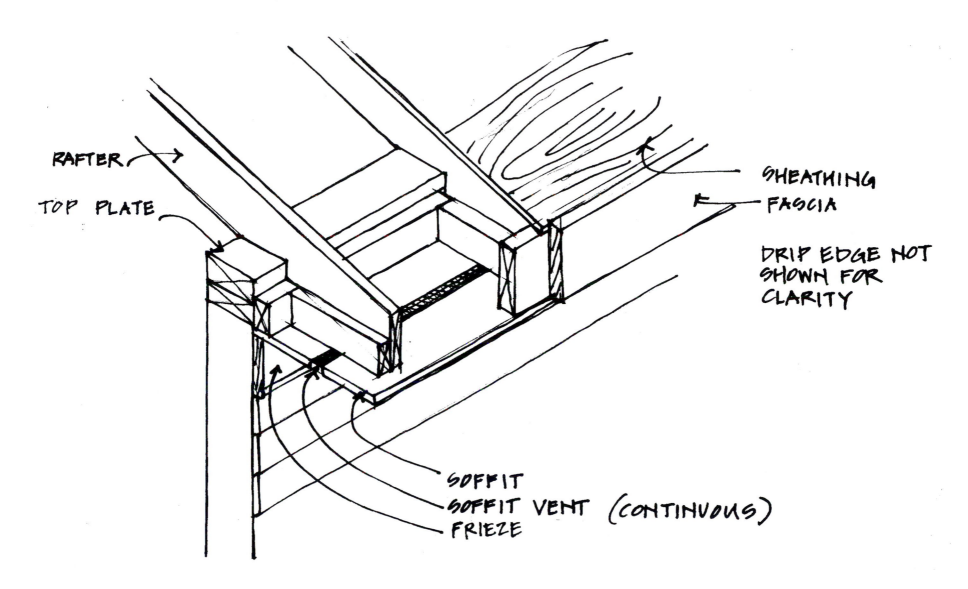

RAFTER

TOP PLATE

SHEATHING

FASCIA

DRIP EDGE NOT
SHOWN FOR
CLARITY

SOFFIT
SOFFIT VENT (CONTINUOUS)
FRIEZE

Figure 9.9 Wood roof framing with boxed soffit and fascia board with continuous ventilation.

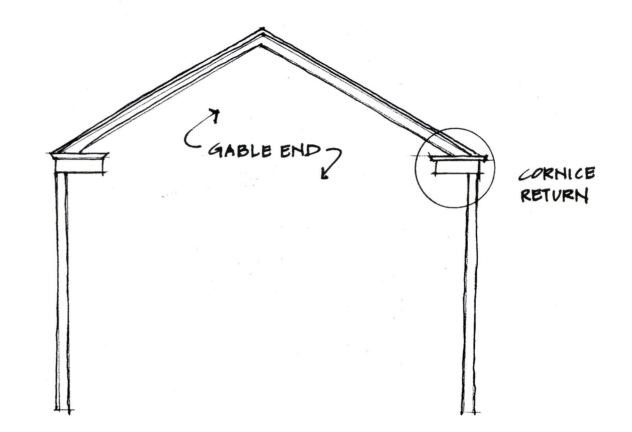

GABLE END

CORNICE RETURN

Figure 9.10
Cornice returns shown on the gable end wall.

Cornice Returns

During the Greek Revival period, the boxed cornices were often returned onto the gable end of the building, thus creating a **cornice return**.

Figure 9.11 Cupola.

Cupola

A small structure located on the roof that allows for ventilation is known as a **cupola**. Originally a functional component, these are often purely decorative in today's construction.

Monitor

A roof **monitor** is a raised section in the middle of the roof that allows for additional lighting in the center of the space. These were commonly used in industrial buildings in the early-to-mid twentieth century.

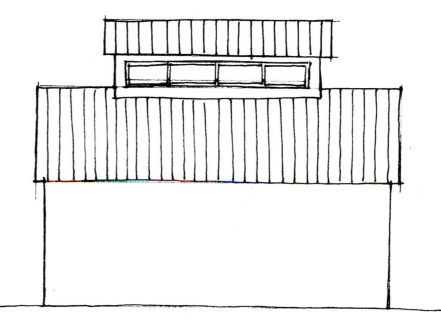

Figure 9.12 Roof monitor.

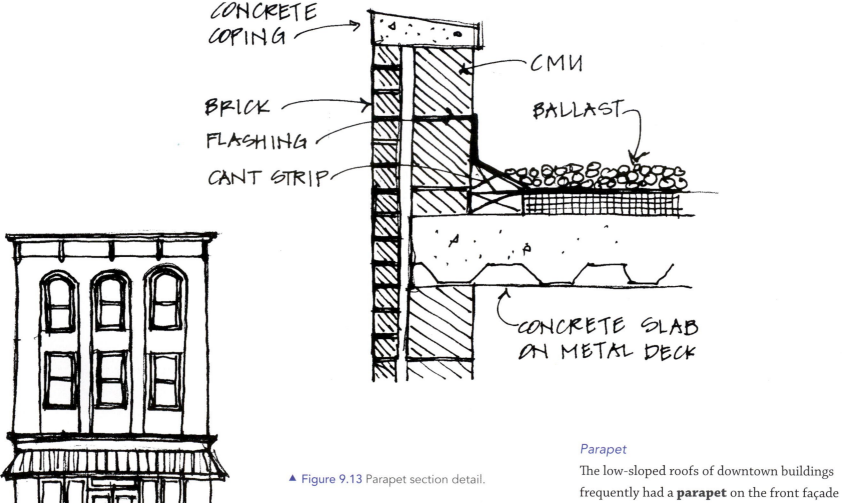

▲ Figure 9.13 Parapet section detail.

◄ Figure 9.14
Downtown Main Street building with parapet.

Parapet

The low-sloped roofs of downtown buildings frequently had a **parapet** on the front façade to mask the roof behind. A parapet is a low wall located above the roof plane.

ROOFING MATERIALS

Several different materials are used to finish roofs. The primary purpose is to shed water away from the roof framing and the interior. The type of finish material that can be used is related directly to the slope of the roof. Low sloped roofs can use only certain materials, such as asphalt shingles, whereas other materials like standing seam metal and slate can be use on a steeply pitched roof.

Flat Roofs

Although no roof is actually flat, the term flat roof is used to describe one that has a very slight slope. On this type of roof, only a rolled membrane roof or a bituminous substance roof should be used. These roof forms are subject to leaking because both water and snow tend to sit on them for long periods of times. In some cases, ballast (or small rounded rocks) may be used on top of the roofing membrane to hold the membrane in place.

Green roofs refer to roofs with live vegetation. These have several advantages including: they absorb rainwater, attract local birds and insects back to the area where the building is, and reduce the overall heat island effect. The heat island effect refers to the condition where the local temperature is higher because heat has been absorbed by roads, sidewalks, and buildings, causing the local area temperature to rise.

Figure 9.15 Green flat roof, Cornwall, England.

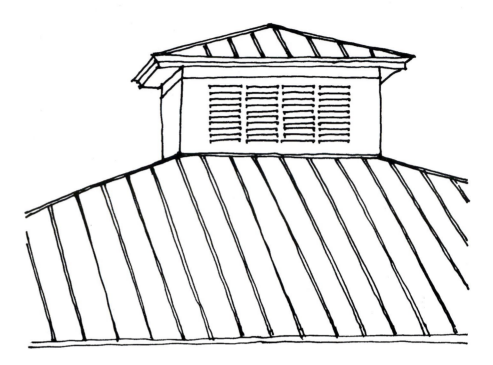

Figure 9.16 Standing seam metal roof.

Low Sloped Roofs

Low sloped roofs refer to those that have a rise of 3 feet in every 12 feet of horizontal distance (3:12) or less. The primary materials that can be used on this type of roof include double-layered asphalt shingles, rolled asphalt, and corrugated metal roofing.

Sloped Roofs

Most materials can be used on roofs with a pitch over 4:12. These include tiles, shingles (wood and metal), and standing seam metal. Slate is recommended for roofs with steeper slopes such as 8:12 and higher. Manufacturer recommendations may vary somewhat depending on the actual material used.

Thatch Roof

Although they are uncommon in North America, thatched roofs are used in other parts of the world. The thatch is composed of dried vegetation that is strapped together to provide a roof shelter.

Figure 9.17 Thatch roof, Veracruz, Mexico.

Figure 9.18 Cathedral ceiling.

SUSTAINABILITY ISSUES AND ROOFING

The primary design consideration for the roof would be to use a lighter color in locations where heat gain is an issue. The lighter the color of the roof, the less heat is absorbed. A second consideration is material choice. Although asphalt is by far the best selling roofing material, it is also a petroleum-based product. Several other more sustainable options are available, including recycled rubber shingles, cement board shingles, sustainably harvested wood products, and recycled metal products.

CEILINGS

CATHEDRAL CEILING/SLOPED CEILING

A ceiling that conforms roughly to the pitch (slope) of the roof is known as a **cathedral ceiling**. First made popular during the 1970s, the cathedral ceiling provides a sense of spaciousness that a flat ceiling may not. The design challenges associated with the cathedral or sloped ceiling include integration of lighting, consideration for adequate heating and cooling, and creation of a sense of human-scale within the space.

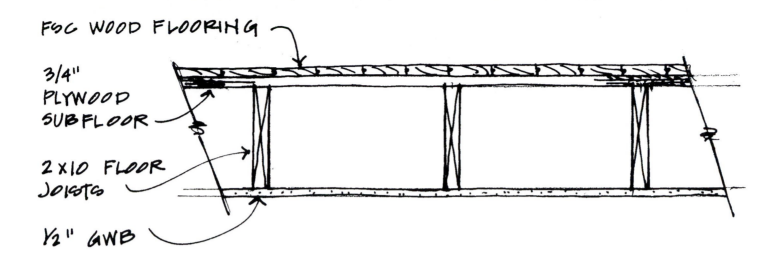

FSC WOOD FLOORING

3/4" PLYWOOD SUBFLOOR

2 X 10 FLOOR JOISTS

1/2" GWB

▲ Figure 9.19 Wallboard ceiling.

▶ Figure 9.20 Plaster ceiling medallion detail.

DIRECTLY APPLIED CEILINGS

Gypsum Wallboard

Within the residential environment, the most common ceiling finish is gypsum wallboard. This material has been described in detail in Chapter 7.

Plaster

As discussed in Chapter 7, plaster is applied in a three-coat system over lath. This finish was the primary wall and ceiling finish prior to the invention of wallboard. In historic buildings, the crown moldings and ceiling medallions in a room where also made of plaster.

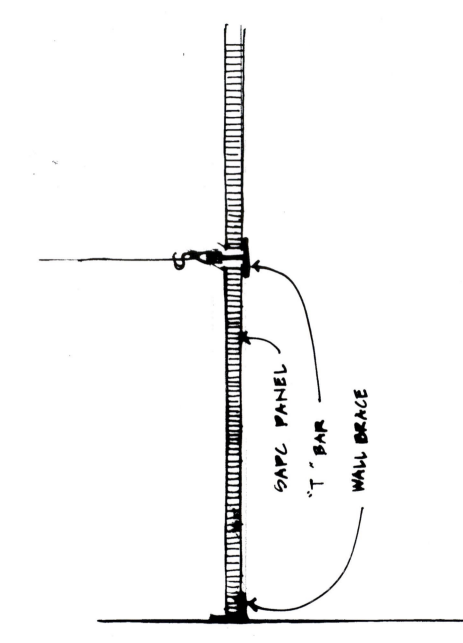

SUSPENDED ACOUSTICAL PANEL CEILINGS (SAPC)

Within the commercial environment, the preferred ceiling treatment is the **suspended acoustical panel ceiling (SAPC)**. The primary reasons for this are twofold: the acoustical ceiling provides noise control in large spaces, and the suspended system allows for ductwork, sprinkler lines, and electrical wiring to occur above the visible ceiling system. Additional advantages include ease of access to utilities and the ability to replace a single damaged tile without redoing the entire ceiling. The standard sizes for the suspended acoustical panel ceiling (SAPC) are 2 feet by 2 feet and 2 feet by 4 feet. A variety of fluorescent light fixtures accommodate these grid sizes, as do mechanical supply registers and return grilles. As such, the SAPC is also the most economical choice available to the commercial client.

Figure 9.21 Typical SAPC detail.

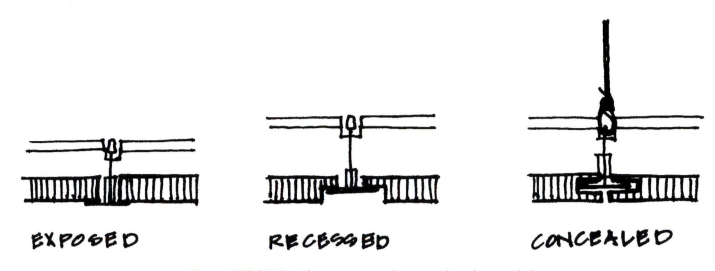

EXPOSED   **RECESSED**   **CONCEALED**

Figure 9.22 SAPC grid types: exposed, recessed, and concealed.

Recycled and Recycled Context/Recyclable

Several factors must be considered for use of a sustainable, suspended ceiling systems.

Ceiling Tile Material

Low-density ceiling materials include fiberglass or mineral fiber. Mineral fibers absorb water and sag over time.

Low Volatile Organic Compounds (VOCs)

Ceiling materials with low or no VOC are available from a variety of manufacturers. These contribute to good indoor air quality because they do not off-gas.

Light Reflectivity

Ceiling systems with a high light reflectivity reduce the amount of artificial lighting required, and thus reduce overall energy consumption within a space.

Ceiling Grid Types

Three basic variations on the grid system that supports the tiles exist.

Exposed T-bar

Recessed T-bar

Concealed grid

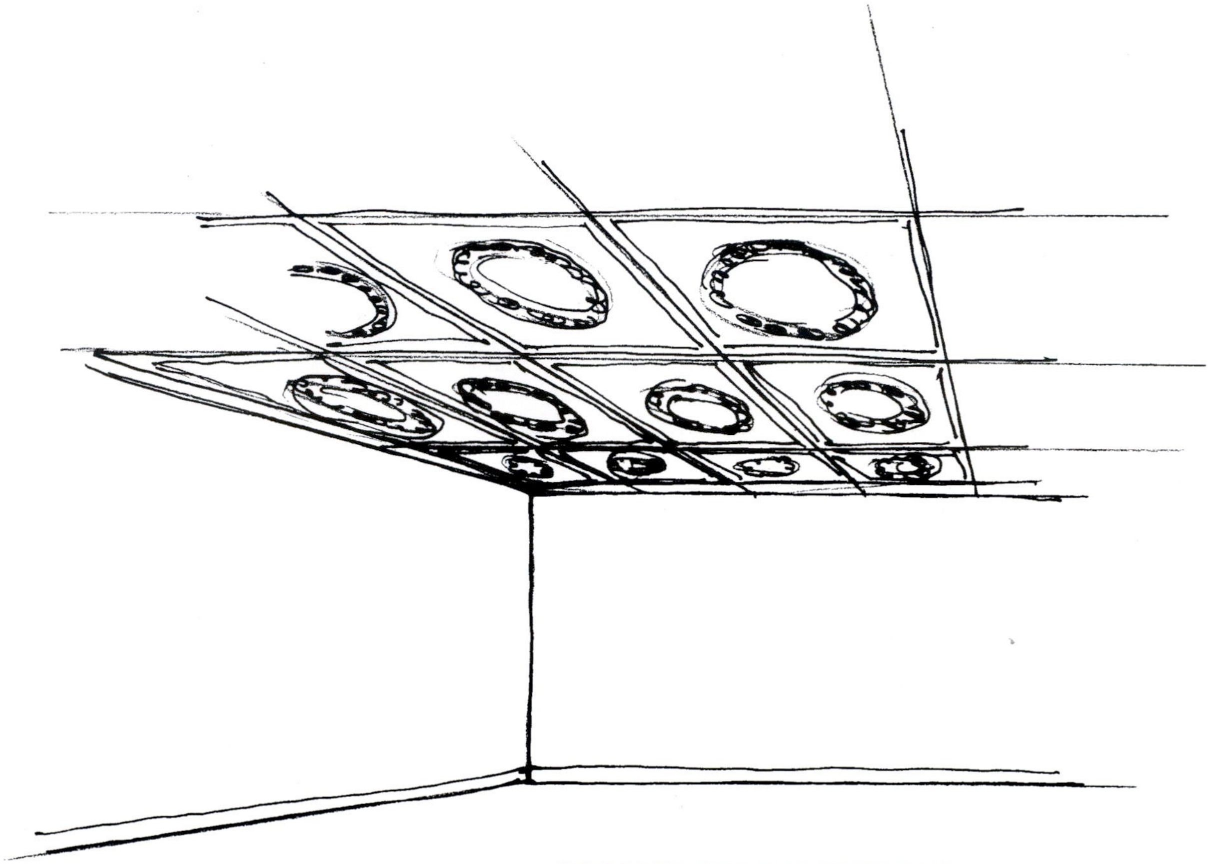

Figure 9.23 Metal ceiling tiles.

DROPPED CEILING SECTIONS

A ceiling grid can hold other types of ceiling tiles in addition to acoustical panels. These include both wood and metal tiles. It should be noted that these materials absorb far less sound than the SAPC system.

Metal tiles are often applied directly to the plaster or drywall using screws. This type of ceiling was common in turn-of-the century commercial interiors, and has experienced resurgent use during the past decade.

EXPOSED STRUCTURE

Designers sometimes want to expose the structure of the ceiling to achieve either a rustic appearance or an industrial interior. Lighting and mechanical systems must be integrated carefully in such an application because all wiring and ductwork will also be exposed.

Metal Structure

When structural steel is left exposed it is subject to both rust and fire. A designer must detail these exposed members to deal with both of these issues.

Wood Structure

Wood beams are commonly left exposed in certain applications. As with steel beams, careful attention to fire prevention and control must be given.

EXPOSED MECHANICAL CEILING

In some designs, it is desirable to have an exposed ceiling where the mechanical and sprinkler systems are visible. Generally, these are painted to match the ceiling color, although this is not necessary. Round ducts are most commonly used when they are to be left exposed. When encased in a ceiling, mechanical ducts are usually insulated on the outside. Therefore, it is important to coordinate exposed duct work with the heating, ventilation, and air conditioning (HVAC) designer to make sure these are insulated internally for a more attractive appearance.

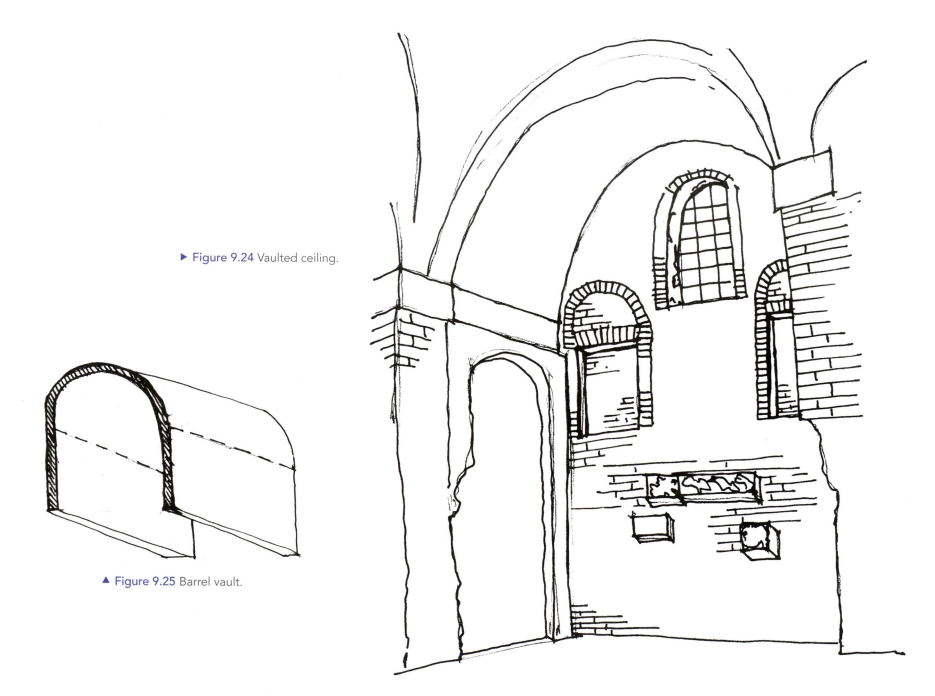

▶ Figure 9.24 Vaulted ceiling.

▲ Figure 9.25 Barrel vault.

CEILING SHAPES

In addition to the cathedral ceiling, other ceiling shapes may also be used. Careful attention must be given to the acoustics within such spaces.

Vaulted Ceiling

Vaulted ceilings have been in use since Roman times and were commonly used in Gothic cathedrals.

Barrel Vault

Barrel vaults also date to the Romans. A barrel vault can be used to enhance any rectangular space.

Dome

Domes have been used to mark monumental spaces since the Roman Empire. The dome provides a central emphasis within a space.

Figure 9.26 Dome with cupola and tower with cupola, Veracruz, Mexico.

INTERIOR DESIGN CONSIDERATIONS

Coordination of lighting with mechanical, sprinkler, and ceiling-mounted equipment such as LCD projectors.

Ideal lighting solutions can be severely impacted by a lack of coordination with the other items.

Acoustics—Noise Control

One of the primary functions of the ceiling plane in a commercial space is to provide acoustical control. Oftentimes, the wall and floor are hard surfaces with very little sound absorption. Thus, the ceiling material is used to control noise within the space.

◄ Figure 9.27a–b A failure to communicate.

▶ Figure 9.28
Acoustical ceiling clouds in an auditorium setting.

Designing the Ceiling

Interior designers use the ceiling plane to delineate space, assist in wayfinding, and enhance the overall conceptual approach of the design intent.

In addition to standard flat ceilings, designers may want to use the ceiling as a design feature to create a sense of movement or otherwise reinforce the design.

RECLAMATION PROGRAMS

Some ceiling manufacturers have created product reclamation programs. An example of this is Armstrong's Ceiling Recycling Program through which 55 million square feet of old ceiling materials have been recycled since 1999, diverting all of these materials from the landfill and saving 10 tons of raw materials.

▶ Figure 9.29 Perkins + Will offices, multi-level wallboard ceiling used to define spaces and for wayfinding. Photo Credit: ArchPhoto, Eduard Hueber.

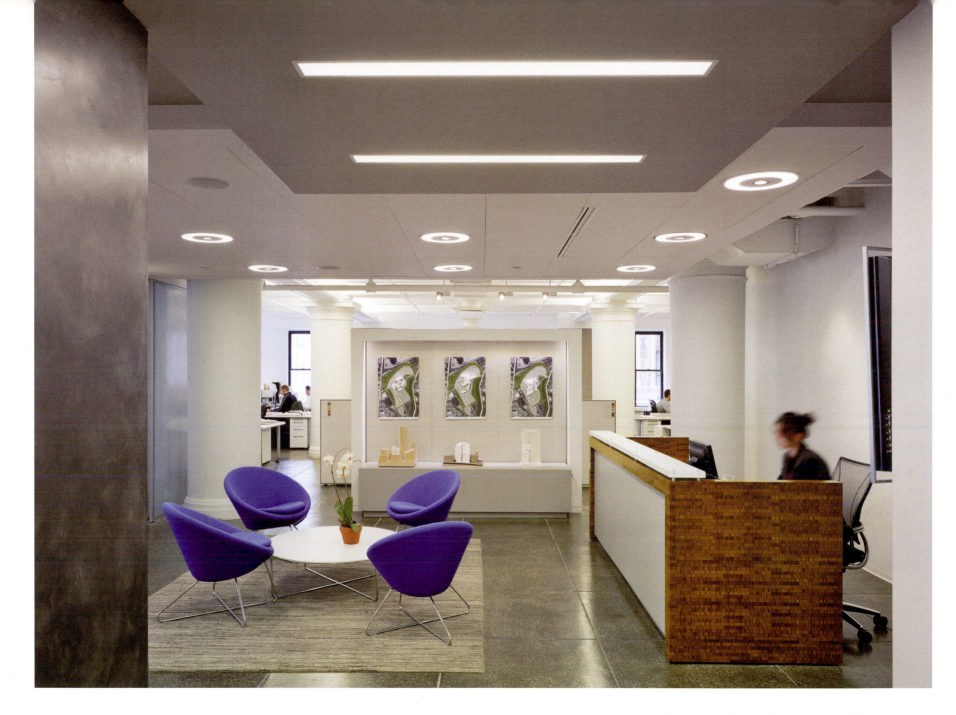

Figure 9.30 Perkins + Will, Haworth Santa Monica Showroom. View of underside of exposed metal deck as finished ceiling. Photo Credit: Marvin Rand, Marvin Rand Photography.

SUMMARY

This chapter has discussed the many different roof shapes and materials as well as the various types of interior finish ceiling materials. Interior design issues related to ceilings and roofs include acoustical considerations, ceiling design, and coordination with other professionals. The following case studies illustrate several different approaches to sustainable ceiling design.

CASE STUDIES

PERKINS + WILL— HAWORTH SHOWROOM, SANTA MONICA, CALIFORNIA

Figure 9.30 illustrates the use of an exposed steel structure and the underside of the metal decking. Light fixtures are suspended from the metal deck. All mechanical is located beneath the access flooring system.

◄ Figure 9.31 Busby Perkins + Will, White Rock Operations Center, salvaged heavy timber roof structure. Photo Credit: Martin Tessler.

▼ Figure 9.32 Busby Perkins + Will, White Rock Operations Center, salvaged heavy timber roof structure. Photo Credit: Martin Tessler.

BUSBY, PERKINS + WILL— WHITE ROCK, VANCOUVER

The White Rock facility includes a reclaimed timber roof decking structure as seen in Figures 9.31 and 9.32. Wood beams and the underside of the roof deck are left exposed in various parts of the design.

RTKL—DC NAVIGATORS BUILDING

The DC Navigators building also uses reclaimed lumber on the interior, but in this instance, as a wall finish as seen in Figure 9.33. The ceiling of this space consists of a combination of wallboard and acoustical surfaces. Multiple levels are created using wallboard and acoustical dropped soffits. Beyond this area of the building and further down the corridor, steel beams are left exposed.

PERKINS + WILL—COFRA BUILDING

The Cofra building includes a variety of ceiling finishes that are often used to highlight the lighting design. In the elevator lobby that leads to the main reception area, a wood slatted ceiling leads visitors from the elevator into the reception space where the ceiling transforms into a wood slatted wall. Circular cut-outs are used to frame the recessed lighting. Supplemental wallboard alcoves along the perimeter of the space contain recessed fluorescent lighting used to graze the wall and highlight their texture.

◀ Figure 9.33 RTKL, DC Navigators, dropped wallboard soffits. Copyright 2008 by RTKL Architects Inc. All rights reserved.

▶ Figure 9.34 Perkins + Will, Cofra office, wood slat ceiling. Photo Credit: ArchPhoto, Eduard Hueber.

Figure 9.35 Perkins + Will, Cofra office, wood slat ceiling. Photo Credit: ArchPhoto, Eduard Hueber.

In the internal corridors, suspended ceiling tiles contain 1-foot-by-4-foot recessed fluorescent fixtures laid perpendicular to the corridor. Both the conference room and break out room feature wood panel ceilings with a combination of recessed lighting and suspended fixtures. The café area has a 2-foot-by-2-foot acoustical ceiling tile grid system with four suspended pendant lights above the tabletop.

Figure 9.36 Perkins + Will, Cofra office, wood ceiling. Photo Credit: ArchPhoto, Eduard Hueber.

281

Figure 9.37 Perkins + Will, Cofra office,
acoustical ceiling tiles in corridor, concealed grid.
Photo Credit: ArchPhoto, Eduard Hueber.

Figure 9.38 Perkins + Will, Cofra office, wood ceiling. Photo Credit: ArchPhoto, Eduard Hueber.

Figure 9.39 Perkins + Will, Cofra office, acoustical ceiling tiles, exposed grid. Photo Credit: Arch-Photo, Eduard Hueber.

283

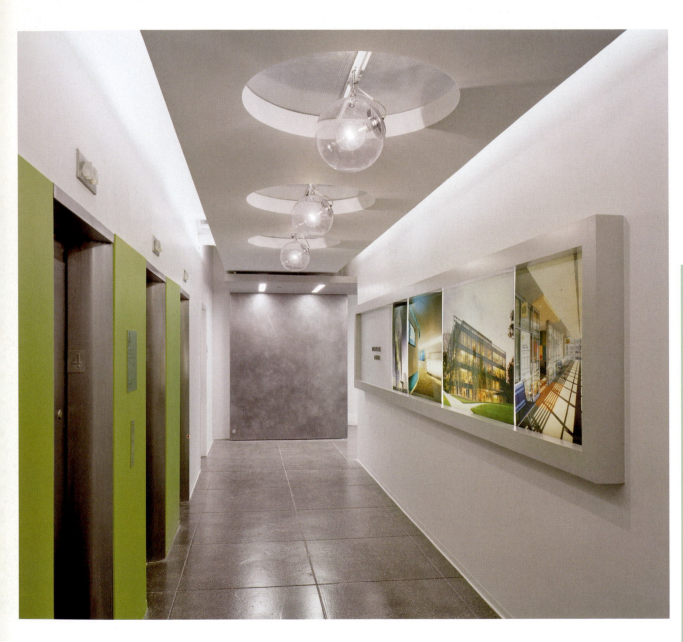

◄ Figure 9.40 Perkins + Will offices, wallboard ceiling design with cut outs for light fixtures and side reveals for lighting. Photo Credit: ArchPhoto, Eduard Hueber.

▶ Figure 9.41 Perkins + Will offices, exposed mechanical and structure painted white in open office. Photo Credit: ArchPhoto, Eduard Hueber.

PERKINS + WILL— NEW YORK OFFICE

The New York office of Perkins + Will uses a variety of creative ceiling solutions. The elevator lobby has recessed fluorescent strip lighting to wash the walls coupled with a suspended wallboard center. Circular areas are cut out of the wallboard to create a recess for suspended globe light fixtures.

The main open office space includes an exposed structure and mechanical systems. All elements of the structure, mechanical, and sprinkler system are painted white. Suspended light fixtures are used to highlight project pin up areas on the perimeter walls and over the desks for ambient lighting.

▼ Figure 9.42 Perkins + Will offices, suspended acoustical panel ceiling with exposed grid in break out room. Photo Credit: ArchPhoto, Eduard Hueber.

▶ Figure 9.43 Perkins + Will offices, wallboard ceiling design with side reveals. Photo Credit: ArchPhoto, Eduard Hueber.

The break out room incorporates a suspended acoustical panel ceiling on a 2–foot-by-2-foot grid with recessed lighting.

The main reception/lobby area has a suspended wallboard ceiling over the seating area with recessed circular fixtures. Accent lighting is used along the perimeter to highlight project models.

The conference room contains a long linear fluorescent light fixture that provides both up and down lighting. Perimeter linear fluorescent wall washers are also integrated into the suspended acoustical panel ceiling system and wash the walls with light.

With each ceiling material transition, a light fixture transition also occurs as seen in Figure 9.45.

287

▲ Figure 9.44 Perkins + Will offices, suspended acoustical panel ceiling with exposed grid in conference room and side reveals. Photo Credit: ArchPhoto, Eduard Hueber.

▶ Figure 9.45 Perkins + Will offices, wallboard ceiling design with cut outs for light fixtures and side reveals for lighting. Photo Credit: ArchPhoto, Eduard Hueber.

KEY TERMS

barrel vault

cathedral ceiling

cornice return

cupola

dome

exposed rafter ends

fascia

green roofs

heat island effect

monitor

parapet

soffit

suspended acoustical panel ceiling (SAPC)

vaulted ceiling

ASSIGNMENTS/EXERCISES

1. Examine your recent design projects. Did you design the ceiling? What could you have done to reinforce your design concept using the ceiling plane? Record this in your sketchbook.

2. Look through current interior design magazines for representative samples of well-designed ceiling planes. See if you can find examples where the ceiling is used as a wayfinding device (not just for hanging signage.)

3. View each of the websites under Additional Resources to find samples for future design projects.

RESOURCES

USG Sustainable Ceiling Resource Center
   www.sustainableceilings.com
Armstrong Ceilings www.armstrong.com
Chicago Metallic www.chicago-metallic.com
Gordon, Inc. www.gordongrid.com

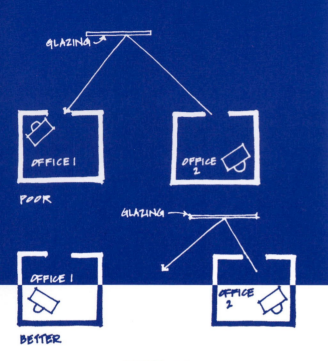

CHAPTER 10

Indoor Environmental Quality: Acoustics and Indoor Air

Good indoor air quality creates healthier and happier building occupants.
Stan Gatland for Environmental Design and Construction, *May 2008*

OBJECTIVES

- Locate open offices for minimal sound transmission and be able to meet client needs for speech privacy
- Describe the importance of good indoor air quality
- Specify materials that support good indoor air quality
- Identify acoustical needs in a space

INTRODUCTION

This chapter addresses indoor air quality and acoustics. Although both of these topics have been addressed in previous chapters, this chapter will address the specifics of each as well as their impact on the health, safety, and welfare of building inhabitants.

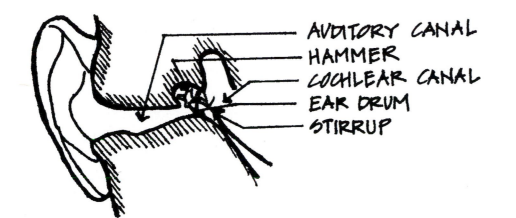

AUDITORY CANAL
HAMMER
COCHLEAR CANAL
EAR DRUM
STIRRUP

HUMAN EAR

Figure 10.1 Diagram of the ear.

ACOUSTICS

Acoustics is the study of sound. How sound moves through a space is a function of the shape of the space and the materials and finishes used within. Unwanted sound is called **noise**. It is the responsibility of the interior designer to anticipate possible sources of noise, and to design spaces that control this potential noise. Privacy is a specific need within interior spaces that can only be provided when sound is blocked from one space into the next.

Sound is generated in pressure oscillations that produce waves and can be measured in hertz. A receiver, such as the ear, receives the pressure and then sound is heard. The range of detectable sound to humans is between 20 and 20,000 hertz (Hz). Frequencies below 20 Hz are called infrasonic and above 20,000 Hz are called ultrasonic.

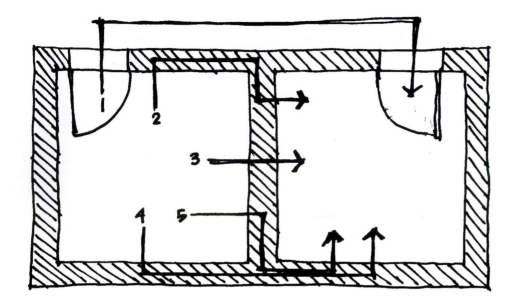

WAY SOUND TRAVELS BETWEEN SPACES

Figure 10.2 Diagram of how sound travels between two adjacent spaces.

Similar to light, sound travels in waves and is, therefore, subject to certain phenomena. Sound waves can be refracted, reflected, diffracted, and diffused. Reflected refers to the return of sound from a surface. As with light waves, a reflected sound wave is mirrored back into the space. Similar to light waves, sound waves can be bent when traveling through a medium, which changes the speed of the sound. Temperature changes can cause this change in speed. Diffraction refers to a sound wave's capability to bend around a barrier or through an opening. Diffusion of a sound wave occurs when the wave encounters an uneven surface and produces a random sound distribution.

In an interior space, walls, floors, and ceilings are detailed to reduce sound transmission to adjacent spaces. Absorbent surfaces help to reduce noise within a space.

Sound pressure is measured in decibels (dBA). The limit of human comfort is about 110 to 120 decibels. Values higher than this can cause permanent damage to the ear.

TABLE 10.1 TYPICAL DECIBELS (dBA) FOR VARIOUS SOUNDS

SOUND LEVEL (dBA)	EVALUATION	SOURCE
0	Threshold of hearing	
10	Just audible	Still night; recording studio
20	Very quiet	Rustling leaves; whisper
40–50	Quiet	Bird calls; private office
60	Moderate	Air conditioning compressor; general office
70	Loud	Heavy traffic; vacuum cleaner
80	Moderately loud	Diesel truck, garbage disposal
90–100	Very loud	Power mower; full symphony; food blender
110–120	Threshold of feeling	Jet flyover; inside propeller plane
130	Threshold of pain	Jet within 500 feet
140	Deafening	Near jet engine, artillery fire

Source: Adapted from p. 52, *Interior Graphic Standards (Student Edition)* by McGowan and Kruse, 2004.

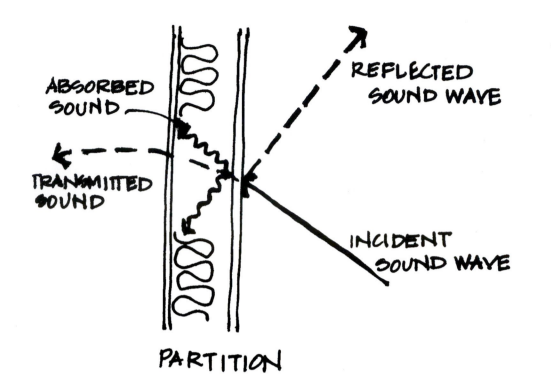

ABSORBED SOUND

REFLECTED SOUND WAVE

TRANSMITTED SOUND

INCIDENT SOUND WAVE

PARTITION

Figure 10.3 Behavior of sound waves within a partition.

PRINCIPLES OF SOUND: CONTROL

Unwanted sound waves can be absorbed. Absorption describes the process by which a sound energy is converted into heat. Part of the sound moving through a partition will be absorbed by the partition. All materials absorb some sound. Typical materials will also be rated with a **noise reduction coefficient (NRC)**.

Insulation is commonly used to absorb sound. Like NRC, all materials have a sound transmission class (STC). The STC refers to the capability of a material to absorb sound, and takes into account the entire frequency spectrum and the association transmission loss (TL) to provide a single number that describes sound transmission of typical human hearing.

Sound waves can also be bent. Redirection refers to purposely directing sound waves into a new direction. This is desirable in rooms where uniform hearing is desired from all locations.

TABLE 10.2 TYPICAL NOISE REDUCTION COEFFICIENTS (NRC)

MATERIAL	NRC
Brick	.00–.05
Carpet on concrete	.20–.30
Carpet on foam pad	.30–.55
Concrete	.00–.35
Cork wall tiles	.30–.70
Cork floor tiles	.10–.15
Drapery (light)	.05–.15
Drapery (heavy)	.60
Glass	.05–.10
Gypsum	.05
Linoleum on concrete	.00–.05
Marble	.00
Plaster	.05
Plywood	.10–.15
Rubber	.05
Seating (occupied)	.80–.85
Steel	.00–.10
Terrazzo	.00
Wood	.05–.15

Source: Adapted from NRC ratings, www.nrcratings.com/nrc.html. Retrieved 10/21/08.

REVERBERATION TIME (RT)

Reverberation describes the sound that is built up in a room over time (echo). This sound can actually begin to distort what is heard if it builds too much. Reverberation can be controlled and different **reverberation times (RT)** are preferred for different facility types. Reverberation time is extremely important when designing auditoriums, classrooms, lecture halls, music rooms, and performance facilities.

PRINCIPLES OF ROOM DESIGN

Partitions

Sound waves travel with little difficulty directly through wall studs from one room to another. Breaking the path of travel of the sound wave can prevent this transmission of sound. Staggered wall studs will help prevent this direct transfer.

Room Volumes

Generally speaking the designer should keep the room volume low when low reverberation times are desired. For example, in music performance halls and other spaces that need higher reverberation times, larger spatial volumes are desirable.

TABLE 10.3 TYPICAL SOUND TRANSFER CLASS (STC) ASSEMBLIES

WALL CONSTRUCTION	STC
4" hollow block, ½" plaster both sides	40
⅜" GWB	26
½" GWB	28
⅝" GWB	29
Two ½" GWB	31
2 × 4 @ 16" o.c., ½" GWB both sides	33

Source: Adapted from Table 13.13.1 Sound Transmission Class (STC) for representative wall constructions, Kinsler, et al, 381.

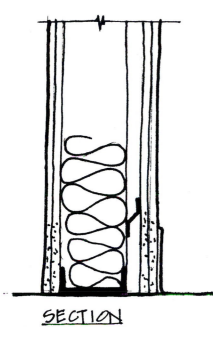

SECTION

Figure 10.4 Section of acoustical partition without staggered studs.

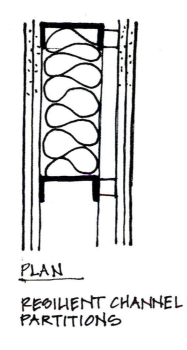

PLAN

RESILIENT CHANNEL PARTITIONS

Figure 10.5 Plan of acoustical partition without staggered studs.

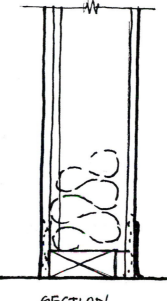

SECTION

Figure 10.6 Section of acoustical partition with staggered studs.

PLAN

STAGGERED STUD PARTITIONS

Figure 10.7 Plan of acoustical partition with staggered studs.

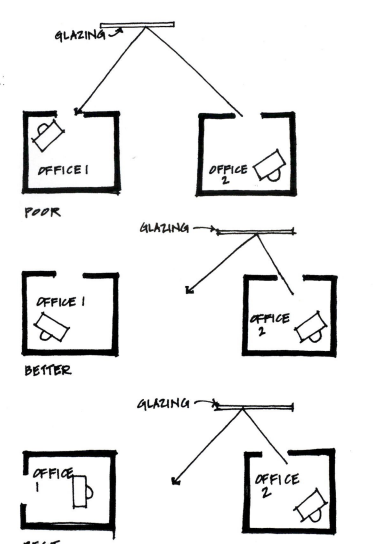

Figure 10.8 Sound transmission plan diagrams—poor, better and best placement.

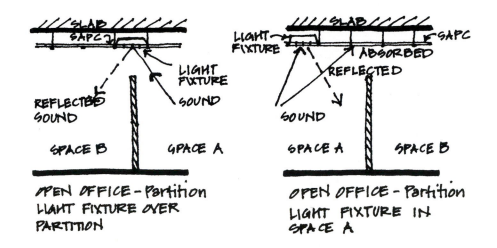

▲ Figure 10.9 Section diagram showing partition placement and light fixture placement.

▼ Figure 10.10 Diagram showing desks with no speech privacy.

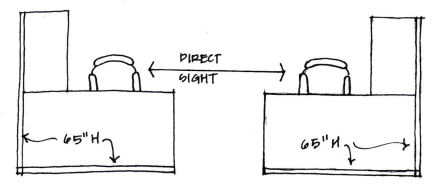

PRIVACY

The open office configuration poses a variety of acoustical challenges with regard to both noise and privacy. Open office acoustical partitions can also be used to reduce unwanted sound between workstations. These systems work best when proper layout is combined with sound-masking white noise and acoustical ceiling tiles. To effectively block unwanted voice transmission, partitions need to be at least five feet high. A six-foot high partition provides a higher sense of privacy, whereas a partition lower than four feet in height cannot prevent sound travel from one cubicle to the next.

Acoustical Partitions (Open Office)

One of the biggest challenges a designer must face is how to control the acoustics in an open office environment. Several systems furniture manufacturers produce a variety of products to assist with this type of design. The layout of the actual workstations is left to the designer; and this determines if the acoustical panels will function effectively.

Figure 10.11 Diagram showing desks with normal speech privacy.

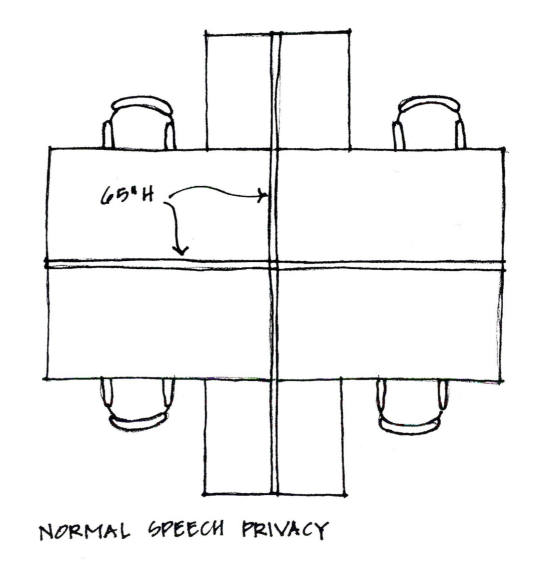

NORMAL SPEECH PRIVACY

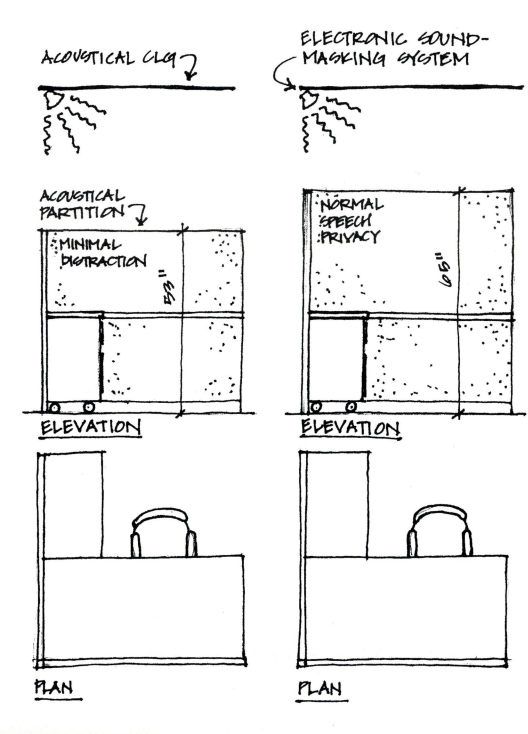

Acoustical Insulation in Partitions

Of particular importance in an office environment is the sound separation of human resources spaces and conference rooms, where personal information could be revealed and confidential conversations may take place. These rooms can be easily sound insulated using a variety of techniques, including full height partitions, acoustical ceilings, and walls with insulation.

Medical Facilities

Recent Health Insurance Portability and Accountability Act (HIPAA) privacy requirements demand that personal medical information be protected. As a result, hospitals have had to institute new methods for patient check-in and release within the medical environment. Sound separation for these areas can be achieved through the use of dividers at the check-in desk or through separate check-in rooms.

Figure 10.12 Plans and elevations with electrical sound masking and varying partition heights—minimal distraction versus normal speech privacy height requirements.

Health Safety and Welfare

Studies show that unwanted noise can lead to a variety of health problems. According to a recent article in *Environmental Health Perspectives* (*EHP*) about the results of a report from the National Institute of Public Health in the Netherlands, which looked at 500 studies of the health effects from noise exposure, "Noise exposure can lead to small increases in blood pressure readings and possibly even increases in cardiovascular disease prevalence..." The article goes on to associate noise with the following physiological effects: hearing loss, myocardial infraction, hypertension, ischemic heart disease, angina pectoria, and other maladies. The report criticizes many of the studies and the methods used. (Weinhold, 2002, 151.) A May 1998 *EHP* article listed some of the chronic effects of environmental noise: waking during the night, bad mood next day (depressed and irritable), ischemic heart disease, psychiatric disorders, annoyance, and poor performance by students with learning disabilities or that used English as a second language (EHP, May 1998, 222).

Passchier-Vermeer and Passchier explain that exposure to noise causes health risks. These risks can include hearing loss, annoyance, heart disease, sleep disturbance, and decreased performance. They suggest that irreversible cognitive impairment in children makes this an important subject for future research (EHP, March 2000, 123).

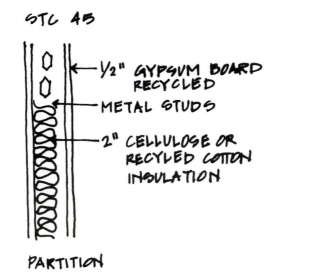

STC 45

— ½" GYPSUM BOARD RECYCLED

— METAL STUDS

— 2" CELLULOSE OR RECYCLED COTTON INSULATION

PARTITION

— RESILIENT CHANNEL
— GLASS FIBER INSULATION
— STUD

— DRYWALL

— DRYWALL

ACOUSTICAL PARTITION

Figure 10.13a–b Wall assembly with STC 45.

SOUND SEPARATION

Absorbing Materials

Interior materials have different sound absorption qualities. Generally, carpeting, acoustical ceiling tiles, and textiles are the most absorbent finishes. From a sustainability point of view, all interior materials should be chosen with regard to their life-cycle properties rather than by performance alone. Many developments in both the carpet and textile industries have made the use of sustainable materials much easier.

Diffusion in Rooms:
Sound Transmission Coefficient (STC)

Different types of spaces need different levels of acoustical control.

Different partition types can achieve these differing acoustical separations. Figures 10.13 through 10.15 show examples of three construction sections composed of sustainable materials that meet STC requirements ranging from 45–55.

STC 50

CONCRETE SLAB
WITH FLY ASH

STC 55

FLOATING FLOOR

Figure 10.14 Floor assembly with STC 50.   Figure 10.15 Floor assembly with STC 55.

TABLE 10.4 RECOMMENDED STC VALUES FOR A RANGE OF SPACE TYPES

ROOM (RECEIVING SOUND)	SOURCE OF SOUND	STC
Offices	Corridor/lobby	50
Offices	Plumbing	55
Bedrooms (hotel)	Adjacent bedroom; hall; plumbing	55
Classroom	Adjacent classroom	45
Classroom	Corridor/lobby	50
Conference room	Office	50
Conference room	Plumbing	55

Source: Adapted from p. 294, *Interior Graphic Standards* by McGowan and Kruse, 2003.

SPECIAL CIRCUMSTANCES

Mechanical systems and heavy equipment are two sources of noise in a building. The noise produced by air ducts can be reduced through proper insulation of the ductwork. Equipment noise can be reduced through a combination of sound insulation between the equipment and other spaces as well as through the use of vibration dampening materials.

Acoustics and Sustainable Design

Recent post occupancy assessments have examined whether LEED-certified buildings and other buildings claiming to be "green" are meeting user needs. In an article for *Architectural Record*, "Looking Back and Moving Forward," author Joann Gonchar, AIA, reveals that one area of frequent dissatisfaction to building users with their new green buildings relates to acoustics. Specifically, in an effort to make natural light available to all occupants, partitions were lowered and acoustical privacy was lost. Thus, when designing for natural light, other strategies besides simply lowering partition heights must be explored to maintain occupant satisfaction levels. Although the article did not explore these other options, some solutions might include central light source from a light well, the use of light shelves to bring natural light further into the space, and locating open offices near the perimeter of the building.

In his article "Acoustic Design for Green Buildings" for the *Environmental Design and Construction Magazine*, Kenneth Roy proposes a solution for acoustical design in green buildings. Specifically, he addresses the new trend for exposed wide-open plans. For this type of space, he recommends acoustical clouds and canopies over specific areas to address noise and privacy issues. Acoustical clouds are flat and come in sizes up to 14 feet by 14 feet, whereas canopies are smaller and curved. Roy also recommends that credits be included in the LEED Rating Systems for acoustical control that would help avoid these problems in future green buildings.

Figure 10.16 (*opposite*) Sketch of ceiling clouds.

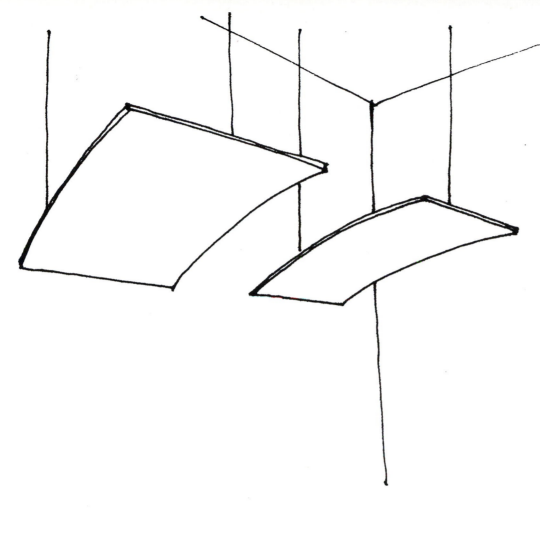

INDOOR AIR QUALITY (IAQ)

The quality of the air inside of a building (**indoor air quality**, or **IAQ**) is impacted by several factors: the HVAC system, the interior materials, the interior furniture, fixtures, and equipment and moisture within a building. Indoor pollutants consist of undesirable substances that make their way into the air supply. These include volatile organic compounds (VOCs) released by indoor products (also known as off-gassing), biological contaminants, minerals, radiation, metals, and water vapor that can lead to mold spores. Proper mechanical design and ventilation are critical to providing fresh air within a space. Although the interior designer does not design the HVAC system, he/she is responsible for interior finishes, fixtures, furnishings, and equipment, and can thus greatly impact the quality of the indoor air quality.

Indoor environmental quality (IEQ) volatile organic compounds may be released into the air by a variety of typical interior furnishings and finishes including new furniture, carpeting and paint. In addition to VOCs, there are several other possible sources of indoor air pollution within a building. These include copy machines, asbestos, cleaners, pesticides, stoves/chimneys/fireplaces, and carbon monoxide that may enter the indoor environment through the use of improperly ventilated appliances including water heaters, furnaces, dryers, and stoves. Mold, radon, and cigarette smoke also add pollution to the indoor environment.

Radon is invisible, tasteless, and odorless, and according to a recent article may be killing as many as 20,000 Americans per year (Kerr, 1988). A bi-product of supernovas, or stellar explosions, radon exists in the ground. It is a bi-product of radium, and results from uranium decay. Radon is released from the ground and is often found in basements and crawl spaces. The gas tends to concentrate. In high concentrations, it has been linked with lung cancer.

Many indoor materials release odors into the environment known as **off-gassing**. Some of these may be toxic. These VOCs can be carcinogenic to human beings, thus endangering the health and welfare of the building's occupants. **Building-related illness (BRI)** is caused by an accumulation of these indoor pollutants and contributes to **Sick building byndrome (SBS)**. BRI can lead to nose, throat, and eye irritation; headaches; nausea; kidney and nervous system damage; and immune system suppression.

Sick Building Syndrome SBS

According to researcher Jan A. Stolwijk, "the sick building syndrome (SBS) is defined as the occurrence of an excessive number of complaints by the occupants of a building" (*Environmental Health Perspectives*, Volume 95, 1991, 99). Among these complaints are a variety of physical discomforts including: nausea, lethargy, dizziness, inability to concentrate, irritation of eyes and throat, and odors. Another term for this type of building condition is *tight building syndrome*. Biological contaminants found in such buildings include mold and bacteria, whereas chemical toxins include VOCs associated with cleaning materials, furniture, and building materials. Tobacco smoke is another source of irritation in the indoor environment.

Building Related Illness (BRI)

Generally, a small percentage of building occupants experience building-related illnesses. Those with preexisting conditions are particularly at-risk.

Legionnaire's Disease

Perhaps the best-known example of BRI is Legionnaire's disease. This disease is associated with buildings that are air-conditioned. When legionella bacteria is allowed to grow within cooling ponds of air-conditioning systems, it can easily be transmitted to building occupants through air ducts. Thus, it is important to drain and treat the cooling pond in addition to regularly maintaining the cleanliness of the duct work and filters.

EFFECTS

As mentioned earlier in this chapter, poor indoor air quality can lead to a variety of physical symptoms ranging from mild to severe reactions. These include irritation of eyes and throat, dizziness, fatigue, and asthma.

TREATMENT

The most efficient method of treatment is to remove the source of the contaminants. Improved ventilation and the use air cleaners and/or air purifiers will also reduce the effect of VOCs.

LIFE-CYCLE ASSESSMENT

The **life-cycle assessment** of a material involves looking at all aspects of the life-cycle: material extraction, where it is made, transportation costs, how long does it last? What happens when it is no longer usable? A complete cradle-to-grave analysis will make it easier to assess the real sustainability of a product.

The embodied energy of a material takes many of these factors into consideration. This is the amount of energy used to create a material from extraction, through production and installation and eventually disposal.

SUMMARY

Interior designers can improve indoor environmental quality in a number of ways. Through the specification of certified low or no VOC interior finishes, the air quality in a space will be better than one with traditional finishes. Also, knowledge of various potential air quality problems can lead to improved maintenance and testing of indoor air. Finally, careful attention to speech privacy and other issues related to sound travel in an interior can substantially improve user perceptions of the space. The following case study demonstrates how acoustical concerns can be addressed.

CASE STUDY

The Bank of Charlotte by Perkins + Will illustrates some standard acoustical design principles as applied within a sustainably designed project. Figure 10.17 shows a typical conference room with acoustical ceiling and doors for sounds separation; Figure 10.18 includes a lounge area with acoustical ceiling for sound absorption. The breakout area employs acoustical ceiling and carpet for sound absorption (Figure 10.19). A breakout space with an acoustical ceiling is shown in Figure 10.20. Figure 10.21 illustrates the main elevator lobby. The sitting area has an acoustical ceiling, and some carpeting and partitions for sound separation and absorption (Figure 10.22).

Figure 10.17 Perkins + Will, Bank of Charlotte, Charlotte, NC, Conference room with acoustical ceiling and doors for sounds separation. Interior Designer & Architect: Perkins + Will; Branded Environments Managing Principal: Eva Maddox; Project Manager: John Morris; Design Principal: Rod Vickroy; Interior Designers: Gardner Vass, Laura Smith, Rebecca Krupp; Planning + Strategies Principal: Janice Barnes; LEED Coordinator: Anne Jackson; Environmental Graphics: Samar Hechaime; Signage and Wayfinding: Chris Mueller. Photo Credit: Steve Hall, Hedrich Blessing Photography.

Figure 10.18 Perkins + Will, Bank of Charlotte, Charlotte, NC. Lounge area with acoustical ceiling for sound absorption. Interior Designer & Architect: Perkins + Will; Branded Environments Managing Principal: Eva Maddox; Project Manager: John Morris; Design Principal: Rod Vickroy; Interior Designers: Gardner Vass, Laura Smith, Rebecca Krupp; Planning + Strategies Principal: Janice Barnes; LEED Coordinator: Anne Jackson; Environmental Graphics: Samar Hechaime; Signage and Wayfinding: Chris Mueller.
Photo Credit: Steve Hall, Hedrich Blessing Photography.

Figure 10.19 Perkins + Will, Bank of Charlotte, Charlotte, NC. Breakout area with acoustical ceiling and carpet for sound absorption. Interior Designer & Architect: Perkins + Will; Branded Environments Managing Principal: Eva Maddox; Project Manager: John Morris; Design Principal: Rod Vickroy; Interior Designers: Gardner Vass, Laura Smith, Rebecca Krupp; Planning + Strategies Principal: Janice Barnes; LEED Coordinator: Anne Jackson; Environmental Graphics: Samar Hechaime; Signage and Wayfinding: Chris Mueller. Photo Credit: Steve Hall, Hedrich Blessing Photography.

Figure 10.20 Perkins + Will, Bank of Charlotte, Charlotte, NC. Group meeting area with acoustical ceiling and doors for sounds separation. Interior Designer & Architect: Perkins + Will; Branded Environments Managing Principal: Eva Maddox; Project Manager: John Morris; Design Principal: Rod Vickroy; Interior Designers: Gardner Vass, Laura Smith, Rebecca Krupp; Planning + Strategies Principal: Janice Barnes; LEED Coordinator: Anne Jackson; Environmental Graphics: Samar Hechaime; Signage and Wayfinding: Chris Mueller. Photo Credit: Steve Hall, Hedrich Blessing Photography.

Figure 10.21 Perkins + Will, Bank of Charlotte, Charlotte, NC. Elevator lobby. Interior Designer & Architect: Perkins + Will; Branded Environments Managing Principal: Eva Maddox; Project Manager: John Morris; Design Principal: Rod Vickroy; Interior Designers: Gardner Vass, Laura Smith, Rebecca Krupp; Planning + Strategies Principal: Janice Barnes; LEED Coordinator: Anne Jackson; Environmental Graphics: Samar Hechaime; Signage and Wayfinding: Chris Mueller. Photo Credit: Steve Hall, Hedrich Blessing Photography.

313

Figure 10.22 Perkins + Will, Bank of Charlotte, Charlotte, NC. Private office with meeting area with acoustical ceiling, some carpeting and partitions for sound separation and absorption. Interior Designer & Architect: Perkins + Will; Branded Environments Managing Principal: Eva Maddox; Project Manager: John Morris; Design Principal: Rod Vickroy; Interior Designers: Gardner Vass, Laura Smith, Rebecca Krupp; Planning + Strategies Principal: Janice Barnes; LEED Coordinator: Anne Jackson; Environmental Graphics: Samar Hechaime; Signage and Wayfinding: Chris Mueller. Photo Credit: Steve Hall, Hedrich Blessing Photography.

KEY TERMS

acoustics

building-related illness (BRI)

decibels (dBA)

diffraction

diffusion

embodied energy

indoor air quality (IAQ)

infrasonic

life-cycle assessment

noise

noise reduction coefficient (NRC)

off-gassing

radon

redirection

refracted

reflected

reverberation time (RT)

sick building syndrome (SBS)

sound transfer coefficient (STC)

transmission loss (TL)

ultrasonic

ASSIGNMENTS/EXERCISES

1. Identify some rooms around you with acoustical problems. Sketch these rooms and record the details. How can you improve the acoustics of the place?

2. Research the life-cycle and embodied energy of some typical building materials: concrete, steel, wood, carpet, and so on. Based on this information, which ones seem to best fit sustainability criteria?

3. Find at least two peer-reviewed journal articles that discuss indoor air quality and record your findings in your sketchbook. What have you learned to improve indoor air quality in your design projects?

4. Analyze a recent design project you have completed and record your ideas for improved acoustics within your design solution.

RESOURCES

Cowen, James. (2000). *Architectural Acoustics Design Guide.* New York: McGraw Hill.

Environmental Health Perspectives, Volume 108, Supplement 1, March 2000, 123.

Environmental Health Perspectives, Volume 106, Number 5, May 1998, 222.

Gatland, S. (2008). "Addressing IAQ: Good Indoor Air Quality Creates Healthier and Happier Building Occupants," *Environmental Design and Construction,* May 2008, 102–104.

Gonchar, Joann. "Looking Back and Moving Forward," *Architectural Record,* February 2008, 161–168.

Kerr, R. (1988). "Indoor Radon: The Deadliest Pollutant," *Science,* Vol. 240, No. 4852 (April 29, 1988), 606–608.

Kinsler, Lawrence, Austin Frey, Alan Coppens, and James Sanders. (2000). *Fundamentals of Acoustics* (4th ed.). New York: John Wiley and Sons.

McGowan, M. and K. Kruse. (2003). *Interior Graphic Standards.* New York: John Wiley and Sons.

Product Crafters. (1984). *Open Plan Office Acoustical Privacy: A Planning Guide.* East Brunswick, NJ: Product Crafters, Inc.

Roy, Kenneth. (2008). "Acoustic Design for Green Buildings" *Environmental Design and Construction Magazine,* March 2008, 44–45.

Stolwijk, Jan A. (1991). "Commentary: Sick Building Syndrome," *Environmental Health Perspectives,* Vol. 95 (Nov. 1991), 99–100.

Weinhold, B. (2002). *Environmental Health Perspectives,* Volume 119, number 3, March 2002, 151.

acoustics.com www.acoustics.com

For sustainable textiles see:

DesignTex, specifically their work with architect William McDonough

Indoor Air Quality Association www.iaqa.org

CHAPTER 11

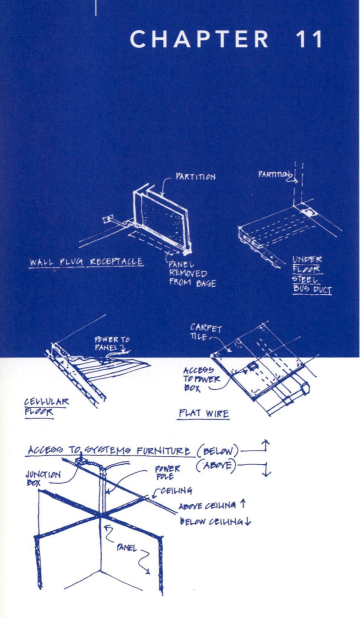

Interior Building Systems

It is notoriously difficult to estimate the overall rate of extinction, but biologists, by using several indirect methods of analysis, generally agree that on the land at least, species are vanishing at a rate one hundred to a thousand times faster than before the arrival of Homo sapiens.

Edward O. Wilson, Consilience: The Unity of Knowledge

OBJECTIVES

- Incorporate appropriate security features into design projects
- Apply the principles of good security design to projects
- Differentiate between the multiple forms of vertical circulation in buildings
- Integrate systems furniture with a building's structure and know how to get power to the systems furniture

INTRODUCTION

This chapter introduces several interior systems that impact the design of a successful interior environment, including data voice and telecommunications systems, energy control systems, security systems, vertical circulation systems, and explains how systems furniture interfaces with the building itself.

DATA, VOICE, AND TELECOMMUNICATIONS

Providing telephone lines and Internet connections are a necessity of the modern interior environment. In addition, many clients also request wireless service resulting in the need for careful placement of wireless routers to ensure equal service throughout a space.

TELECONFERENCING

Some clients may want teleconferencing capabilities. The room in which this takes place must accommodate a projection screen—more than likely a large plasma or LCD screen—and a calling device that will be centrally placed and through which people can call out to another site and speak. If the room setting is a conference room, phone jacks should be provided at the center of the conferencing table with the screen at one end of the room.

Figure 11.1
Conference room with audio-visual technology.

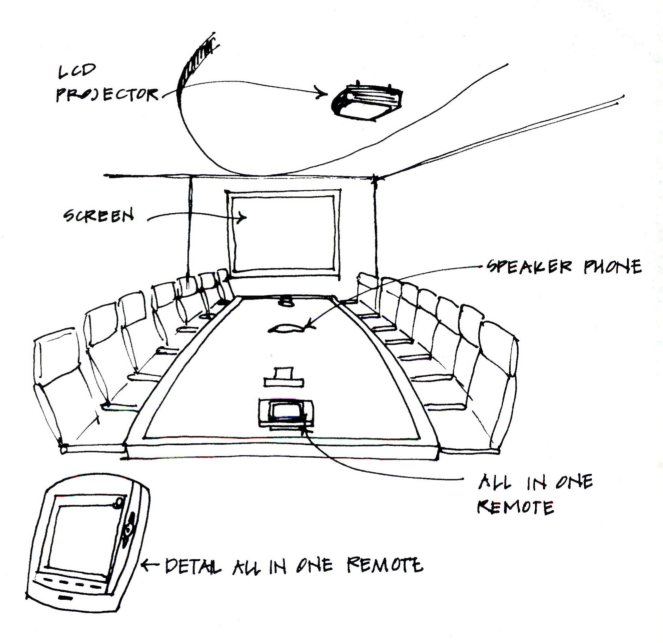

LCD PROJECTOR

SCREEN

SPEAKER PHONE

ALL IN ONE REMOTE

← DETAIL ALL IN ONE REMOTE

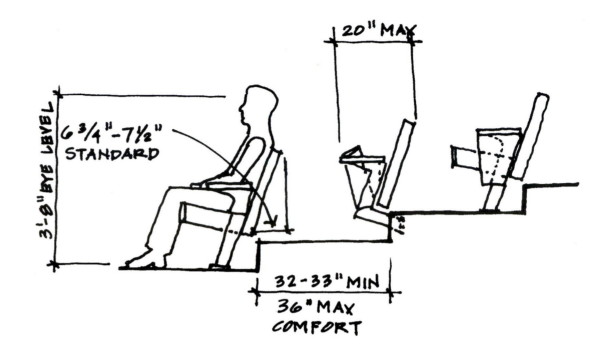

Figure 11.2 Sight lines in a theater/auditorium.

AUDIO VISUAL SYSTEMS

PROJECTION SPACE PLANNING REQUIREMENTS/VISUAL SIGHT LINES

One of the primary issues when installing audio-visual systems is to make sure all occupants of the space are able to see the image being projected. Depending on the size of the space, this may involve staggering the seats (in a small space) or creating different seating levels (in a larger space). The floor can either be ramped or stepped to created many levels so that everyone has a clear view of the image area. Some rules of thumb for placing the screen include: the closest viewer should be no more the two times the height of the screen (two-and-a-half times is preferred), and the top of the screen should form an angle of no more than 30 degrees from the horizontal sight line of the viewer.

ACOUSTICS

Another key component of the audio-visual environment is enabling the attendee to hear clearly. The size and shape of the space as well as the interior materials will greatly impact the ability of people to hear. Soundproofing between adjacent spaces is also critical.

ENERGY CONTROL

To create a truly sustainable building requires careful monitoring systems to regulate and control energy usage. A complete energy control system will address HVAC and lighting.

SECURITY

Since September 11, 2001, building security has become a preeminent issue in building design. Specific types of spaces require differing types of security controls. Examples of security intensive interiors include hospitals (especially maternity and delivery wards), retail spaces, banks, courthouses, jails, Alzheimer/dementia facilities, airports, and many other building types. Added to this list in recent years have been schools (high school and middle schools) and colleges and universities. In today's society, people expect a certain level of safety from the built environment. Very few project types do not require special security design. Security systems range from space planning issues such as sight lines and barriers within a space to actual alarm and control systems such as metal detectors. Designers need to be aware of both types of security interventions.

SPACE PLANNING ISSUES AND VISUAL CONTROL

How a space is organized can contribute to the overall sense of security. In multiple applications, visual control of the environment needs to be included. For example, in a retail environment, the sales force needs to be able to monitor both the cash registers and checkout area as well as entrances and exits. A variety of tag and alarm systems are used in larger retail settings. Similarly, hotel front desk personnel need encompassing views of hotel lobbies and, in some cases, elevators. Elevator access can also be controlled through the use of key cards. In healthcare facilities, visual access to patient rooms contributes to proper nursing care. In areas with newborns, heightened security measure may be needed including door alarms to supplement visual monitoring. Alzheimer and dementia care facilities also benefit from the inclusion of door alarms to alert the staff when a patient has left the area unknowingly.

SECURITY CONTROL SYSTEMS

Security systems are divided into three basic types: perimeter systems, area or room systems, and surveillance systems. Perimeter systems are used to monitor a building perimeter and include devices such as magnetic contacts at windows and doors, glass break protectors, and screen alarms. Area or room security measures include detectors (infrared, audio, ultrasonic, and microwave) as well as pressure sensors and photoelectric beams. Surveillance systems include access control systems such as biometric control systems using finger print, hand print, or retinal scans, card readers, numbered keyboards, and punch card access such as those used in hotels.

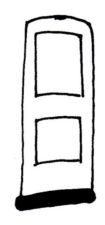

Store Alarm Systems

Most retail stores have some type of **store alarm system**. Oftentimes, these are stationary anti-theft detection devices coupled with tags or scan codes that create an audio sound and sometimes a visual alarm when a customer tries to leave the store without checking out.

Figure 11.3 Anti-theft device for retail.

MORTISE CYLINDER

▲ Figure 11.4 Photograph of a typical fire door.

▼ Figure 11.5 Sketch of gates as found in a shopping mall.

Audio Security Alarms

Audio security alarms can be attached to fixed anti-theft devices, doors, and other mechanisms, and are designed to alert personnel within the facility if someone is attempting to leave a facility with unpurchased items or enter an area where they are not permitted. An example would be exiting through a fire exit.

Lockdown Systems

A **lockdown system** is used when it is desirable to lock down a specific area in the event of an emergency or after hours of operation. These are commonly used in prisons. Other applications include high schools and shopping malls. Oftentimes both schools and malls have some areas that are used after common hours of operation. In this instance a variety of metal gates or other devices may be used to close off those areas that are closed.

Figure 11.6 Photograph of a typical burglar alarm.

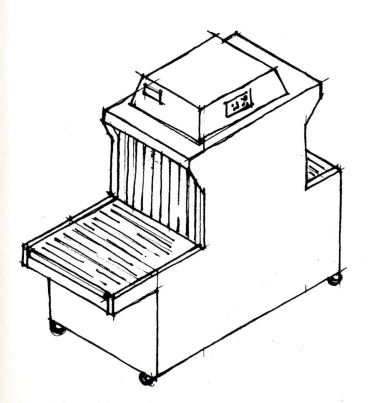

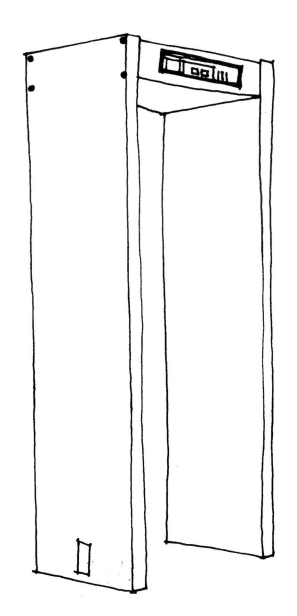

Burglar Alarms

Burglar alarms are used in many building types. These alarms vary widely in how they are installed and how they operate. Some may be wired only to doors and sound an alarm when a person enters the space. Others may be hardwired to a security company that is alerted in the event of a fire, unauthorized entry, and other situations. Some systems require authorized people to enter codes or a security scan card to disarm them. Others are manually disarmed.

Metal Detectors

Metal detectors are commonly used in several specific instances including airport security, government buildings, and courthouses. They may also be used in many other applications. The metal detector generates a pulse of energy that creates a magnetic field. Large pieces of metal cause the system to set off an audio and visual alarm alerting personnel to check for guns and other unauthorized metallic objects.

▶ Figure 11.7 Sketch of metal detector.

◀ Figure 11.8 X-ray machine.

Wand Scanners

In the event a metal detector alarm goes off, the second level of security is often the **wand scanner**. These are hand-held devices that security personnel use to identify the actual location of the metal that has set off the alarm on a person's physical body.

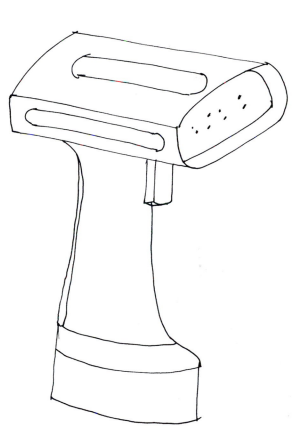

Figure 11.9 Wand scanner.

According to security expert, David Shelton, "The best security is to remove opportunity" (2008). From an interior design perspective, this includes eliminating nooks and crannies and places for people to hide or go unobserved. Access control systems coupled with human resources can handle most internal security concerns. Mass alert systems can be used to notify building occupants of security breaches. All of these security measures are best integrated during the initial stages of the design process.

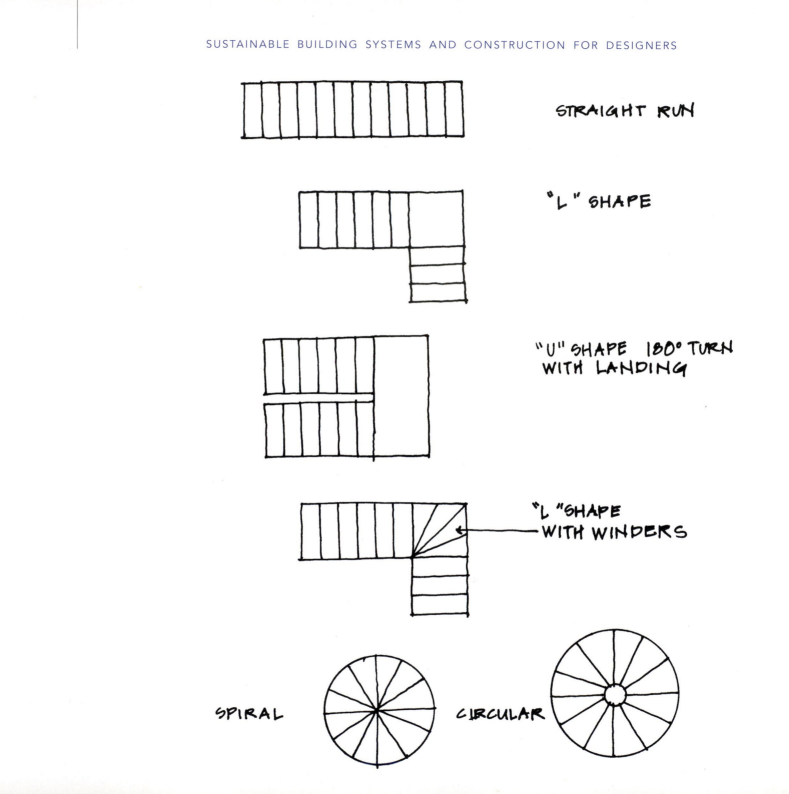

STRAIGHT RUN

"L" SHAPE

"U" SHAPE 180° TURN WITH LANDING

"L" SHAPE WITH WINDERS

SPIRAL

CIRCULAR

CONVEYING SYSTEMS: VERTICAL CIRCULATION

The way in which people and objects move from floor to floor or level to level within a space is through the use of different types of vertical circulation. These include stairs, elevators, escalators, and ladders.

STAIRS

Stairs can be configured in several different ways. The layout of the stair will determine the amount of space required on each floor to accommodate the stair.

Stair Design

The building codes regulate the specific sizes of stair treads and riser heights as well as the overall width of the stair for specific occupancies. A mathematical relationship between these two determines the comfort of the stairs.

Stairs are constructed from many materials. The three most common construction materials include wood, metal, and concrete.

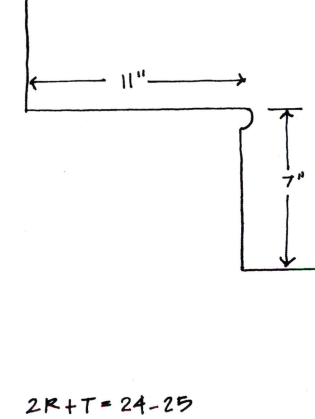

$$2R + T = 24 - 25$$
$$2(T) + 11 =$$
$$14 + 11 = 25$$

◀ Figure 11.10 Stair configurations.

▲ Figure 11.11 Typical rise tread relationship.

Figure 11.12 Sketch showing wood stair components.

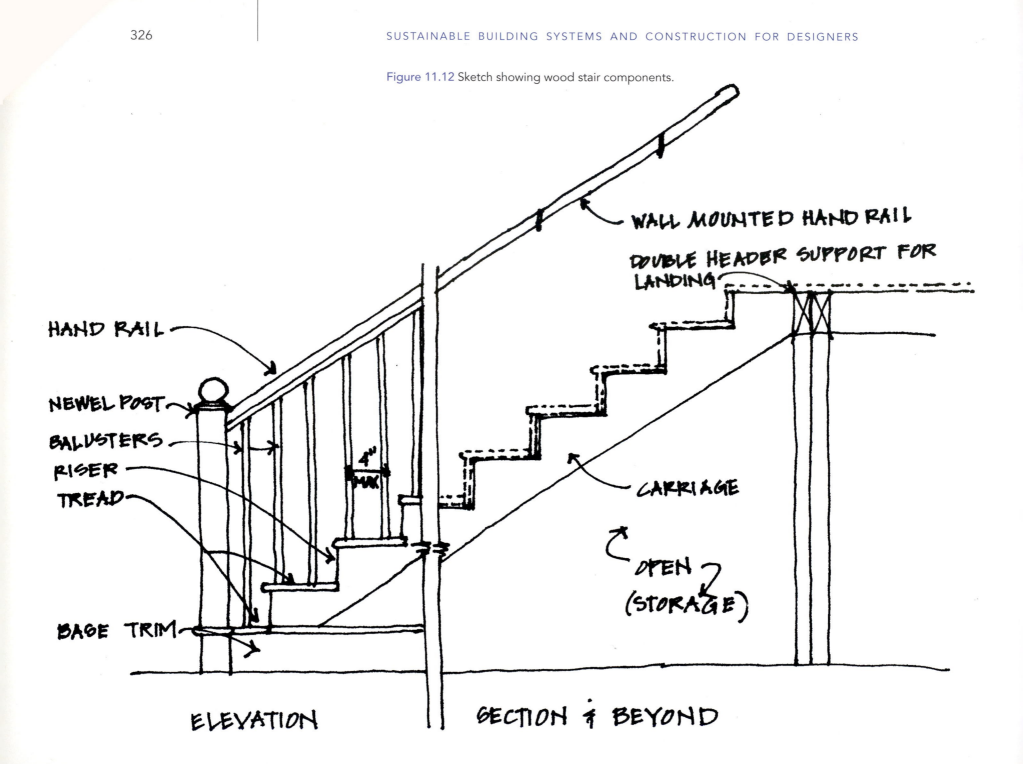

WALL MOUNTED HAND RAIL

DOUBLE HEADER SUPPORT FOR LANDING

HAND RAIL

NEWEL POST

BALUSTERS

RISER

TREAD

4" MAX

CARRIAGE

OPEN (STORAGE)

BASE TRIM

ELEVATION

SECTION & BEYOND

Stair Terminology

The manner in which stairs are constructed is similar for wood and steel stairs. The terminology for each of the constituent parts varies somewhat.

Concrete stairs create a series of individual concrete members, each of which acts as a simple beam. As with all concrete beams, these concrete members must be reinforced with steel rebar.

The risers of a set of stairs may be either open or closed. Codes regulate which occupancy types can utilize open risers.

Figure 11.13 Sketch showing steel stair components.

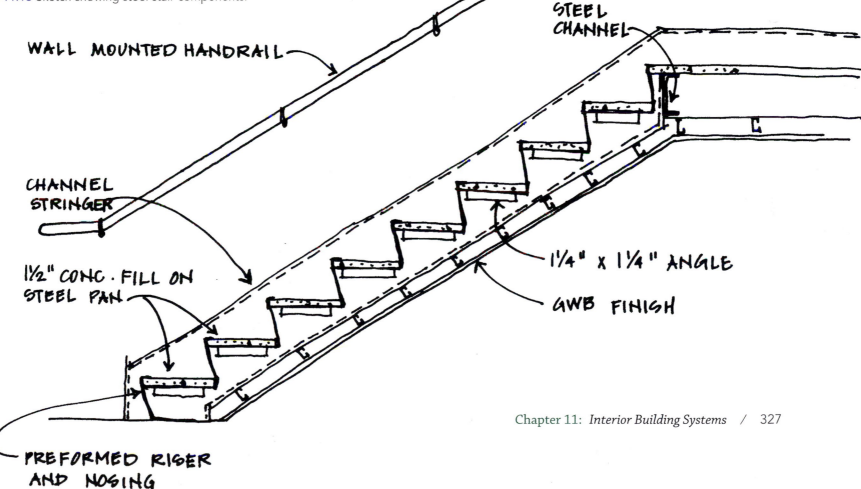

WALL MOUNTED HANDRAIL

STEEL CHANNEL

CHANNEL STRINGER

1½" CONC. FILL ON STEEL PAN

1¼" x 1¼" ANGLE

GWB FINISH

PREFORMED RISER AND NOSING

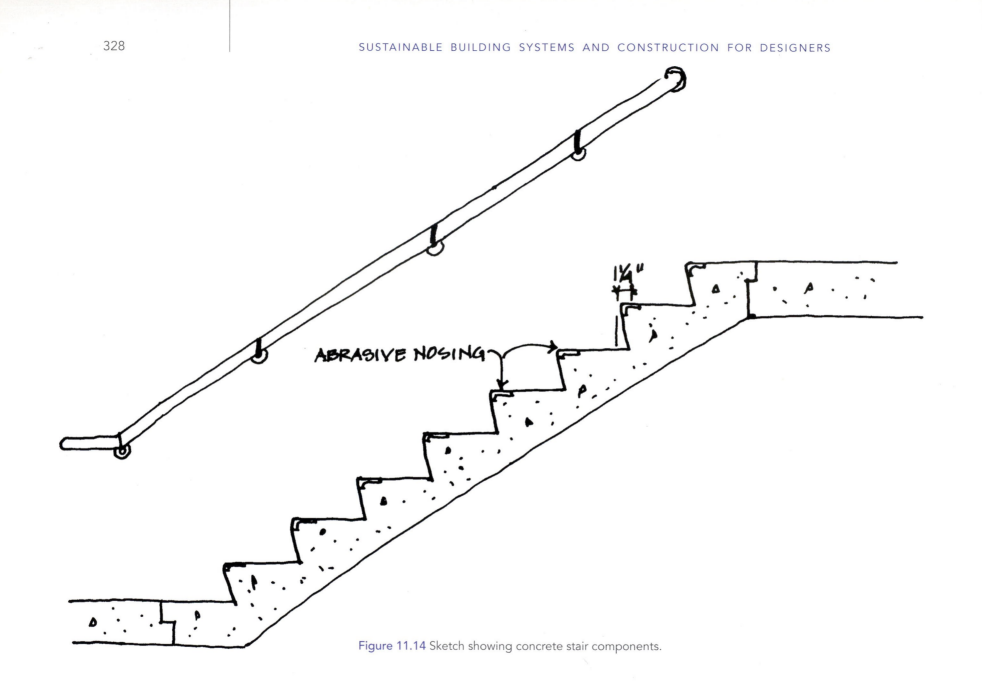

1¼"

ABRASIVE NOSING

Figure 11.14 Sketch showing concrete stair components.

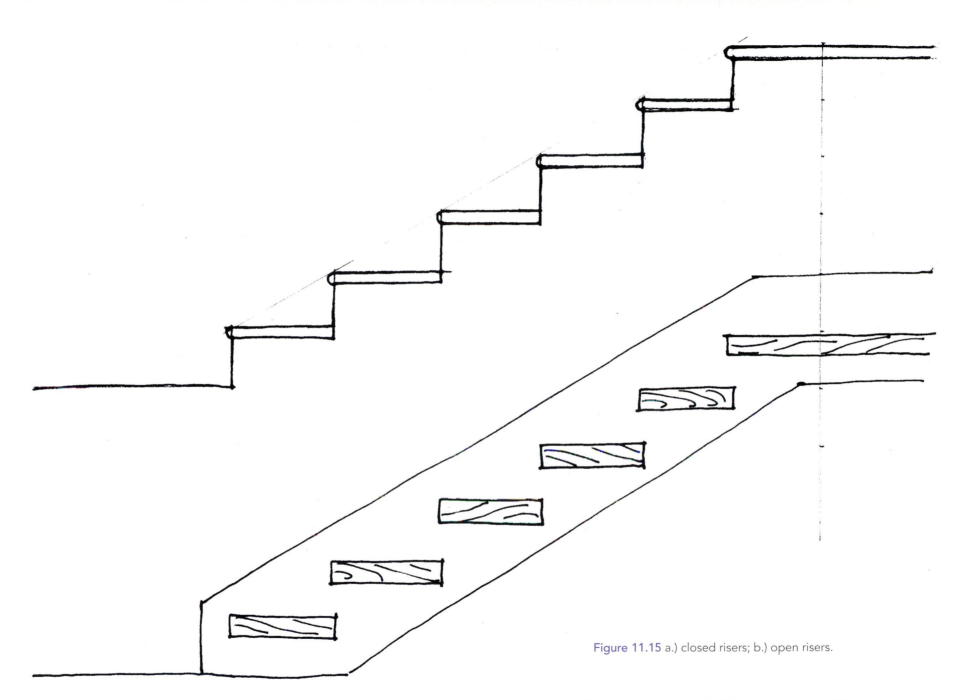

Figure 11.15 a.) closed risers; b.) open risers.

Guard Rails versus Hand Rails

Guard rails are defined by the building code as the horizontal restraining railings that are located at landings and the top of stairs. Hand rails follow the slope of the stairs themselves.

Figure 11.16
Photograph showing a handrail and a guardrail.

ELEVATORS

Most multilevel buildings include some form of elevator. There are two basic types of elevators: hydraulic and electric. Electric elevators require a rooftop mechanical room for the cable traction system that pulls the elevator up. This type of elevator is faster than a hydraulic and is typically used in high-rise buildings (over 60 to 70 feet). When only a couple of floors exist, a hydraulic elevator is more commonly used. This type of elevator requires a piston and a space beneath the elevator for the piston to push the elevator up from floor to floor.

Recent developments in elevator technology have resulted in the introduction of the machine roomless elevator. These gearless traction type elevators are comparable in energy use to current standard electric elevators, but use less metal and other materials resulting in less embodied energy. LED lighting can also reduce the use of power needed for illumination (Smiley, 2008).

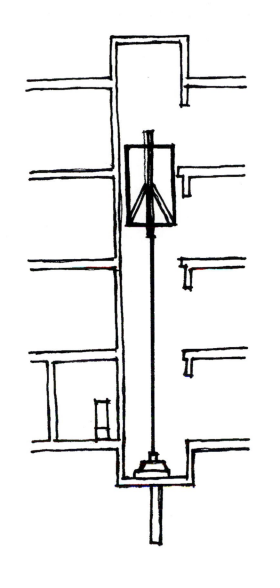

▲ Figure 11.17 Hydraulic elevator section.

▶ Figure 11.18 Electric elevator section.

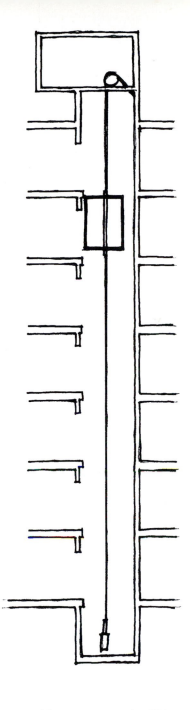

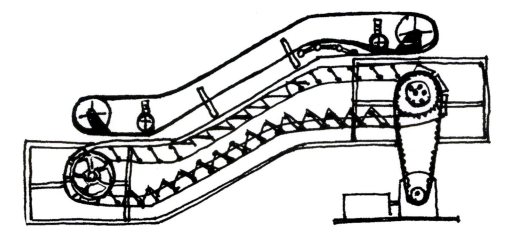

Figure 11.19 Section through a typical escalator.

ESCALATORS

An escalator is a mechanical stair that runs on a continuous belt. These are used to avoid having to climb a stair and can continuously accommodate users, unlike an elevator that must wait in between uses. The basic components of an escalator include a structural truss, an upper module step and handrail drive system, a lower module, a top and bottom landing platform, a step chain, tracks, escalator steps and a handrail. The geometry of an escalator should not exceed a 30 degree angle. The standard stair widths are 24, 32, and 40 inches (Tetlow, 2008).

LADDERS

Ladders are generally used in one of two ways within a building: in a residential building as access to a loft or attic space, or in a commercial space to access the rooftop. In either case, the ladder is not a public form of vertical circulation. The ladder is used because it requires far less floor space than any other form of vertical transportation and is the least expensive option as well.

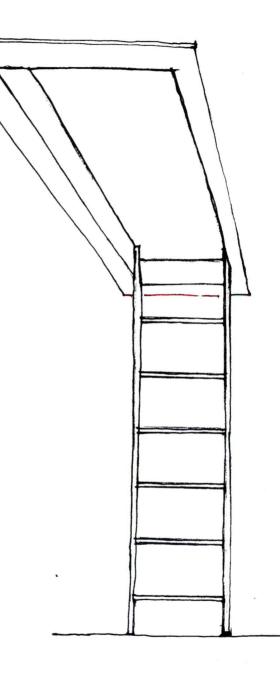

Figure 11.20 Ladder to the roof.

SYSTEMS FURNITURE

Systems furniture provides flexibility within an open office space. By providing panel-based movable offices, interior spaces can be constantly reconfigured to address client needs. Additional benefits of the systems furniture approach include maximizing the number of occupants in a given square footage as well as creating opportunities for team-based interactive environments between and around cubicles.

Despite a nearly infinite array of configurations, systems furniture does require careful interface with the building itself.

The first fully cradle to cradle systems furniture system is the Answer system by Steelcase. The system includes multiple sustainable features:

- Power solution is PVC free and meets reduction of hazardous substances (RoHS) requirements and waste of electric and electronic equipment (WEEE) criteria.
- The Think chair used with the system is 98 percent recyclable whereas the Move side chairs are 99 percent recyclable. Both can be disassembled into their component parts in five minutes.
- The DesignTex panel fabrics are made of 100 percent recycled polyester.
- The panels themselves are 100 percent reusable and easy to disassemble.
- Metal finishes are 100 percent solvent free, the system is PVC free, and the wood components are made from Forest Stewardship Council (FSC)– and the Sustainable Forestry Initiative (SFI)–certified woods finished with water-based top coats (Steelcase).

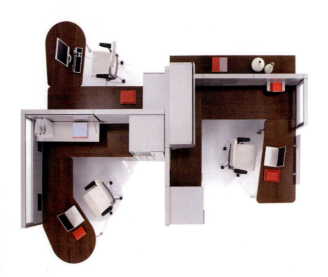

Figure 11.21
"Answer" systems furniture configuration.
Courtesy of Janet Davis, Steelcase.

Figure 11.22
"Answer" systems furniture configuration.
Courtesy of Janet Davis, Steelcase.

Figure 11.23
"Answer" systems furniture configuration.
Courtesy of Janet Davis, Steelcase.

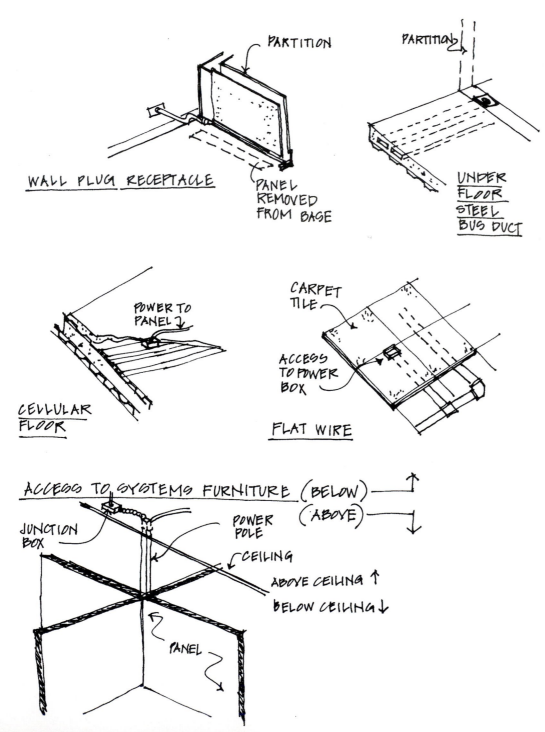

POWERING SYSTEMS FURNITURE

Because systems furniture panels are electrified, a source of power must be connected to the panel. This can be done in a variety of ways, including through the use of access flooring, power poles, wall receptacles, and other floor-based delivery mechanisms. Providing data and voice telecommunication lines presents a similar set of issues and solutions.

INTERFACE WITH BUILDING SHELL

Although system furniture panels are thin, they must still be carefully integrated with a building's fenestration to avoid running panels into windows or in front of windows. Additionally, panel placement in relation to electric lighting will impact user performance within a space as well as the acoustics within and between cubicles.

Figure 11.24
Ways of powering systems furniture in a building.

SIGNAGE AND WAYFINDING

Wayfinding describes the process by which a building provides visual cues to an occupant about how to navigate through the various spaces. This can be done in several ways, oftentimes through a combination of design decisions. These can include ceiling design elements and the shape and orientation of built-in furniture pieces as well as those that are movable. Floor patterns may be used as well as paint schemes to identify specific areas.

Related to wayfinding and equally important in helping people find their way through a building is the signage. An ideal signage solution alerts people to where they are and where they are going from the time they approach a building until they leave. Signage has also become a way to achieve LEED innovation credit. In this instance signage is used to educate building users about the sustainable features of a building.

One of the most important types of signage in a building is the exit signage. Exit signs are required by the building code, which also specifies their location and frequency of use. These signs are used to lead people safely to an exit in the event of an emergency.

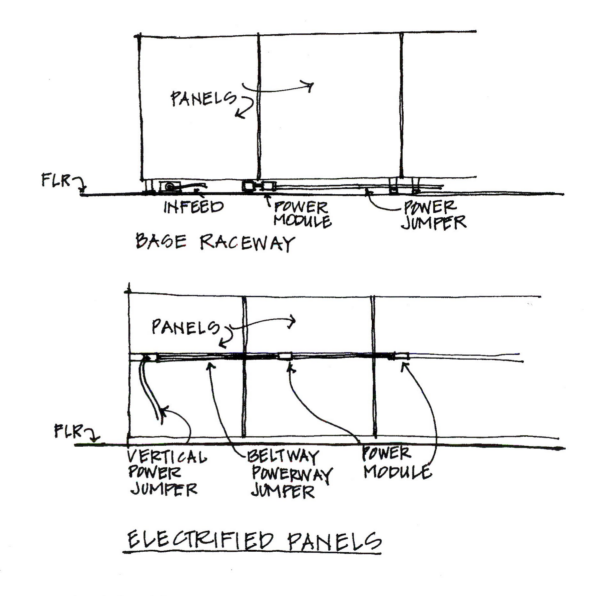

Figure 11.25 Electrified panel diagrams.

SUMMARY

This chapter covered vertical circulation systems, wayfinding and signage, and an introduction to the many forms of building security. The following case studies illustrate examples of some of these items.

CASE STUDIES

Two projects by Perkins + Will are used to illustrate a few of the concepts discussed in this chapter.

Figure 11.26 shows systems furniture in an open office setting powered using a raised floor system; Figure 11.27 illustrates a closed office setting powered through the wall. The Cofra Offices project also uses signage as an educational tool to describe the building systems and green building features (Figure 11.28).

The Haworth Showroom in Calgary, Alberta, demonstrates how a monumental, straight-run stair can be used as a point of emphasis within the design solution. FSC woods highlight the spaces and are used on both the ceiling and wall surfaces. They complement the sustainable carpet tiles, suspended ceiling systems and fluorescent lighting to create a serene interior space with panoramic views to the exterior (Figures 11.29 through 11.32).

▶ Figure 11.26 (*opposite*) Perkins + Will, Cofra offices, systems furniture in an open office setting powered using a raised floor system. Photo Credit: ArchPhoto, Eduard Hueber.

OUR HVAC AND LIGHTING CONTROLS SYSTEMS WORK
IN A COORDINATED WAY WITH OUR SHADING SYSTEM
TO AUTOMATICALLY MAXIMIZE THE USE OF NATURAL,
INSTEAD OF ARTIFICIAL, LIGHT FOR ILLUMINATION. THIS
ALSO REDUCES THE NEED FOR AIR CONDITIONING BY
MINIMIZING SOLAR HEAT GAIN. THE SYSTEM WILL BE
PERIODICALLY ADJUSTED BY A "COMMISSIONING AGENT"
FOR MAXIMUM OCCUPANT COMFORT.

**COMMISSIONING
AND CONTROLS**

OUR HVAC EQUIPMENT IS ALL ENERGY STAR RATED, USES
NON CFC REFRIGERANTS AND HAS MORE ADJUSTABILITY
BY OCCUPANTS THAN MOST SYSTEMS. IN ADDITION, THE
SYSTEM ADJUSTS THE AMOUNT OF OUTDOOR AIR FLOW
BASED ON CO2 SENSORS.

**HEATING
VENTILATING AND
AIR CONDITIONING**

◄ Figure 11.27 Perkins + Will, Cofra offices, systems furniture in a closed office setting powered through the wall. Photo Credit: ArchPhoto, Eduard Hueber.

▲ Figure 11.28 Perkins + Will, Cofra offices, signage used as an educational tool to describe the buildings systems and green building features. Photo Credit: ArchPhoto, Eduard Hueber.

Figure 11.29 Perkins + Will, Haworth Showroom, Calgary, open straight run entry stairs.
Photo Credit: Nick Merrick, Hedrich Blessing Photography.

▲ Figure 11.30 Perkins + Will, Haworth Showroom, Calgary, open straight run entry stairs. Photo Credit: Nick Merrick, Hedrich Blessing Photography.

▶ Figure 11.31 Perkins + Will, Haworth Showroom, Calgary. Photo Credit: Nick Merrick, Hedrich Blessing Photography.

Figure 11.32 Perkins + Will, Haworth Showroom, Calgary. **Photo Credit:** Nick Merrick, Hedrich Blessing Photography.

KEY TERMS

audio alarms

burglar alarms

lockdown system

metal detectors

signage

store alarm system

wand scanner

wayfinding

ASSIGNMENTS/EXERCISES

1. Analyze a recent design project you have completed. Where should security be integrated? Sketch possible solutions in your sketchbook.

2. Find three examples of security retrofits where security measures have been added after initial construction. How might these have been integrated at the beginning? Why were they added?

RESOURCES

Nadel, B. (2004). *Building Security: Handbook for Architectural Planning and Design.* New York: John Wiley and Sons.

Shelton. P.D. (2008). "Security Integrated into Building Design," *Architech,* April 2008, 6-8.

Smiley, P. (2008). "Sustainable Design Innovations in Vertical Transportation," *Archi-Tech,* April 2008. Retrieved from www.architechmag.com/articles/detail.aspx?contentID=5937 on October 8. 2008.

Smiley. P., and J. Grenlaw. (2008). "Sustainable Design Innovations in Vertical Transportation," *Architech,* April 2008.

Steelcase Product Literature, MBDC Cradle to Cradle Certified, Silver Level.

Tetlow, K. (2008). "Escalator Basics Today: How to Plan, Design and Update," *Architectural Record,* October 2008, 171–175.

CHAPTER 12

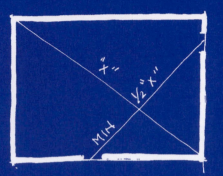

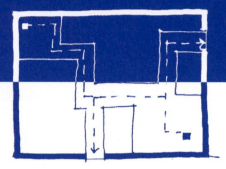

*SOME EXCEPTIONS MAY APPLY

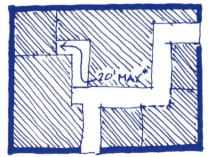

Regulations

Interior design is a multi-faceted profession in which creative and technical solutions are applied within a structure to achieve a built interior environment. These solutions are functional, enhance the quality of life and culture of the occupants, and are aesthetically attractive. Designs are created in response to and coordinated with the building shell, and acknowledge the physical location and social context of the project. Designs must adhere to code and regulatory requirements, and encourage the principles of environmental sustainability. The interior design process follows a systematic and coordinated methodology, including research, analysis and integration of knowledge into the creative process, whereby the needs and resources of the client are satisfied to produce an interior space that fulfills the project goals.
National Council for Interior Design Qualification (www.ncidq.org)

OBJECTIVES

- Differentiate among codes, voluntary programs, ADA, and testing agencies
- Apply the basic building code provisions to design projects
- Identify the phases of a design project

INTRODUCTION

The difference between a licensed or certified design professional and a regulated professional is that the regulated professional must comply with local, state, and federal regulations or risk losing his/her status as a professional. Regulations with regard to certification and licensure vary from state to state and province to province. The very first task an educated professional must do is to find out what regulations are in place within the jurisdiction where he/she is working. This applies to professional regulations as well as pertinent building codes.

PHASES OF A DESIGN PROJECT

The phases of a design project recognized by both the American Institute of Architects (AIA) and the American Society of Interior Designers (ASID) contract documents are discussed in the following sections.

PROGRAMMING

During the programming phase, the designer will interview the client(s), and create a user needs assessment and spatial analysis of what is required for the project. Background research and case studies are collected during this phase. From a regulatory perspective it is important to determine the occupancy type and identify all applicable codes and statutes that apply to the project locale. Under AIA contracts, programming is an additional service and is not included in the Standard Form of Agreement.

SCHEMATIC DESIGN

Preliminary design of the project is done during the schematic design phase. The design team will ordinarily produce a series of solutions that are presented to the client until all parties accept a solution. During this time, the design team will conduct occupancy calculations, determine the required number of exits, and delineate the egress path, making sure that it is under the maximum travel distance permitted.

DESIGN DEVELOPMENT

Development of the design solution includes all selections for the project and the changes needed to implement the actual materials and finishes. During this phase, the design team will design hour-rated partition types, do all door, glass, and finishes selections in compliance with the building code requirements.

CONTRACT DOCUMENTS

The design team creates a final set of construction documents that includes all drawings and specifications during this phase. The cover sheet of the drawings contains information about all applicable codes used to design the project as well as a map to the location, and contact information for the primary designer.

CONSTRUCTION ADMINISTRATION

Going to the site to make sure the project is being constructed consistent with the design intent of the project occurs during construction administration. Frequently this is covered under a separate contract.

BUILDING CODES

Building codes date back to ancient times and are in place to protect the public. The first code, the Code of Hammurabi, dates to 2000 B.C. The first building code in the United States was created in Chicago in 1875 following a major fire in the city. Until recently, there were several different codes in use across the United States and Canada. In 2000, the International Building Code was first published, and has been adopted in nearly every state in the United States. It is important for design professionals to be aware, however, that not all states are using the latest version of the IBC. Additionally, states may choose to adopt a given code and then amend it at the state level.

The International Building Code (IBC) regulates all construction types except single-family residential design, which fall under the International Residential Code (IRC.) The IBC is organized to provide designers and contractors with all of the information they need to create a minimally competent, safe building. Building code usage is not synonymous with good design.

Generally, the code is divided into 35 chapters that begin with the overall issues of a building, proceed into specific issues related to egress, construction, and building systems, and end with information regulating specific materials and the tests that they must meet to be safe.

An interior designer works as part of a team and should be well versed in all sections of the code pertaining specifically to interior design. These include use group and occupancy classification; detailed requirements based on use and occupancy; types of construction; fire-resistance-rated construction; interior finishes; means of egress; accessibility; and the interior environment. It is helpful if designers are also familiar with all other sections of the building code in order to be an informed member of the team.

TABLE 12.1 CHAPTERS OF THE INTERNATIONAL BUILDING CODE (IBC)

CHAPTER	SUBJECT	CHAPTER	SUBJECT
Chapter 1	Administration	Chapter 18	Soils and Foundations
Chapter 2	Definitions	Chapter 19	Concrete
Chapter 3	Use and Occupancy Classification	Chapter 20	Aluminum
Chapter 4	Special Detailed Requirements Based on Occupancy	Chapter 21	Masonry
		Chapter 22	Steel
Chapter 5	General Building Heights and Areas	Chapter 23	Wood
Chapter 6	Types of Construction	Chapter 24	Glass and Glazing
Chapter 7	Fire-Resistance-Rated Construction	Chapter 25	Gypsum Board and Plaster
Chapter 8	Interior Finishes	Chapter 26	Plastic
Chapter 9	Fire Protection Systems	Chapter 27	Electrical
Chapter 10	Means of Egress	Chapter 28	Mechanical Systems
Chapter 11	Accessibility	Chapter 29	Plumbing Systems
Chapter 12	Interior Environment	Chapter 30	Elevators and Conveying Systems
Chapter 13	Energy Efficiency	Chapter 31	Special Construction
Chapter 14	Exterior Walls	Chapter 32	Encroachments into the Public Right-of-Way
Chapter 15	Roof Assemblies and Rooftop Structures	Chapter 33	Safeguards During Construction
Chapter 16	Structural Design	Chapter 34	Existing Structures
Chapter 17	Structural Tests and Special Inspections	Chapter 35	Referenced Standards

Source: Adapted from the *International Building Code* 2006.
Note: Always refer to the actual code book.

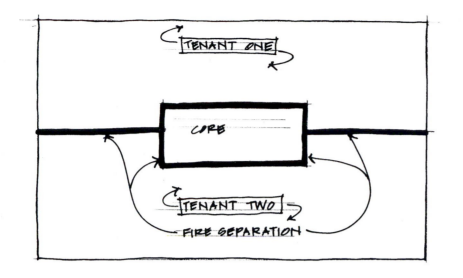

Each jurisdiction adopts its own codes. It is important to know which codes have been adopted in the locale of the project. The use of and familiarity with various parts of the code are important to different phases of the project. Although this is a fluid process and all codes are used during all phases of a project, generally speaking the use of codes is consistent with the following: During the programming phase, the initial use groups and occupancies for the project will be determined. As the design team moves to schematic design, issues of egress help to shape the interior space. During design development, accessibility and interior finishes may cause slight changes to the overall design.

Figure 12.1a–b Compartmentalization.

COMPARTMENTALIZATION

Large spaces must be subdivided in order to create separate compartments for smoke containment. This process, by which sections of a building are closed off during a fire or other emergency, is called compartmentalization. This involves not only fire-rated walls, but also the overall planning mechanisms by which a designer creates separate areas within a building.

EXITS REQUIRED

EXIT LOCATIONS

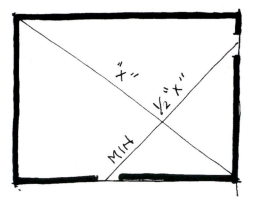

TRAVEL DISTANCE

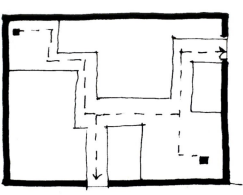

DEAD END
CORRIDOR

* SOME
EXCEPTIONS
MAY APPLY

FIRE SEPARATION

Different uses within a building as well as egress corridors, doors, and stairs must maintain specific fire-rated separations in compliance with Chapter 10 of the IBC. Chapter 10 regulates the entire path of egress for all occupants of a building to safely evacuate from the building in the event of an emergency. This includes egress width, means of illumination of the path, doors, gates and turnstiles, stairways and handrails, ramps, exit signs, guardrails, and horizontal and vertical exits.

Figure 12.2 Fire separation.

MOVEMENT

Movement along the path of egress and throughout the building is addressed in the following areas by the IBC: egress stairs, corridors, and exits.

DETECTION

Fire detection equipment is used to detect smoke and/or fire within a building. This includes many components such as smoke and fire alarms with both audio signals and visual strobes.

▲ Figure 12.3 Path of egress.

▶ Figure 12.4 Photograph of a typical fire alarm.

SUPPRESSION

Fire suppression equipment is used to extinguish a fire. Apparatus include fire hoses, hand-held fire extinguishers, standpipe systems, and sprinklers within a building.

Sprinkler Systems

The use of sprinkler systems in a building allow for longer travel distances to emergency exits in some instances. Although a fire-suppression specialist often designs these systems, it is important to understand some general rules regarding the placement of sprinkler heads. For light hazard spaces, a sprinkler head is required every 200 square feet (not hydraulic) or 225 square feet (hydraulic). In a space with wood ceiling joists, a sprinkler head is required every 130 square feet. The maximum distance from any wall should be 7 feet 6 inches while the minimum distance is 4 feet. When an object, such as a column, obstructs the sprinkler head distribution pattern, the sprinkler head should be placed a minimum of three times the maximum dimension of the object. For example, the sprinkler heads near a 12-inch-by-8-inch column should be at least 3 feet away from the column.

Figure 12.5
Photograph of a fire extinguisher case.

INTERIOR FINISHES

Chapter 8 of the IBC addresses the requirements for interior finishes. One of the most important elements of this chapter is Table 803.5: Interior Wall and Ceiling Finish Requirements by Occupancy. This table provides guidance as to what class of material is required by specific occupancy depending on whether the building is sprinklered.

TABLE 12.2 SAMPLE FINISHES REQUIREMENTS FROM THE IBC

	SPRINKLERED			NONSPRINKLERED		
GROUP	Exit enclosure and exit passageway	Corridor	Rooms and enclosed spaces	Exit enclosure and exit passageway	Corridor	Rooms and enclosed spaces
B	B	C	C	A	B	C
H	B	B	C	A	A	B
I-1	B	C	C	A	B	B
I-2	B	B	B	A	A	B
I-3	A	A	C	A	A	B
I-4	B	B	B	A	A	B

Source: Adapted from the *International Building Code* 2006.
Note: Always refer to the actual code book.

AMERICANS WITH DISABILITIES ACT (ADA)

The **Americans with Disabilities Act** (ADA) is part of a Federal statute originally enacted in 1990. The ADA specifies how every public building must provide equal opportunity access for people with a variety of disabilities. This includes not only people confined to a wheelchair, but also those with hearing and seeing impairments. The integration of ADA compliance within an interior affects many decisions that the designer will make.

Compliant Route

A compliant route consists of the entire route from the site into the building and to all areas within the building.

Ramps

The maximum slope of an ADA complaint ramp is 1:12. Any time a design includes multiple floor heights, equal access for the movement impaired must be provided.

Doors

To provide a 32-inch clear opening through a doorway, a 36-inch door is required. In addition to proper door size, the required clearances on both the push side and pull side of a door must also be provided.

Figure 12.6
Photograph of an ADA Compliant door.

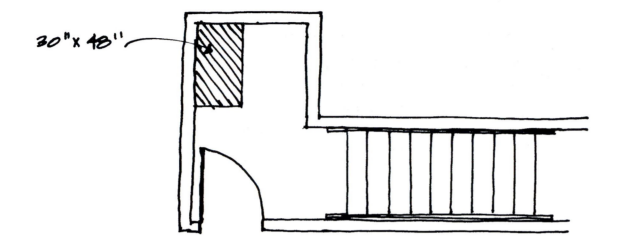

30" x 48"

Elevators and Areas of Refuge

Although there is some research currently being conducted regarding the use of elevators as a mean of egress, it is still the generally accepted practice that the elevators will not be used during a building evacuation. This means that someone confined to a wheelchair is forced to wait in a stair hall to be rescued. This area, located at the top landing within the stair hall or adjacent to it, is called an area of refuge. These areas need to be equipped with a call system for communication between the disabled and rescue personnel.

A 5-foot turning radius is required for a change in path direction.

▲ Figure 12.7 Diagram for area of refuge in a stairway.

▼ Figure 12.8 Diagram of a five-foot turning radius.

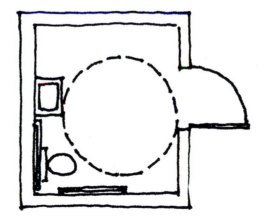

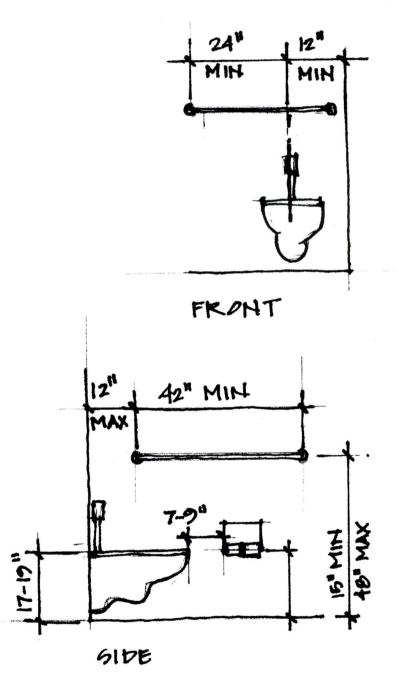

FRONT

SIDE

Restrooms

Public restroom facilities must also be ADA compliant. This number is determined based on the occupancy of the building, with a minimum of one accessible bathroom in each building. ADA compliant features required include grab bars; a compliant lavatory with compliant hardware; a compliant water closet; compliant stall; a lowered or slanted mirror; and the appropriate compliant accessories such as a paper towel holder or hand dryer.

Signage

Signage in a public building must include Braille for the visually impaired as well as symbols for the hearing impaired.

Figure 12.9
Placement of ADA bathroom accessories.

Figure 12.10a–b Signage for ADA.

INTERNATIONAL SYMBOL OF ACCESSIBILITY

TTY PICTOGRAM

TELEPHONE PICTOGRAM

EAR PICTOGRAM

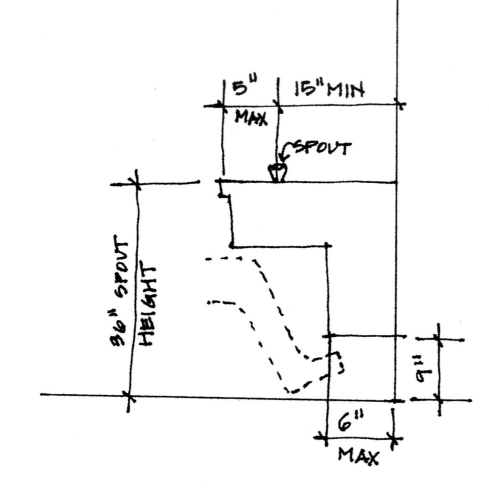

Projections

The ADA prohibits projections in excess of 7 inches into any egress corridor for protection of the seeing impaired.

Figure 12.11 ADA-compliant water fountain.

INDUSTRY-SPECIFIC REGULATIONS

Depending on the specific project type, additional regulations may be applied. An excellent example is healthcare design where specific medical requirements may be in place based on the corporation for whom the project is designed. Another example of a project type with its own set of regulations is work completed for the military (army, navy, air force, or marines) and federal, state, and local governmental agencies.

Life Safety Code

The **Life Safety Code** is published by the National Fire Protection Association, and provides additional requirements for life safety in the event of a fire including fumes, smoke, and panic. In addition to initial construction, the Life Safety Code also addresses maintenance and operation to reduce the risk of fire in a building. The current edition of the Life Safety Code is 2008 with revisions occurring every two years.

TESTING AGENCIES

ANSI

American National Standards Institute (ANSI) supports the accrediting of programs that assess standard compliance. The organization was founded in 1918 and is a not-for-profit organization that is the voice of U.S. standards and conformity assessments protecting the health and safety of people.

UL

Underwriters Laboratory (UL) tests product compliance with standards. UL has developed over 100 safety standards for a variety of consumer products.

ASTM

The **American Society for Testing and Materials (ASTM)**, commonly referred to as ASTM, is an international testing society and is composed of scientists and engineers who test and create standards for safer products and services around the world. ASTM is best known for its work in standardizing safe manufacturing practices.

LEED

The U.S. Green Building Council's (USGBC) Leadership in Energy and Environmental Design (LEED) Rating Systems are voluntary in many parts of the country. Although some jurisdictions have written a requirement to follow the LEED system in their public buildings, this sort of legal adoption is the exception not the rule.

LEED AP

A person who takes and passes the LEED examination is called a **LEED Accredited Professional** and is entitled to use LEED AP after their name.

When a building meets LEED criteria, it becomes a LEED Certified building. Thus, people are accredited and buildings are certified. The following list includes all of the LEED Rating Systems:

- LEED NC: LEED for New Construction
- LEED CI: LEED for Commercial Interiors
- LEED NH: LEED for New Homes
- LEED Core and Shell
- LEED for Schools
- LEED for Healthcare
- LEED for Retail
- LEED EB: LEED for Existing Buildings
- LEED for Neighborhood Development

(Note: At the time of this book, the LEED Rating Systems are in the process of undergoing a major restructuring.)

Secretary of the Interior's
Standards for Historic Preservation

When working on historic buildings, particularly those with significance, a designer should be aware of the **Secretary of the Interior's Standards for Historic Preservation**. These are the gold standard by which work on historic buildings is judged. Compliance with these standards can lead to tax credits for buildings listed on the National Register of Historic Places, and can also lead to delisting of such properties if the work is done improperly. In addition to the Standards themselves, there are also several Preservation Briefs that describe in detail how to work with historic buildings.

KEY TERMS

Americans with Disabilities Act (ADA)

American National Standards Institute (ANSI)

American Society for Testing and Materials (ASTM)

International Building Code (IBC)

International Residential Code (IRC)

LEED Accredited Professional

LEED Certified

Life Safety Code

Secretary of the Interior's Standards for Historic Preservation

Underwriter's Laboratory (UL)

ASSIGNMENTS/EXERCISES

Record all findings for the following in your course sketchbook:

1. Find the statewide building code requirements in your state. Check with the local building inspector to see if there are other regulations you must know about.

2. Go to the National Park Service website at www.nps.org and locate the Secretary of the Interior's Standards and the Preservation Briefs.

3. Do a code analysis of your current design project. What have you done correctly? Where do you have violations? What could you do to improve your project?

4. Assess the accessibility of the buildings you use every day. Are there features that no longer meet ADA requirements? Sketch a corrected solution.

RESOURCES

American National Standards Institute (www.ansi.org)

American Society for Testing and Materials (www.astm.org)

Americans with Disabilities Act (www.ada.gov/)

Ching, D.K., and S. Winkel. (2007). *Building Codes Illustrated: A Guide to Understanding the 2006 International Building Code*. New York: John Wiley and Sons.

Harmon, S., and K. Kennon. (2008). *The Codes Guidebook for Interiors*. 4th ed. New York: John Wiley and Sons.

International Code Council (www.iccsafe.org)

National Fire Protection Association (www.nfpa.org)

National Park Service (www.nps.gov)

U.S. Green Building Council (www.usgbc.org)

Yatt, B. (1998). *Cracking the Codes: An Architect's Guide to Building Regulations*. New York: John Wiley and Sons.

CHAPTER 13

Case Studies

"I believe we are as capable as any organism—capable of healing the earth and creating conditions conducive to life. If that is what we ask our buildings to do, if that is the function that we select, then that is what we will turn our prodigious design imaginations to. And we will have plenty of help finding examples of how to do this right outside our window. It starts as soon as we decide to see solutions that have been there—scampering, slithering, buzzing, and blooming—all along.

Janine Benyus, "A Good Place to Settle: Biomimicry, Biophilia, and the Return of Nature's Inspiration to Architecture" in Biophilic Design

OBJECTIVES

After reading this chapter you will be able to see how firms as well as other students have integrated sustainable design into their projects.

INTRODUCTION

This chapter incorporates sustainable projects by firms and students to demonstrate the principles and practices outlined in this book as expressed in design projects by various designers.

CASE STUDY 1

UNITED STATES GREEN BUILDING COUNCIL HEADQUARTERS BUILDING—

PERKINS + WILL (WASHINGTON, D. C.) LEED CI—PLATINUM

The U.S. Green Building Council (USGBC) headquarters building sought to highlight sustainable design strategies consistent with LEED certification and the mission of the organization. The design team was charged to promote productivity within the organization. The design solution maximized daylight and views. The interior finishes include salvaged wood, glass, and wood millwork as well as bamboo, linoleum, and cork. Whenever possible, materials were sourced locally (within a 500-mile radius of the project).

▲ Figure 13.1 United States Green Building Council Headquarters Building, Perkins + Will, Washington, D.C. Design Principal: Holly Briggs, AIA, LEED AP. Design Team: Gretchen Leigh, NCIDQ, LEED AP, David Cordell, NCIDQ, CID, LEED AP. Photo Credit: Prakash Patel, www.prakashpatel.com

▶ Figure 13.2 United States Green Building Council Headquarters Building, Perkins + Will, Washington, D.C. Design Principal: Holly Briggs, AIA, LEED AP. Design Team: Gretchen Leigh, NCIDQ, LEED AP, David Cordell, NCIDQ, CID, LEED AP. Photo Credits: Prakash Patel, www.prakashpatel.com

▲ Figure 13.3 United States Green Building Council
Headquarters Building, Perkins + Will, Washington, D.C. Design
Principal: Holly Briggs, AIA, LEED AP. Design Team: Gretchen
Leigh, NCIDQ, LEED AP, David Cordell, NCIDQ, CID, LEED AP.
Photo Credit: Prakash Patel, www.prakashpatel.com

▶ Figure 13.4 United States Green Building Council
Headquarters Building, Perkins + Will, Washington, D.C. Design
Principal: Holly Briggs, AIA, LEED AP. Design Team: Gretchen
Leigh, NCIDQ, LEED AP, David Cordell, NCIDQ, CID, LEED AP.
Photo Credit: Prakash Patel, www.prakashpatel.com

CASE STUDY 2
TELUS HOUSE—

BUSBY PERKINS + WILL (VANCOUVER, BRITISH COLUMBIA) LEED NC - GOLD

The Telus House project consisted of a two-phase intervention. The first phase entailed extensive interior and exterior renovations of an existing building to meet sustainability goals. The second phase involved a seismic upgrade and the integration of a new atrium space. The client required continued occupancy of the building throughout this process. The project includes a series of innovative sustainable design solutions including existing building reuse, a double-glazed atrium, a high-performance exterior façade with integrated photovoltaic panels, and sustainable interior finishes. A raised access flooring system is used throughout to allow individual control over HVAC. Likewise, operable windows allow individual control over fresh air.

Figure 13.5 Telus House, Busby Perkins + Will, Vancouver, British Columbia. Photo Credit: Martin Tessler.

Figure 13.6 Telus House, Busby Perkins + Will, Vancouver, British Columbia. Photo Credit: Martin Tessler.

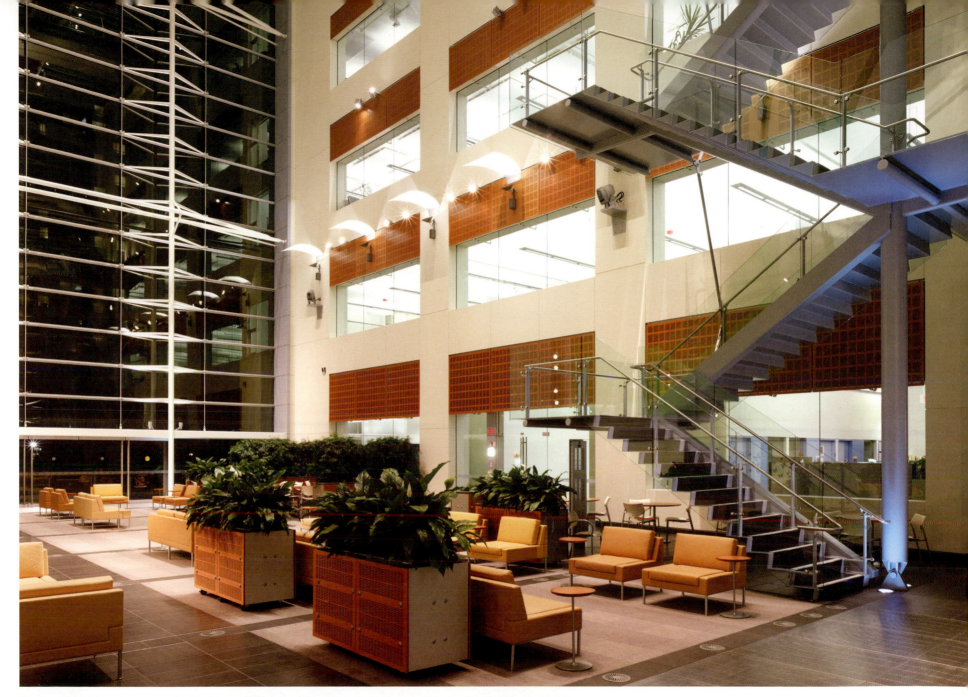

Figure 13.7 Telus House, Busby Perkins + Will, Vancouver, British Columbia. Photo Credit: Martin Tessler.

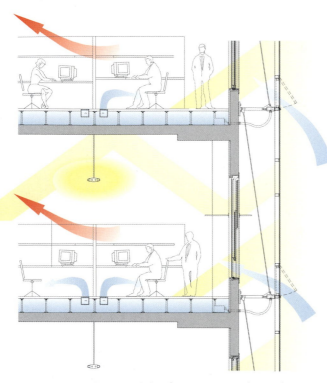

▲ Figure 13.8 Telus House, Busby Perkins + Will, Vancouver, British Columbia. Photo Credit: Martin Tessler.

▶ Figure 13.9 Telus House, Busby Perkins + Will, Vancouver, British Columbia. Photo Credit: Martin Tessler.

► Figure 13.10 Telus House, Busby Perkins + Will, Vancouver, British Columbia.
Photo Credit: Martin Tessler.

▼ Figure 13.11 Telus House, Busby Perkins + Will, Vancouver, British Columbia.
Photo Credit: Martin Tessler.

▲ Figure 13.12 Newark Center for Health Sciences & Technology, Perkins + Will, Ohlone College, Silicon Valley, California. **Photo Credit: Robert Canfield Photography.**

▶ Figure 13.13 (*opposite*) Newark Center for Health Sciences & Technology, Perkins + Will, Ohlone College, Silicon Valley, California. **Photo Credit: Robert Canfield Photography.**

CASE STUDY 3
NEWARK CENTER FOR HEALTH SCIENCES & TECHNOLOGY—

PERKINS + WILL (OHLONE COLLEGE, SILICON VALLEY, CALIFORNIA) LEED NC - PLATINUM

The overall sustainable approach to this project addressed both how the center could contribute to the surrounding environment and how the environment contributed to the center, making it an integral part of the regional eco-system. This was accomplished through sustainable site interventions such as soil remediation, water efficient strategies wherein drought tolerant plants were used, passive cooling and high-performance mechanical systems, materials with low embodied energy, and an education program within the building.

375

▲ Figure 13.16 Newark Center for Health Sciences & Technology, Perkins + Will, Ohlone College, Silicon Valley, California. Photo Credit: Robert Canfield Photography.

▶ Figure 13.17 Newark Center for Health Sciences & Technology, Perkins + Will, Ohlone College, Silicon Valley, California. Photo Credit: Robert Canfield Photography.

▲ Figure 13.14 Newark Center for Health Sciences & Technology, Perkins + Will, Ohlone College, Silicon Valley, California. Photo Credit: Robert Canfield Photography.

◀ Figure 13.15 Newark Center for Health Sciences & Technology, Perkins + Will, Ohlone College, Silicon Valley, California. Photo Credit: Robert Canfield Photography.

CASE STUDY 4
PERKINS + WILL OFFICES—

PERKINS + WILL (SEATTLE, WASHINGTON) LEED CI - PLATINUM

One of two interior projects in the country to obtain LEED CI at the Platinum level, the Seattle office of Perkins + Will showcases sustainable strategies for interior design. Located within a 1912-era building, the new office complex included several sustainable interventions: All existing windows were replaced with operable windows, the original timber-frame ceiling structure was exposed, and natural daylight was allowed to suffuse the interior spaces. The finalized interior uses 40 percent less water than would a comparable space, and the lighting strategy is 46 percent more efficient than a typical interior. In addition, 98 percent of the construction waste was diverted from the landfill through recycling. Local materials were used for 40 percent of the building interior.

Figure 13.18–13.22 (*clockwise from opposite left*)
Perkins + Will offices, Perkins + Will, Seattle, Washington.
Photo Credit: Benjamin Benschneider.

CASE STUDY 5

HAWORTH SHOWROOM—

PERKINS + WILL (CHICAGO, ILLINOIS) LEED CI PILOT PROGRAM

The Haworth Showroom in Chicago demonstrates Haworth's commitment to sustainable design through its use of GREENGUARD certified products—products containing both post-industrial and post-consumer recycled content, and use of FSC woods. The showroom encompasses sustainability from a variety of perspectives: economic, environmental, and social. The workspaces within the showroom demonstrate the complete integration of modular walls and furniture; raised flooring systems with HVAC; lighting; sound; and data voice.

The design team sought to provide a lighting solution that was both flexible and as integrated with architectural elements as possible. Randy Burkett Lighting Design, Inc. provided a lighting design solution that was fully integrated with Haworth's furniture, floor, and wall products. The solution also met Gold-level LEED Certification criteria. For example, the project includes a lighting load that was 40 percent less than Chicago's energy code. To achieve these goals, T5 fluorescent lamps were used in conjunction with compact fluorescent,

LED, and halogen systems. Daylight harvesting strategies combined with occupancy sensors and dimmers led to an effective energy efficient solution (DiLouie, 2008).

Figures 13.23 and 13.24 illustrate the large reflecting pool designed to provide a restorative element to the environment. Ceiling mounted MR16 lamps accent the 1,200-square-foot pool. Individual offices, as shown in Figure 13.25, include wooden slat walls to create a sense of privacy.

Display walls as seen in Figure 13.26 flank the entry door. Haworth's access flooring features are demonstrated through the use of glass flooring (Figure 13.27). Concealed and integrated lighting combined with river rocks and water are used to create a peaceful and serene interior space, as seen in Figure 13.28. Natural elements (Figure 13.29) portray the sense of repose the designers hoped to supplement the workspace and provide workers with a holistic environment within which they would be satisfied.

Figure 13.23 Haworth Showroom, Perkins + Will, Chicago, Illinois.
Large reflecting pool designed to provide a restorative element to
the environment. Design: Perkins + Will.

▲ Figure 13.24 Haworth Showroom, Perkins + Will, Chicago, Illinois. Large reflecting pool designed to provide a restorative element to the environment. Photo Credit: Craig Dugan, Hedrich Blessing Photography.

▶ Figure 13.25 (*opposite*) Haworth Showroom, Perkins + Will, Chicago, Illinois. Photo Credit: Craig Dugan, Hedrich Blessing Photography.

▲ Figure 13.26 Haworth Showroom, Perkins + Will, Chicago, Illinois. Display walls on either side flank the entry door. **Photo Credit: Steve Hall, Hedrich Blessing Photography.**

▶ Figure 13.27 (*opposite*) Haworth Showroom, Perkins + Will, Chicago, Illinois. Access flooring features are demonstrated through the use of glass flooring. **Photo Credit: Craig Dugan, Hedrich Blessing Photography.**

385

Figure 13.28 Haworth Showroom, Perkins + Will, Chicago, Illinois. Concealed and integrated lighting combined with river rocks and water are used to create a peaceful and serene interior space. Photo Credit: Steve Hall, Hedrich Blessing Photography.

Figure 13.29 Haworth Showroom, Perkins + Will, Chicago, Illinois. Natural elements portray the sense of repose the designers hoped to supplement the workspace and provide workers with a holistic environment within which they would be satisfied. Photo Credit: Craig Dugan, Hedrich Blessing Photography.

CASE STUDY 6
SALVAGGIO RESIDENCE—

STUDIO27ARCHITECTURE (WASHINGTON, D.C.)

This 650-square-foot residential addition demonstrates the use of sustainable materials in a bedroom, bathroom, and sitting room application. Located within a typical WDC row house, this upper-level space incorporates a series of platforms and wall screen in glass and wallboard to create a sense of ritual and privacy. The maple floors are sustainably harvested wood and have a low-VOC finish. The architects salvaged the existing historic structure and interior shell, and created a series of contours and folds highlighted by two glass volumes within the existing shell. All spaces have access to daylight and views. Perimeter high-efficient T5 lamps and fixtures that are hidden from view supplement daylighting. A tankless high-efficiency toilet is used in the newly added bathroom.

◀ Figure 13.30 (*opposite*) Salvaggio Residence, studio27architecture, Washington, D.C. Photo Credit: Anice Hoachlander, Hoachlander Davis Photography, LLC.

▲ Figure 13.31 Salvaggio Residence, studio-27architecture, Washington, D.C. Photo Credit: Anice Hoachlander, Hoachlander Davis Photography, LLC.

▲ Figure 13.32 Salvaggio Residence, studio27architecture, Washington, D.C.
Photo Credit: Anice Hoachlander, Hoachlander Davis Photography, LLC.

▶ Figure 13.33 Salvaggio Residence, studio27architecture, Washington, D.C.
Photo Credit: Anice Hoachlander, Hoachlander Davis Photography, LLC.

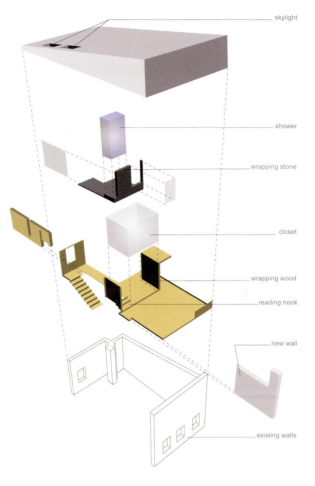

skylight

shower

wrapping stone

closet

wrapping wood

reading nook

new wall

existing walls

e x p l o d e d   i s o m e t r i c

▲ Figure 13.34 Salvaggio Residence, studio27architecture, Washington, D.C.
Photo Credit: Anice Hoachlander, Hoachlander Davis Photography, LLC.

◄ Figure 13.35 Salvaggio Residence, studio27architecture, Washington, D.C.
Photo Credit: Anice Hoachlander, Hoachlander Davis Photography, LLC.

STUDENT PROJECTS CASE STUDIES

WHOLE FOODS MARKET, AMRITA RAJA

The inspiration for this project was the city map of Austin, Texas, where the building for the Whole Foods Market was to be headquartered. The designer intended to create a dialogue between the headquarters building and the city. Organized along interior "streets," separate "neighborhoods" were created inside the space. Sustainable materials were used throughout, including concrete with fly ash, linoleum, salvaged wood flooring, and steel beams and cork walls.

Figure 13.36 Whole Foods Market, Amrita Raja, Project Title Page.

"whole foods, whole people, whole planet."

Whole Foods Market was founded in Austin, Texas in 1980. Since then, the company has continued to emphasize their "declaration of interdependence." They insist that "quality is a state of mind" and measure success in the happiness of their Team Members.

As such, the design for an extension of Whole Foods Market's headquarters Austin aims to remember the company's history while looking to the future. The site was chosen to reflect this intention. The design incorporates technology into the meeting spaces for the three teams working at the office (accounting, marketing and real estate).

The company's pride in quality is reflected in the design's intent to create a quality of working life by including public spaces in the office's core, such as meditation rooms, a gym, a library and a kitchen, that all service the "whole" body.

Sustainable principles govern the design, while images of the company's product, food, become the primary signage and graphic language. In this way, the design reflects the company's motto, "Whole Foods, Whole People, Whole Planet."

the company

Figure 13.37 Whole Foods Market, Amrita Raja, Project Statement.

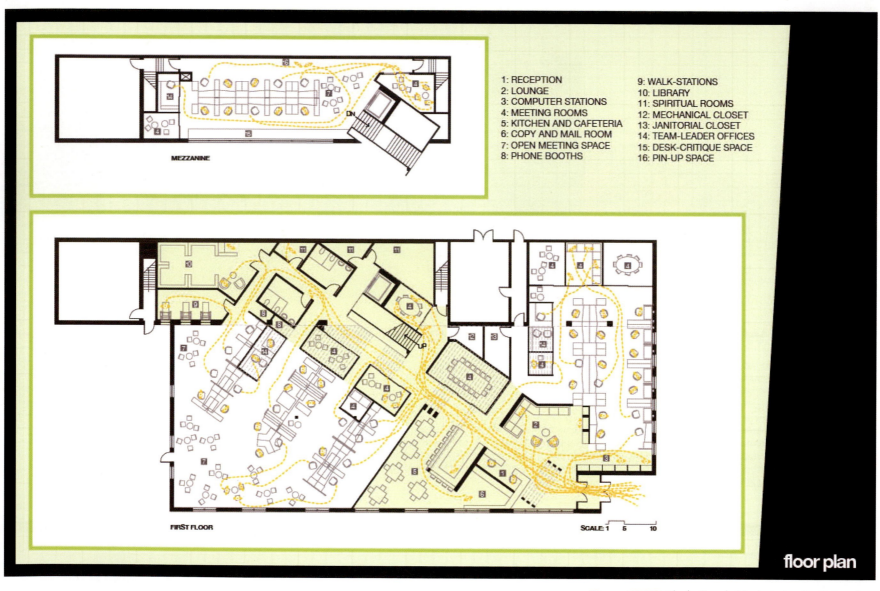

MEZZANINE

1: RECEPTION
2: LOUNGE
3: COMPUTER STATIONS
4: MEETING ROOMS
5: KITCHEN AND CAFETERIA
6: COPY AND MAIL ROOM
7: OPEN MEETING SPACE
8: PHONE BOOTHS

9: WALK-STATIONS
10: LIBRARY
11: SPIRITUAL ROOMS
12: MECHANICAL CLOSET
13: JANITORIAL CLOSET
14: TEAM-LEADER OFFICES
15: DESK-CRITIQUE SPACE
16: PIN-UP SPACE

FIRST FLOOR

SCALE: 1   5   10

floor plan

Figure 13.38 Whole Foods Market, Amrita Raja, plan.

Figure 13.39 Whole Foods Market, Amrita Raja, reception.

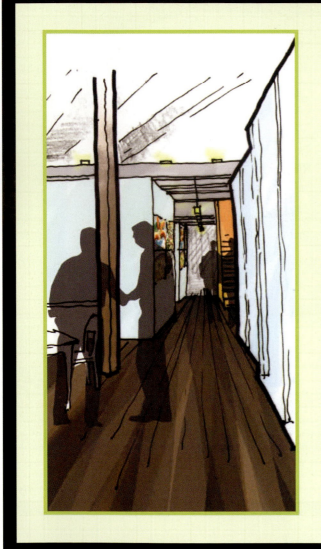

The indoor street is the connection between Austin's Warehouse District and Whole Food Market's corporate office. It is the path team members take to approach any public space within the structure (such as meeting rooms of varying scales and rest rooms).

The street is also accessible to the public after the office closes. This provides a direct relationship between the work community and the greater community of Austin. The access to private quarters can be limited through gates along the street perimeter.

indoor street

Figure 13.40 Whole Foods Market, Amrita Raja, corridor.

meeting space

Figure 13.41 Whole Foods Market, Amrita Raja, meeting space.

The office hosts three teams, each with team-specific spaces. The real estate team, for example, has pin-up space for projects on the boards and work-stations for individual team members.

open-office

Figure 13.42 Whole Foods Market, Amrita Raja, open office.

W. L. GORE, BRITNEY BISHOP

A space designed to create a sense of equality and creativity, the Gore headquarters building integrates natural lighting throughout. Workstations consist of Steelcase's MDBC Silver Cradle to Cradle certified Montage line, and Leap and Think task chairs. Teragren bamboo flooring is used throughout the space in conjunction with Shaw carpeting in the breakout spaces. These specific carpet tiles are 100 percent sustainable, with Ecoworx non-PVC backing. Both the fiber and backing systems are MBDC Cradle-to-Cradle Silver level certified. The gymnasium space features Expanko rubber flooring in black and charcoal. Sustainable fabric lines by Maharam and Arc Com are used on all upholstered items.

Designed By: Britney Bishop
Located in the Heart of Washington D.C.
W.L. Gore Corporate Design Office

Figure 13.43 W.L. Gore, Britney Bishop, cover page.

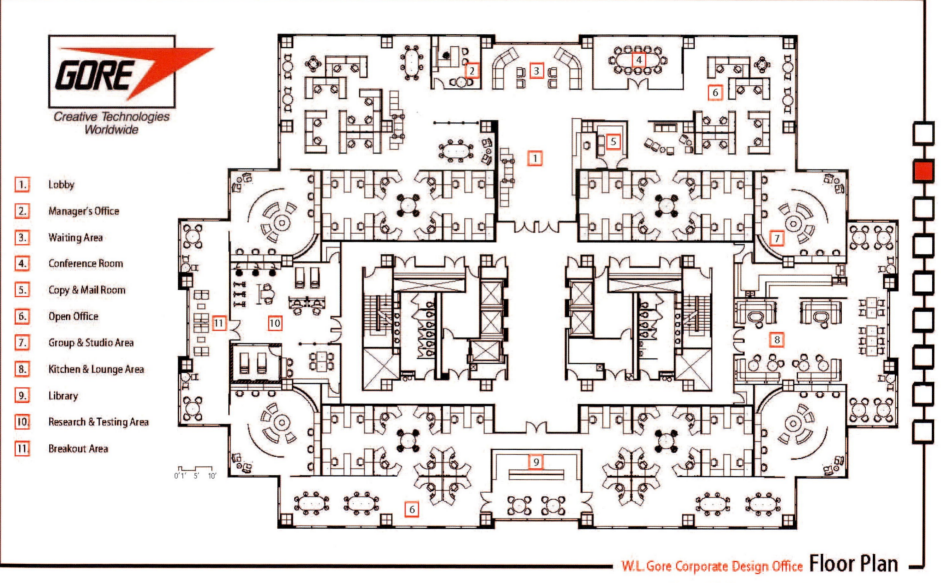

GORE
*Creative Technologies
Worldwide*

1. Lobby
2. Manager's Office
3. Waiting Area
4. Conference Room
5. Copy & Mail Room
6. Open Office
7. Group & Studio Area
8. Kitchen & Lounge Area
9. Library
10. Research & Testing Area
11. Breakout Area

0' 1' 5'   10'

W.L. Gore Corporate Design Office **Floor Plan**

Figure 13.44 W.L. Gore, Britney Bishop, plan.

In order to effectively achieve a corporate design office for the company W.L. Gore, inventor of Gore Tex, it was necessary to understand their brand & aesthetic desires. Located in the heart of Washington D.C., the client requested that the concept of sustainable design be incorporated into their work environment. Because W.L. Gore's products are centered around the notion of high functionality themselves, I wanted to create a space that was functional for their collaborative work style, while mirroring their unique corporate structure.

Since the people at W.L. Gore pride themselves on being a company that maximizes individual potential and nourishes an environment where creativity can flow freely, I wanted this corporate office design to be representational of both open collaboration and equality when organizing the spaces. As soon as one enters the lobby of the office, he/she is immediately drawn towards the outer rim of the plan, the windows. I have designed the main circulation pathways around the exterior of the plan so that all can experience the wonderful views of downtown Washington D.C., thus emphasizing the concept of equality amongst the employees. Seating areas are located along the main circulation path to allow for less formal meetings of employees. Organized around the four open office areas are larger group and studio spaces where employees can present their design ideas more freely. Here, in the group and studio area, the formation of space revolves around a central point that then directs one's attention to the moveable white boards at the front of the room, thus creating a chance for critique and collaboration.

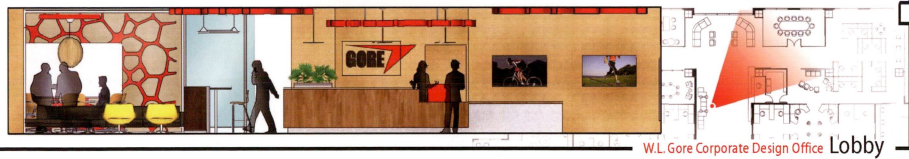

W.L. Gore Corporate Design Office **Lobby**

Figure 13.45 W.L. Gore, Britney Bishop, concept.

401

Out in the open office, groups of workstations are organized around a smaller centralized space. The orientation of workstations is designed to promote instantaneous sharing of ideas through unique clustering, thus getting away from the typical row and column organization. In order to capture the natural daylight entering the space through the floor to ceiling windows that line the exterior, the workstations were designed as low as possible in order to allow the natural light to penetrate even further into the core of the space, while still preserving individual privacy. By creating a space where natural light reaches into the center of the space reduces the need for artificial lighting, while also reinforcing the company's notion of equality.

The workstations specified within the open office areas are from a Steelcase line called Montage® which is *MBDC Silver Cradle to Cradle^CM Certified*, as well as being *SCS Indoor Advantage^TM Indoor Air Quality Certified*. Steelcase's Leap® and Think® task/work chairs are used throughout the space, which are also *MBDC Silver Cradle to Cradle^CM Certified* and *SCS Indoor Advantage^TM Certified*. The Teragren bamboo flooring in the lobby and open office areas is a rapidly renewable resource that is sustainably harvested and can contribute to LEED® MR Credit 6: Rapidly Renewable Materials.

A	Teragren Bamboo Flooring Flat Grain Caramelized
B	Steelcase Leap Chair
C	Maharam Kvadrat, Tinta #454
D	Steelcase Wood Veneer Natural Walnut #3714

W.L. Gore Corporate Design Office Open Office

Figure 13.46 W.L. Gore, Britney Bishop, open office.

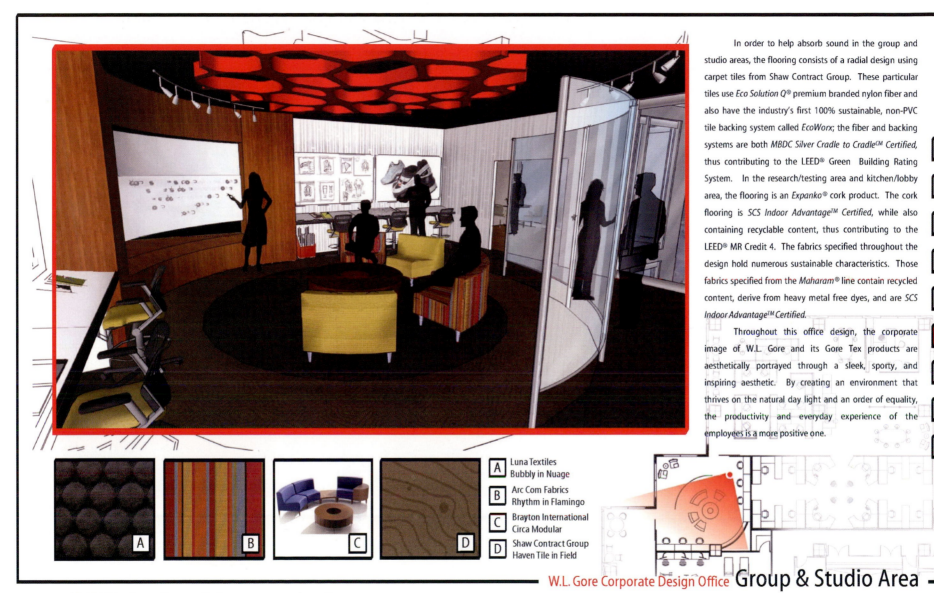

In order to help absorb sound in the group and studio areas, the flooring consists of a radial design using carpet tiles from Shaw Contract Group. These particular tiles use *Eco Solution Q*® premium branded nylon fiber and also have the industry's first 100% sustainable, non-PVC tile backing system called *EcoWorx*; the fiber and backing systems are both *MBDC Silver Cradle to Cradle*ᶜᴹ *Certified*, thus contributing to the LEED® Green Building Rating System. In the research/testing area and kitchen/lobby area, the flooring is an *Expanko*® cork product. The cork flooring is *SCS Indoor Advantage*™ *Certified*, while also containing recyclable content, thus contributing to the LEED® MR Credit 4. The fabrics specified throughout the design hold numerous sustainable characteristics. Those fabrics specified from the *Maharam*® line contain recycled content, derive from heavy metal free dyes, and are *SCS Indoor Advantage*™ *Certified*.

Throughout this office design, the corporate image of W.L. Gore and its Gore Tex products are aesthetically portrayed through a sleek, sporty, and inspiring aesthetic. By creating an environment that thrives on the natural day light and an order of equality, the productivity and everyday experience of the employees is a more positive one.

A — Luna Textiles Bubbly in Nuage

B — Arc Com Fabrics Rhythm in Flamingo

C — Brayton International Circa Modular

D — Shaw Contract Group Haven Tile in Field

W.L. Gore Corporate Design Office Group & Studio Area

Figure 13.47 W.L. Gore, Britney Bishop, group and studio area.

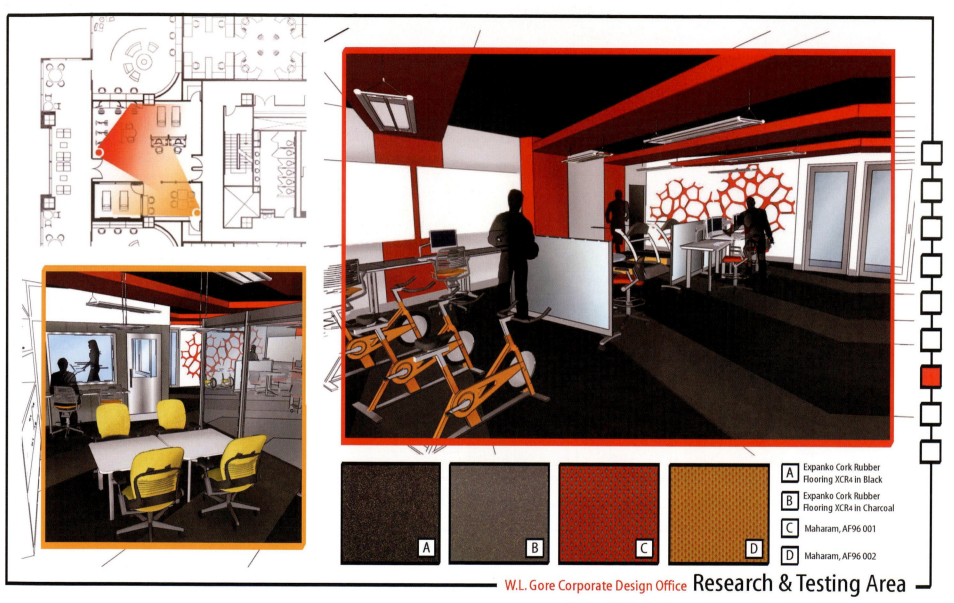

A	Expanko Cork Rubber Flooring XCR4 in Black
B	Expanko Cork Rubber Flooring XCR4 in Charcoal
C	Maharam, AF96 001
D	Maharam, AF96 002

W.L. Gore Corporate Design Office **Research & Testing Area**

Figure 13.48 W.L. Gore, Britney Bishop, research and testing area.

A — Expanko Cork Floors
Castello

B — Maharam, Squarely in Dolphin

C — Bix System by Metro

D — Arc Com Fabrics
Rhythm in Circus

W.L. Gore Corporate Design Office Kitchen & Lounge Area

Figure 13.49 W.L. Gore, Britney Bishop, kitchen and lounge area.

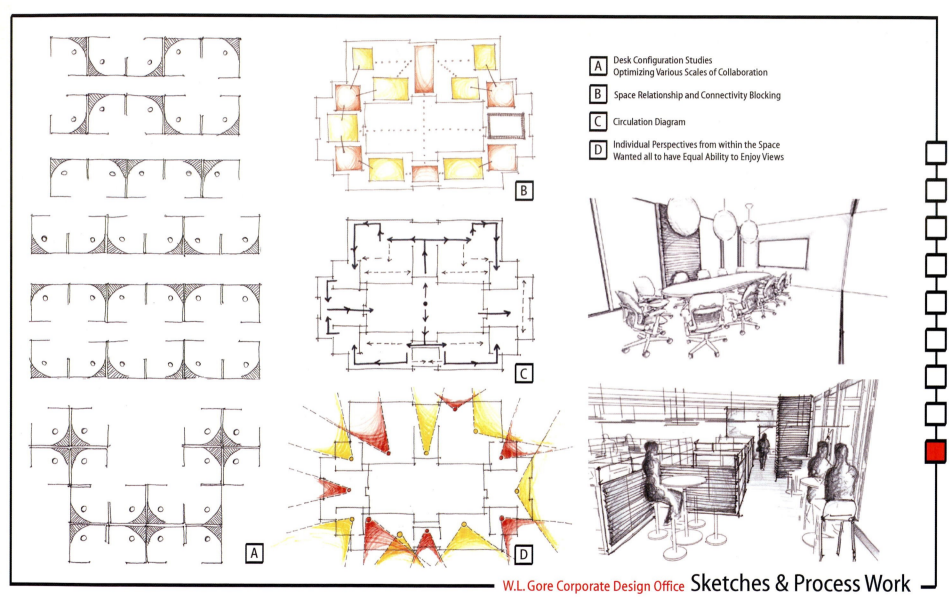

A   Desk Configuration Studies
Optimizing Various Scales of Collaboration

B   Space Relationship and Connectivity Blocking

C   Circulation Diagram

D   Individual Perspectives from within the Space
Wanted all to have Equal Ability to Enjoy Views

W.L. Gore Corporate Design Office Sketches & Process Work

Figure 13.50 W.L. Gore, Britney Bishop, process work.

UNIFY THE SPACE LIKE A FOREST

STEVE HYUNJUN CHANG

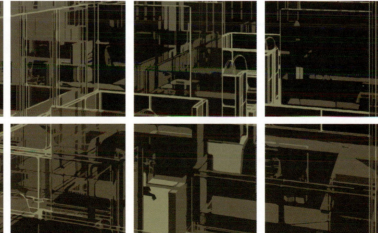

D'SIGN LAB, HYUN JUN CHANG

This design project was inspired by the verticality of a forest. A variety of sustainable finishes are combined to create the forest-inspired interior space including 3-form, bamboo, locally cultivated slate tiles, low VOC paint, and sustainable systems furniture from Steelcase and Knoll.

Figure 13.51 D'Sign Lab, Steve Hyun Jun Chang, cover page.

407

VERTICAL LINE

GREEN

UNIFORMATION

HORIZONTAL MOVEMENT

The forest consists of many different types of living creatures. However, they creature a uniform and beautiful natural scenary. The forest makes beautiful vertical line arrangements of trees and horizontal movements of paths.

There are the staffs from four different countries in this firm, but they are working in one unified space with same goal. This space should be like a beautiful forest that is GREEN and a UNIFIED place.

FOREST

01
PROJECT CONCEPT

Figure 13.52 D'Sign Lab, Steve Hyun Jun Chang, concept page.

VERTICAL LINE

HORIZONTAL MOVEMENT

GREEN

UNIFORMATION

ENTER

BLOCKING

Existing plan had some structural columns in the space. Therefore, it was important to deal with these columns by intergrating the most columns. Also, the design staffs from 4 different countries (Brazil, China, India and US) should be distinguished but also they need to be unified as one group of design team. That was the basic concept of the plan. The corridor / hallway on the center is symbolizing the path in the forest.

Rest rooms and kitchen areas are separated from each other because Rest rooms are for both guests and staffs but kitchen is just for the staffs.

Figure 13.53 D'Sign Lab, Steve Hyun Jun Chang, blocking.

The plan is built up more like to be practical and represent design concept. But the basic layout of spaces is similar to the block diagram. The elevator and the stairs to the loft are added within the space for library. The rest rooms have additional 4" walls along the existing walls for plumbing issue.

The main hall path in the middle and circulating paths around the design studios make a nice traffic line in the space.

BUILD-UP

BUILD-UP

03

HORIZONTAL MOVEMENT

GREEN

UNIFORMATION

VERTICAL LINE

Figure 13.54 D'Sign Lab, Steve Hyun Jun Chang, preliminary.

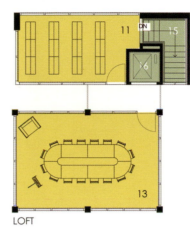

MAIN FLOOR

LOFT

DESIGNERS	**PUBLIC**
01 DESIGN STUDIO	10 LIBRARY 1st FLOOR
02 PROJECT MANAGERS	11 LIBRARY 2nd FLOOR
03 KITCHEN / REST AREA	12 RECEPTION
04 PRINTING AREA	13 CONFERENCE ROOM
ADMINISTRATIONS	**FACILITIES / OTHERS**
05 PRINCIPAL OFFICES	14 REST ROOMS
06 BUSINESS MANAGER	15 STAIRS / MECHANICAL ROOM
07 PUBLIC RELATION	16 ELEVATOR
08 ACCOUNTANT	17 STORAGES / CLOSETS
09 STAFF MEMBER	18 PIN-UP BOARD

– – – LOFT AREA

FURNITURE PLAN

04

Figure 13.55 D'Sign Lab, Steve Hyun Jun Chang, floor plan.

MAIN FLOOR

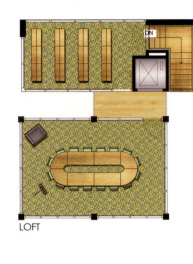

LOFT

MATERIAL FINISHES

05
FINISH PLAN

Figure 13.56 D'Sign Lab, Steve Hyun Jun Chang, finishes plan.

Reception area is the first space where the guests meet. Reception area should be designed to welcome the guests and should show the concept of the space.

By using the natural material finishes - like woods and black slate - and colors, the reception area is following the concept of the forest, and the horizontal wood boards on the wall and the vertical lines on the glass panels of the design studio also explain the concept.

RECEPTION

KEY MAP

PERSPECTIVE

06

RECEPTION

MATERIAL FINISHES

ELEVATION

Figure 13.57 D'Sign Lab, Steve Hyun Jun Chang, reception.

PERSPECTIVE

CONFERECE ROOM

Conference room is a space where both guests and staffs use. Conference room is a part of public space but it is also necessary to be very private. Therefore, conference room is placed on the loft, so both guests and the staffs can access easily. The sound absorption of the room is increased by using the acoustical glass and the carpet.

CONFERENCE ROOM

07

MATERIAL FINISHES

FURNITURES

BERUER   CORBUSIER   KNOLL STUDIO PROPELLER

KEY MAP

Figure 13.58 D'Sign Lab, Steve Hyun Jun Chang, conference room.

Main hall in the center of the space is a path which directly connects from the library to the administration offices.
The glass panels around the design studios have vertical lines which represent the shape of the woods in the forest.
Wood floor and the green vertical stripes have a purpose to make people feel like walking in the forest.

MAIN HALL

KEY MAP

PERSPECTIVE

MATERIAL FINISHES

ELEVATION

MAIN HALL VIEW

08

Figure 13.59 D'Sign Lab, Steve Hyun Jun Chang, main hall.

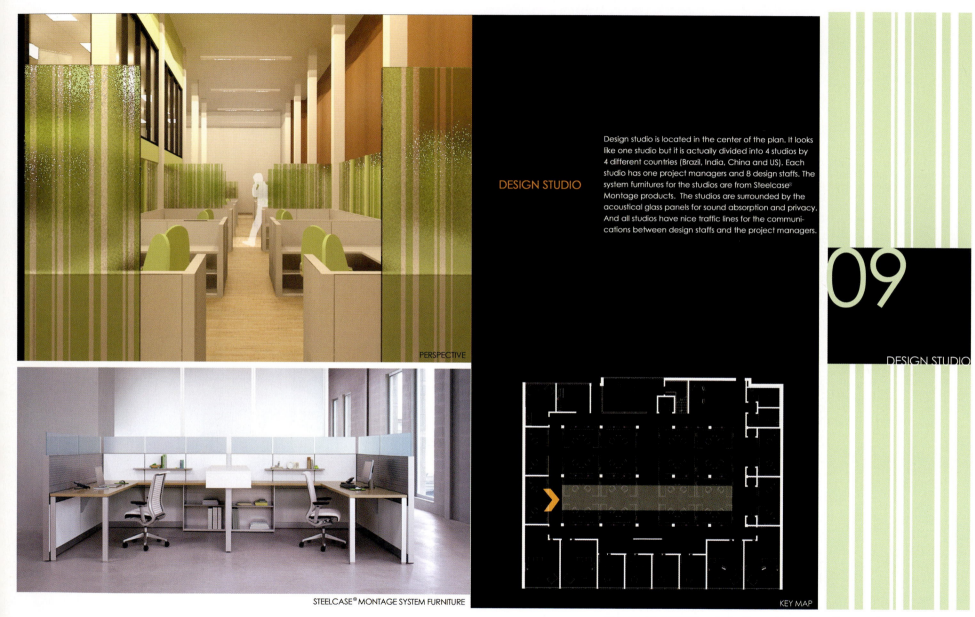

DESIGN STUDIO

Design studio is located in the center of the plan. It looks like one studio but it is actually divided into 4 studios by 4 different countries (Brazil, India, China and US). Each studio has one project managers and 8 design staffs. The system furnitures for the studios are from Steelcase® Montage products. The studios are surrounded by the acoustical glass panels for sound absorption and privacy. And all studios have nice traffic lines for the communications between design staffs and the project managers.

PERSPECTIVE

STEELCASE® MONTAGE SYSTEM FURNITURE

KEY MAP

09
DESIGN STUDIO

Figure 13.60 D'Sign Lab, Steve Hyun Jun Chang, design studio.

Administration offices are more private than the other spaces. Since these people are more focused on business and management, this space is classfied by brown wood color tone. It shows that this space is more private.

2 principals' offices are located on the each side and other business staffs' offices are on the center. For their privacy and sound absorption, the walls are acoustically structured with acoutic wood panels.

ADMINISTRATION OFFICES

PERSPECTIVE

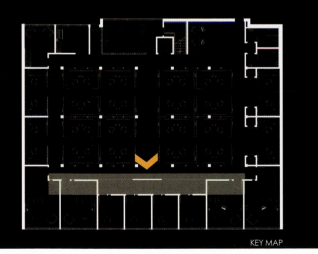

KEY MAP

ELEVATION

10

ADMINISTRATION OFFICES

Figure 13.61 D'Sign Lab, Steve Hyun Jun Chang, administrative offices.

(PRINCIPAL OFFICE) PERSPECTIVE

(LIBRARY 2nd FLOOR) PERSPECTIVE

PRINCIPAL OFFICE & LIBRARY

KEY MAP

PRINCIPAL OFFICE & LIBRARY

Principal office is an executive office. It must be private. The walls are covered with acoustical wood panels for the sound absorption. The executive desk is from Steelcase® Wood Solution product.

Library is located on both main floor and loft. People can access to the 2nd floor of the library by the stairs and the elevator. Library is also a place where both guests and staffs use.

Figure 13.62 D'Sign Lab, Steve Hyun Jun Chang, principal's office.

SHARE, LAUREN SHAW

Inspired by the concept of collage, this design project integrates many of the tasks of daily living under one roof to reduce the environmental impact of the employees. The plan incorporates a gymnasium and shower room as well as a lounge area for employees. Sustainable finishes include Steelcase systems furniture, 3-form panels, Maharam sustainable textiles, and bamboo flooring.

Figure 13.63
Share, Lauren Shaw, table of contents.

419

Figure 13.64 Share, Lauren Shaw, plan.

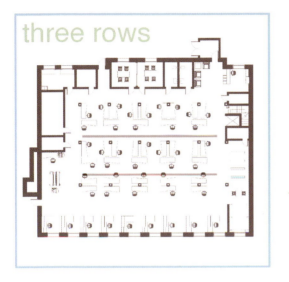

three rows

small groups

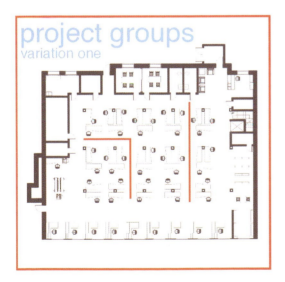

project groups
variation one

project groups
variation two

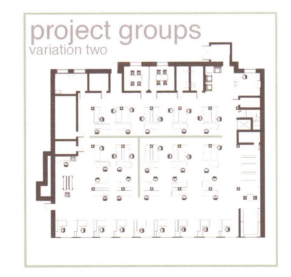

Figure 13.65 Share, Lauren Shaw, groupings.

panels = collage

Mobile upholstered panels are used throughout the building to create the visual effect of a collage. Each panel is upholstered in a different fabric, but has a color that coordinates with the rest of the studio design. Not only do these panels create a pleasing visual effect, they also allow for total flexability within the space and have the ability to give portions of the studio a completely different feel. To the left, thie diagrams show possible forms that the space could take using the panel system. The panels allow for privacy and greater productivity by allowing different work groups to meet in an isolated environment

03

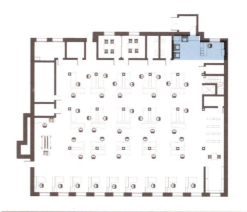

reception area

A reception area is the first chance to make a positive impression on a visitor. This layout is simple and easy to navigate, and the use of color scheme is simple so as not to immediately overwhelm the visitor. Upon first entering the building, the first thing a visitor sees is the reception desk. Built in filing is integrated in to the custom built desk to keep important information at the receptionist's fingertips. The back wall features the firm's name illuminated and cast in stainless steel. To the right, one sees the waiting area. Here, past projects are displayed on the back wall.

04

Figure 13.66 Share, Lauren Shaw, reception.

Figure 13.67 Share, Lauren Shaw, studio.

share.

design.

team.

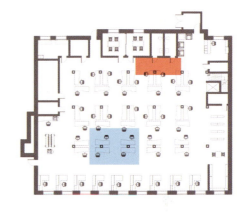

studio & balcony

The studio space consists one of large, open area. The columns create a grid on which the desks can be placed and the partitions can move within to create smaller, more intimate areas. Depending on the number of panels used and one's position within the studio, the panels create a "collage" effect due to the different fabric textures and colors. Each designer has a desk that is easy to move and storage that is independent of the desk and mobile as well. There are multiple pinup areas situated around the perimeter of the studio for informal presentations. The second story balcony is visible from the floor level and is bordered by transparent 3 form panels.

05

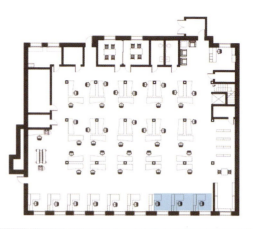

admin. & principal offices

The administration and principal offices are not enclosed in order to promote teamwork and involvement within all positions in the firm. When privacy is needed, employees may use the mobile upholstered panels to create partitioned spaces. The panels may be easily accessed and stored against the wall or in a closet, and are also used throughout the studio space to create the illusion of a collage. Each personal office space includes ample storage and surface area on which to work. Additional storage may be located in the data storage/archive room.

store.

work.

observe.

Figure 13.68 Share, Lauren Shaw, administration and principals.

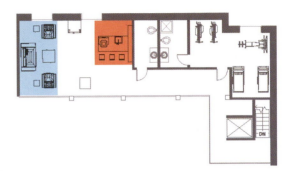

connect.

revitalize.

Figure 13.69 Share, Lauren Shaw, lounge.

lounge & kitchen

The second story loft serves as a retreat and meeting place for busy designers to escape the stresses of everyday life. During the day, employees can stop by the lounge for a coffee break, quick meal, or a brief chat with other coworkers. It is the perfect atmosphere for the designers to unwind and take some time out of the hectic workday to get to know one another. With a beautiful view of the city, comfortable furnishings, and television, the lounge has everything one needs to sit back and relax alone or within a group. Its location directly adjacent to the fully equipped kitchen is convenient and creates the opportunity for after work dinner parties and get togethers.

07

reception
offect
solichair

prandina quad

kitchen

lem piston stool

plate lamp

moco kitchen

studio

steelcase universal
storage

steelcase mobile
work surface

offices

bertoia chair

vitra petal clock

teca lamp

lounge

caboche lamp

habitat utah chair

west elm table

mdf italia sofa

bisazza labrinto

2+ areas

durodesign
bamboo floor

maharam:
blink fabric

maharam:
field fabric

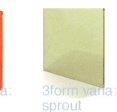

fritz hansen
oxford chair

3form varia:
firefly

3form varia:
sprout

3form varia:
surf

Figure 13.70 Share, Lauren Shaw, accessories.

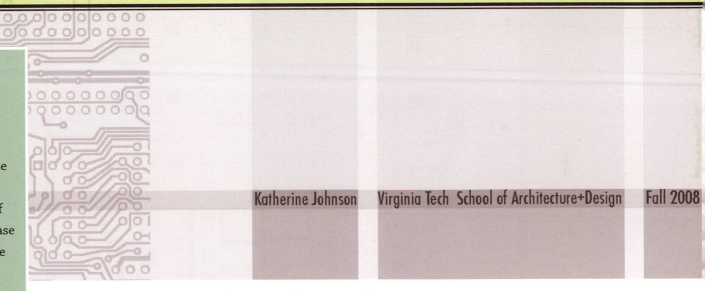

ARCH D
architecture interior industrial landscape

Soho Corporate Headquarters
454 BROOME STREET
NEW YORK, NY 10013

Katherine Johnson   Virginia Tech School of Architecture+Design   Fall 2008

SOHO CORPORATE HEADQUARTERS, KATHERINE JOHNSON

The interiors of this design office were inspired by the dynamic flow of energy. The interior expresses a high tech approach to design that is enhanced through the use of interior cables, brick, and concrete. Steelcase furniture is used throughout, including the Think chair and Groupwork by Turnstone. Cork flooring and sustainable textiles provide acoustical surfaces to complement the hard concrete and brick interiors.

Figure 13.71 Soho Corporate Headquarters, Katherine M. Johnson, cover.

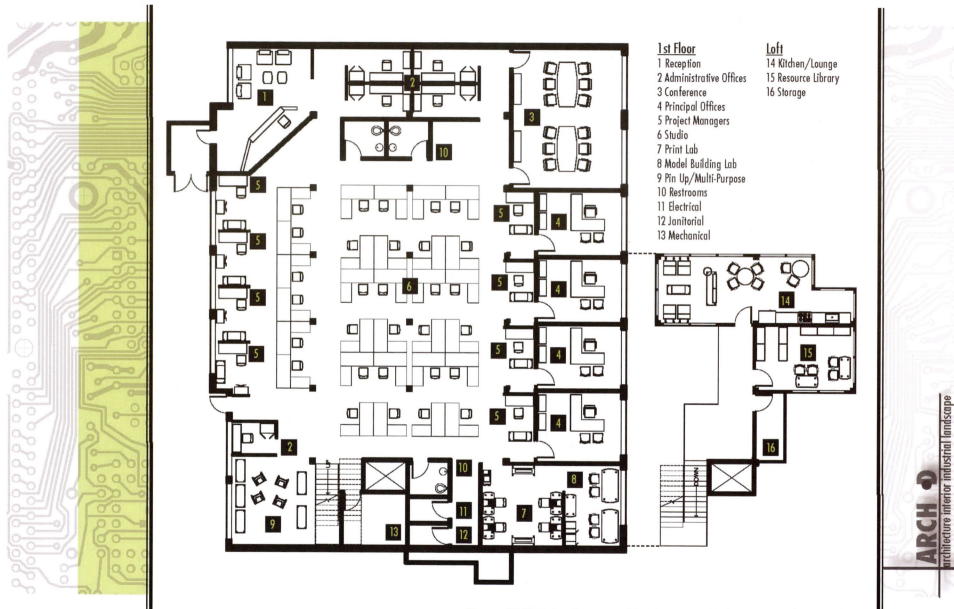

1st Floor
1 Reception
2 Administrative Offices
3 Conference
4 Principal Offices
5 Project Managers
6 Studio
7 Print Lab
8 Model Building Lab
9 Pin Up/Multi-Purpose
10 Restrooms
11 Electrical
12 Janitorial
13 Mechanical

Loft
14 Kitchen/Lounge
15 Resource Library
16 Storage

Figure 13.72 Soho Corporate Headquarters, Katherine M. Johnson, plan.

• RECEPTION

• Brick • Concrete • 3form: lime • 3form: seaweed • Steelcase: Archipelago by Metro

Figure 13.73 Soho Corporate Headquarters, Katherine M. Johnson, reception.

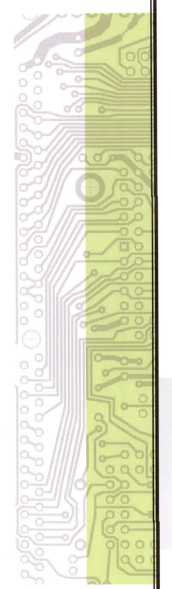

• **STUDIO**

• Steelcase:
Think Chair

• Steelcase:
Groupwork by Turnstone

• lastra by Flos

Figure 13.74 Soho Corporate Headquarters, Katherine M. Johnson, studio.

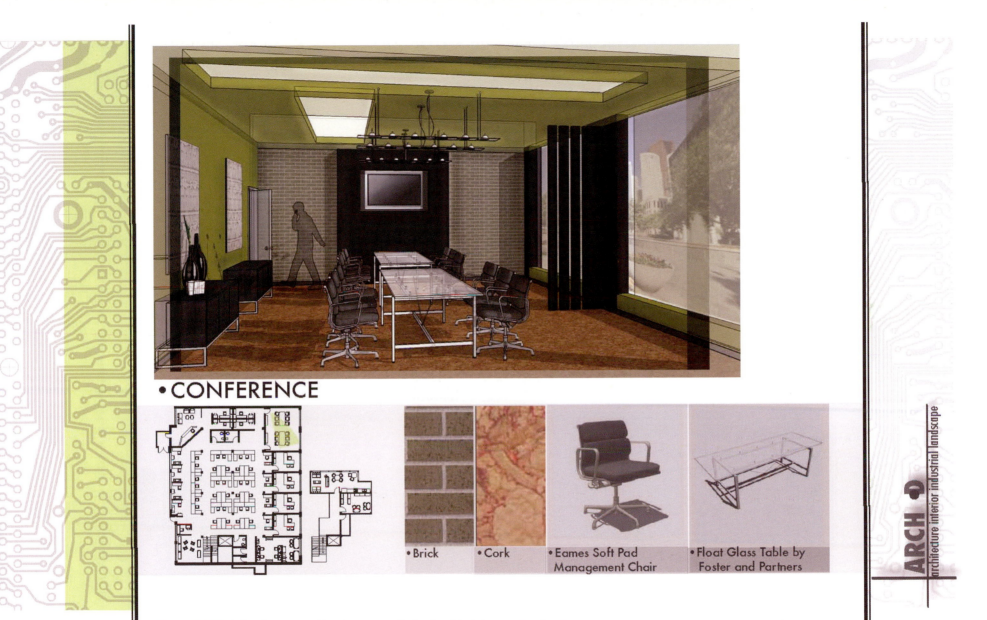

• CONFERENCE

• Brick • Cork • Eames Soft Pad Management Chair • Float Glass Table by Foster and Partners

Figure 13.75 Soho Corporate Headquarters, Katherine M. Johnson, conference.

• OFFICE: PRINCIPAL

• Gigi Chair by Knoll

• Tolomeo Table Lamp by Artemide

• Carve Office Set by Topdeq

Figure 13.76 Soho Corporate Headquarters, Katherine M. Johnson, office.

• PIN UP/MULTI-PURPOSE

• Concrete

• 3form: lime

• Steelcase: Bix by Metro

• Steelcase: Scoop by Turnstone

Figure 13.77 Soho Corporate Headquarters, Katherine M. Johnson, pin-up.

CUSTOM FURNITURE: Reception Desk

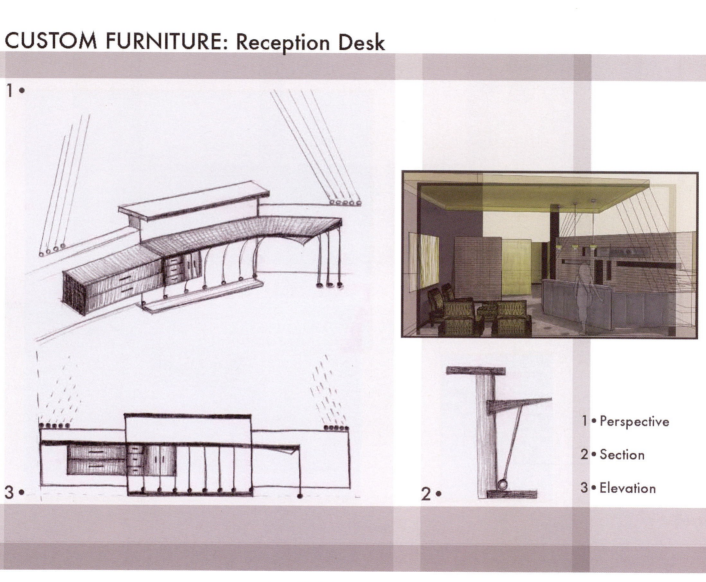

1 • Perspective

2 • Section

3 • Elevation

ARCH
architecture interior industrial landscape

Figure 13.78 Soho Corporate Headquarters, Katherine M. Johnson, custom desk.

RESOURCES

DiLouie, Craig. (2008). "Dramatic efficiency: Energy-efficient lighting design emphasizes integration, flexibility at showroom," *Archi-Tech,* April 2008, 14-20.

Index